Sixth Workshop on Building and Using Comparable Corpora 2013

Sofia, Bulgaria
8 August 2013

ISBN: 978-1-62993-011-4

Printed from e-media with permission by:

Curran Associates, Inc.
57 Morehouse Lane
Red Hook, NY 12571

Some format issues inherent in the e-media version may also appear in this print version.

Printed by Curran Associates, Inc. (2013)

Association for Computational Linguistics
209 N. Eighth Street
Stroudsburg, Pennsylvania 18360

Phone: 1-570-476-8006
Fax: 1-570-476-0860

acl@aclweb.org

Additional copies of this publication are available from:

Curran Associates, Inc.
57 Morehouse Lane
Red Hook, NY 12571 USA
Phone: 845-758-0400
Fax: 845-758-2634
Email: curran@proceedings.com
Web: www.proceedings.com

Introduction to BUCC 2013

Comparable corpora are collections of documents that are comparable in content and form in various degrees and dimensions. This definition includes many types of parallel and non-parallel multilingual corpora, but also sets of monolingual corpora that are used for comparative purposes. Research on comparable corpora is active but used to be scattered among many workshops and conferences. The workshop series on "Building and Using Comparable Corpora" (BUCC) aims at promoting progress in this exciting emerging field by bundling its research, thereby making it more visible and giving it a better platform.

Following the five previous editions of the workshop which took place in Africa (LREC'08 in Marrakech), America (ACL'11 in Portland), Asia (ACL-IJCNLP'09 in Singapore), Europe (LREC'10 in Malta) and also on the border between Asia and Europe (LREC'12 in Istanbul), the workshop this year is co-located with ACL'13 in Sofia, Bulgaria. The main theme for the current edition is "Terminology mining". We have received 27 submissions, accepted 10 oral presenations and 7 posters, including four oral presentations on the special topic.

We would like to thank all people who in one way or another helped in making this workshop once again a success. Our special thanks go to Hinrich Schütze for accepting to give the invited presentation, to the members of the program committee who did an excellent job in reviewing the submitted papers under strict time constraints, and to the ACL'13 workshop chairs and organizers. Last but not least we would like to thank our authors and the participants of the workshop.

Serge Sharoff, Reinhard Rapp, Pierre Zweigenbaum

Organizers:

Serge Sharoff, University of Leeds, UK (Chair)
Reinhard Rapp, Universities of Mainz, Germany, and Aix-Marseille, France
Pierre Zweigenbaum, LIMSI, CNRS, Orsay, and ERTIM, INALCO, Paris, France

Invited Speaker:

Hinrich Schütze, Ludwig-Maximilians-Universität München, Germany

Scientific Committee:

Caroline Barriere (Computer Research Institute of Montreal, Canada)
Chris Biemann (TU Darmstadt, Germany)
Hervé Déjean (Xerox Research Centre Europe, Grenoble, France)
Kurt Eberle (Lingenio, Heidelberg, Germany)
Andreas Eisele (European Commission, Luxembourg)
Gregory Grefenstette (Exalead, Paris, France)
Silvia Hansen-Schirra (University of Mainz, Germany)
Hitoshi Isahara (Toyohashi University of Technology)
Kyo Kageura (University of Tokyo, Japan)
Natalie Kübler (Université Paris Diderot, France)
Philippe Langlais (Université de Montréal, Canada)
Dragos Munteanu (Language Weaver, US)
Emmanuel Morin (Université de Nantes, France)
Lene Offersgaard (University of Copenhagen, Denmark)
Reinhard Rapp (Université Aix-Marseille, France)
Serge Sharoff (University of Leeds, UK)
Mandel Shi (Xiamen University, China)
Michel Simard (National Research Council Canada)
Richard Sproat (OGI School of Science & Technology, US)
Dragos Stefan Munteanu (Language Weaver, Inc., US)
Justin Washtell (365 Media Inc, US)
Michael Zock (Laboratoire d'Informatique Fondamentale, CNRS, Marseille)
Pierre Zweigenbaum (LIMSI-CNRS, France)

Table of Contents

Conference Program

Session: Invited talk

9:00–10:00 *Three dimensions of comparable corpora: same or different language, given or inferred comparability, means to an end or end in itself*
Hinrich Schütze

Session: (10:00-12:30) Terminology

10:00–10:30 *Cross-lingual WSD for Translation Extraction from Comparable Corpora*
Marianna Apidianaki, Nikola Ljubešić and Darja Fišer

Coffee break: (10:30-11:00)

11:00–11:30 *Bilingual Lexicon Extraction via Pivot Language and Word Alignment Tool*
Hong-seok Kwon, Hyeong-won Seo and Jae-hoon Kim

11:30–12:00 *Using WordNet and Semantic Similarity for Bilingual Terminology Mining from Comparable Corpora*
Dhouha Bouamor, Nasredine Semmar and Pierre Zweigenbaum

12:00–12:30 *A Comparison of Smoothing Techniques for Bilingual Lexicon Extraction from Comparable Corpora*
Amir Hazem and Emmanuel Morin

Session: (14:00-15:00) Comparable corpora

14:00–14:30 *Finding More Bilingual Webpages with High Credibility via Link Analysis*
Chengzhi Zhang, Xuchen Yao and Chunyu Kit

14:30–15:00 *A modular open-source focused crawler for mining monolingual and bilingual corpora from the web*
Vassilis Papavassiliou, Prokopis Prokopidis and Gregor Thurmair

Session: (15:00-15:30) Posters with Booster Session

15:00–15:03 *Building basic vocabulary across 40 languages*
Judit Acs, Katalin Pajkossy and Andras Kornai

15:04–15:07 *Scientific registers and disciplinary diversification: a comparable corpus approach*
Elke Teich, Stefania Degaetano-Ortlieb, Hannah Kermes and Ekaterina Lapshinova-Koltunski

15:08–15:11 *Improving MT System Using Extracted Parallel Fragments of Text from Comparable Corpora*
Rajdeep Gupta, Santanu Pal and Sivaji Bandyopadhyay

15:12–15:15 *VARTRA: A Comparable Corpus for Analysis of Translation Variation*
Ekaterina Lapshinova-Koltunski

8 August 2013 (continued)

15:16–15:19 *Building Ontologies from Collaborative Knowledge Bases to Search and Interpret Multilingual Corpora*
Yegin Genc, Elizabeth Lennon, Winter Mason and Jeffrey Nickerson

15:20–15:23 *Using a Random Forest Classifier to recognise translations of biomedical terms across languages*
Georgios Kontonatsios, Ioannis Korkontzelos, Sophia Ananiadou and Jun'ichi Tsujii

15:24–15:27 *Comparing Multilingual Comparable Articles Based On Opinions*
Motaz Saad, David Langlois and Kamel Smaili

Coffee break: (15:30-16:00)

Session: (16:00-18:00) Comparable corpora

16:00–16:30 *Mining for Domain-specific Parallel Text from Wikipedia*
Magdalena Plamada and Martin Volk

16:30–17:00 *Gathering and Generating Paraphrases from Twitter with Application to Normalization*
Wei Xu, Alan Ritter and Ralph Grishman

17:00–17:30 *Learning Comparable Corpora from Latent Semantic Analysis Simplified Document Space*
Ekaterina Stambolieva

17:30–18:00 *Chinese–Japanese Parallel Sentence Extraction from Quasi–Comparable Corpora*
Chenhui Chu, Toshiaki Nakazawa and Sadao Kurohashi

Cross-lingual WSD for Translation Extraction from Comparable Corpora

Marianna Apidianaki
LIMSI-CNRS
Rue John Von Neumann
BP 133, 91403
Orsay Cedex, France
marianna@limsi.fr

Nikola Ljubešić
Dept. of Information Sciences
University of Zagreb
Ivana Lučića 3, HR-10000
Zagreb, Croatia
nljubesi@ffzg.hr

Darja Fišer
Department of Translation
University of Ljubljana
Aškerčeva 2, SI-1000
Ljubljana, Slovenia
darja.fiser@ff.uni-lj.si

Abstract

We propose a data-driven approach to enhance translation extraction from comparable corpora. Instead of resorting to an external dictionary, we translate source vector features by using a cross-lingual Word Sense Disambiguation method. The candidate senses for a feature correspond to sense clusters of its translations in a parallel corpus and the context used for disambiguation consists of the vector that contains the feature. The translations found in the disambiguation output convey the sense of the features in the source vector, while the use of translation clusters permits to expand their translation with several variants. As a consequence, the translated vectors are less noisy and richer, and allow for the extraction of higher quality lexicons compared to simpler methods.

1 Introduction

Large-scale comparable corpora are available in many language pairs and are viewed as a source of valuable information for multilingual applications. Identifying translation correspondences in this type of corpora permits to construct bilingual lexicons for low-resourced languages, and to complement and reduce the sparseness of existing resources (Munteanu and Marcu, 2005; Snover et al., 2008). The main assumption behind translation extraction from comparable corpora is that a source word and its translation appear in similar contexts (Fung, 1998; Rapp, 1999). So, in order to identify a translation correspondence between the two languages, the contexts of the source word and the candidate translation have to be compared. For this comparison to take place, the same vector space has to be produced, which means that the vectors of the one language have to be translated in the other language. This generally assumes the availability of a bilingual dictionary which might however not be the case for some language pairs and domains. Moreover, the classic way in which a dictionary is put into use, which consists in translating vector features by their first translation in the dictionary, neglects semantics. We expect that a method capable of identifying the correct sense of the features and translating them accordingly could contribute to producing cleaner vectors and to extracting higher quality lexicons.

In this paper, we show how source vectors can be translated into the target language by a cross-lingual Word Sense Disambiguation (WSD) method which exploits the output of data-driven Word Sense Induction (WSI) (Apidianaki, 2009), and demonstrate how feature disambiguation enhances the quality of the translations extracted from the comparable corpus. This study extends our previous work on the topic (Apidianaki et al., 2012) by applying the proposed methods to a comparable corpus of general language (built from Wikipedia) and optimizing various parameters that affect the quality of the extracted translations. We expect the disambiguation to have a beneficial impact on the results given that polysemy is a frequent phenomenon in a general, mixed-domain corpus. Our experiments are carried out on the English-Slovene language pair but as the methods are totally data-driven, the approach can be easily applied to other languages.

The paper is organized as follows: In the next section, we present some related work on bilingual lexicon extraction from comparable corpora. Section 3 presents the data used in our experiments and Section 4 provides details on the approach and the experimental setup. In Section 5, we report and discuss the obtained results before concluding and presenting some directions for future work.

2 Related work

The traditional approch to translation extraction from comparable corpora and most of its extensions (Fung, 1998; Rapp, 1999; Shao and Ng, 2004; Otero, 2007; Yu and Tsujii, 2009; Marsi and Krahmer, 2010) presuppose the availability of a bilingual lexicon for translating source vectors into the target language. A translation candidate is generally considered as correct if it is an appropriate translation for at least one sense of the source word in the dictionary, which often corresponds to its most frequent sense. An alternative consists in considering all translations provided for a word in the dictionary but weighting them by their frequency in the target language (Prochasson et al., 2009; Hazem and Morin, 2012). The high quality of the exploited handcrafted resources, combined to the skewed distribution of the translations corresponding to different word senses, often lead to satisfying results. Nevertheless, the applicability of the methods is limited to languages and domains where bilingual resources are available. Moreover, by promoting the most frequent sense/translation, this approach neglects polysemy. We believe that feature disambiguation can lead to the production of cleaner vectors and, consequently, to higher quality results.

The need to bypass pre-existing dictionaries has been addressed by Koehn and Knight (2002) who built the initial seed dictionary automatically, based on identical spelling features between English and German. Cognate detection has also been used by Saralegi et al. (2008) for extracting word translations from English-Basque comparable corpora. The cognate and seed lexicon approaches have been successfully combined by Fišer and Ljubešić (2011) who showed that the results with an automatically created seed lexicon, based on language similarity, can be as good as with a pre-existing dictionary. But all these approaches work on closely-related languages and cannot be used as successfully for language pairs with little lexical overlap, such as English and Slovene, which is the case in this experiment.

Regarding the translation of the source vectors, we use contextual information to disambiguate their features and translate them using clusters of semantically similar translations in the target language. A similar idea has been implemented by Kaji (2003) who performed sense-based word clustering to extract sets of synonymous translations from comparable corpora with the help of a bilingual dictionary.

Using translation clusters permits to expand feature translation and to suggest multiple semantically correct translations. A similar approach has been adopted by Déjean et al. (2005) who expand vector translation by using a bilingual thesaurus instead of a lexicon. In contrast to their work, the method proposed here does not rely on any external knowledge source to determine word senses or translation equivalents, and is thus fully data-driven and language independent.

3 Resources

3.1 Comparable corpus

The comparable corpus from which the bilingual lexicon will be extracted is a collection of English (EN) and Slovene (SL) texts extracted from Wikipedia. The February 2013 dumps of Wikipedia articles were downloaded and cleaned for both languages after which the English corpus was tokenized, part-of-speech (PoS) tagged and lemmatized with the TreeTagger (Schmid, 1994). The same pre-processing was applied to the Slovene corpus with the ToTaLe analyzer (Erjavec et al., 2010) which uses the TnT tagger (Brants, 2000) and was trained on MultextEast corpora. The Wikipedia corpus contains about 1.5 billion tokens for English and almost 24 million tokens for Slovene.

In previous work, we applied our approach to a specialized comparable corpus from the health domain (Apidianaki et al., 2012). The results were encouraging, showing how translation clustering and vector disambiguation help to improve the quality of the translations extracted from the comparable corpus. We believe that the positive impact of this approach will be more significant on lexicon extraction from a general language comparable corpus, in which polysemy is more prominent.

3.2 Parallel corpus

The parallel corpus used for clustering and word sense induction consists of the Slovene-English parts of Europarl (release v6) (Koehn, 2005) and of JRC-Acquis (Steinberger et al., 2006) and amounts to approximately 35M words per language. A number of pre-processing steps are applied to the corpus prior to sense induction, such

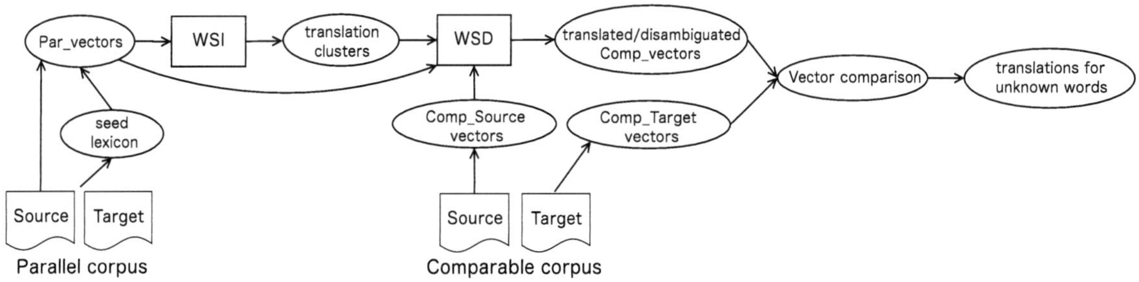

Figure 1: Translation extraction from comparable corpora using cross-lingual WSI and WSD.

as elimination of sentence pairs with a great difference in length, lemmatization and PoS tagging with the TreeTagger (for English) and ToTaLe (for Slovene) (Erjavec et al., 2010). Next, the corpus is word-aligned with GIZA++ (Och and Ney, 2003) and two bilingual lexicons are extracted, one for each translation direction (EN–SL/SL–EN). To clean the lexicons from noisy alignments, the translations are filtered on the basis of their alignment score and PoS, keeping only translations that pertain to the same grammatical category as the source word. We retain only intersecting alignments and use for clustering translations that translate a source word more than 10 times in the training corpus. This threshold reduces data sparseness issues that affect the clustering and eliminates erroneous word alignments. The filtered EN-SL lexicon contains entries for 6,384 nouns, 2,447 adjectives and 1,814 verbs having more than three translations in the training corpus.

The parallel corpus, which contains EU texts, is more specialized than the comparable corpus built from Wikipedia. This is not the ideal scenario for this experiment; domain adaptation is important for the type of semantic processing we want to apply as there might be a shift in the senses present in the two corpora. However, as EU texts often contain a lot of general vocabulary, we expect that this discrepancy will not strongly affect the quality of the results.

3.3 Gold standard

We evaluate the quality of the bilingual lexicons extracted from the comparable corpus by comparing them to a gold standard lexicon, which was built from the aligned English (Fellbaum, 1998) and Slovene wordnets (Fišer and Sagot, 2008). We extracted all English synsets from the Base Concept sets that belong to the Factotum domain and contain literals with polysemy levels 1-5 and their Slovene equivalents which have been validated by a lexicographer. Of 1,589 such synsets, 200 were randomly selected and used as a gold standard for automatic evaluation of the method proposed in this paper.

4 Experimental setup

4.1 Overview of the method

Figure 1 gives an overview of the way information mined from the parallel training corpus is exploited for discovering translations of source (English) words in the comparable corpus. The parallel corpus serves to extract an English-Slovene seed lexicon and source language context vectors (Par_vectors) for the Slovene translations of English words. These vectors form the input to the Word Sense Induction (WSI) method which groups the translations of an English word into clusters.

The clusters of semantically related Slovene translations constitute the candidate senses which, together with the Par_vectors, are used for disambiguating and translating the vectors extracted from the source (English) side of the comparable corpus (Comp_source). The translated vectors are then compared to the ones extracted from the target language (Slovene) side of the comparable corpus (Comp_target) and the best translations are selected, for a list of unknown words. All steps of the proposed method illustrated in Figure 1 will be detailed in the following sections.

4.2 Translation clustering

The translations of the English words in the lexicon built as described in 3.2 are clustered according to their semantic proximity using a cross-lingual Word Sense Induction method (Apidianaki, 2008). For each translation T_i of a word w, a vector is built from the content word co-

Language	POS	Source word	Slovene sense clusters
EN–SL	**Nouns**	sphere	{krogla}_*(geometrical shape)* {sfera, področje}_*(area)*
		address	{obravnava, reševanje, obravnavanje}_*(dealing with)* {naslov}_*(postal address)*
		portion	{kos}_*(piece)* {obrok, porcija}_*(serving)* {delež}_*(share)*
		figure	{številka, podatek, znesek}_*(amount)* {slika}_*(image)* {osebnost}_*(person)*
	Verbs	seal	{tesniti}_*(to be water-/airtight)* {zapreti, zapečatiti}_*(to close an envelope or some other container)*
		weigh	{pretehtati}_*(consider possibilities)* {tehtati, stehtati}_*(check weight)*
		educate	{poučiti}_*(give information)* {izobraževati, izobraziti}_*(give education)*
		consume	{potrošiti}_*(spend money/goods)* {uživati, zaužiti}_*(eat/drink)*
	Adjs	mature	{zrel, odrasel}_*(adult)* {zorjen, zrel}_*(ripe)*
		minor	{nepomemben}_*(not very important)* {mladoleten, majhen}_*(under 18 years old)*
		juvenile	{nedorasel}_*(not adult/biologically mature yet)* {mladoleten, mladoletniški}_*(not 18/legally adult yet)*
		remote	{odmaknjen, odročen}_*(far away and not easily accessible)* {oddaljen daljinski}_*(controlled from a distance (e.g. remote control))*

Table 1: Entries from the English-Slovene sense cluster inventory.

occurrences of w in the parallel sentences where it is translated by T_i. Let N be the number of features retained for each T_i from the corresponding source contexts. Each feature F_j ($1 \leq j \leq N$) receives a total weight with a translation T_i, $\text{tw}(F_j, T_i)$, defined as the product of the feature's global weight, $\text{gw}(F_j)$, and its local weight with that translation, $\text{lw}(F_j, T_i)$. The global weight of a feature F_j is a function of the number N_i of translations (T_i's) to which F_j is related, and of the probabilities (p_{ij}) that F_j co-occurs with instances of w translated by each of the T_i's:

$$\text{gw}(F_j) = 1 - \frac{\sum_{T_i} p_{ij} \log(p_{ij})}{N_i} \quad (1)$$

Each p_{ij} is computed as the ratio of the co-occurrence frequency of F_j with w when translated as T_i to the total number of features seen with T_i:

$$p_{ij} = \frac{\text{cooc\_frequency}(F_j, T_i)}{N} \quad (2)$$

The local weight $\text{lw}(F_j, T_i)$ between F_j and T_i directly depends on their co-occurrence frequency:

$$\text{lw}(F_j, T_i) = \log(\text{cooc\_frequency}(F_j, T_i)) \quad (3)$$

The pairwise similarity of the translations is calculated using the Weighted Jaccard Coefficient (Grefenstette, 1994).

$$WJ(T_m, T_n) = \frac{\sum_j \min(tw(T_m, F_j), tw(T_n, F_j))}{\sum_j \max(tw(T_m, F_j), tw(T_n, F_j))} \quad (4)$$

The similarity score of each translation pair is compared to a threshold locally defined for each w using an iterative procedure. The threshold (T) for a word w is initially set to the mean of the scores (above 0) of its translation pairs. The set of translation pairs of w is then divided into two sets ($G1$ and $G2$) according to whether they exceed, or are inferior to, the threshold. The average of scores of the translation pairs in each set is computed ($m1$ and $m2$) and a new threshold is calculated that is the average of $m1$ and $m2$ ($T = (m1 + m2)/2$). The new threshold serves to separate again the translation pairs into two sets, a new threshold is calculated and the procedure is repeated until convergence.

The semantically similar translations of w are grouped into clusters. Translation pairs with a score above the threshold form initial clusters that might be further enriched provided that there exist additional strongly related translations. Clustering stops when all translations of w are clustered and all their relations have been checked. An important feature of the algorithm is that it performs soft clustering, so translations can be found in different clusters. The final clusters are characterized by global connectivity, i.e. all their elements are linked by pertinent relations.

Table 1 gives examples of clusters obtained for English words of different PoS with clear sense distinctions in the parallel corpus. For each English word, we provide the obtained clusters of Slovene translations including a description of the sense described by each cluster. For instance, the translations for the adjective *minor* from the training corpus (*nepomemben*, *mladoleten* and *majhen*) are grouped into two clusters describing its two senses: {nepomemben} - "not very important" and {mladoleten, majhen} - "under 18 years old". The resulting cluster inventory contains 13,352 clusters in total, for 8,892 words. 2,585 of the words (1,518 nouns, 554 verbs and 513 adjectives) have more than one cluster.

In the next section, we explain how the clusters and the corresponding translation vectors are used for disambiguating the source language vectors extracted from the comparable corpus.

4.3 Cross-lingual vector comparison

4.3.1 Vector building

We build context vectors in the two languages for nouns occurring at least 50 times in the comparable corpus. The frequency threshold is important for the lexicon extraction approach to produce good results. As features we use three content words to the left and to the right of the retained nouns, stopping at the sentence boundary, without taking into account their position. Log-likelihood is used to calculate feature weights.

In the reported experiments we focus on the 1,000 strongest features. A portion of these features is disambiguated for each headword, depending on the availability of clustering information. We observed that disambiguating a smaller amount of features yielded similar results and including additional features did not improve the results.

4.3.2 Vector translation and disambiguation

Translation correspondences between the two languages of the comparable corpus are identified by comparing the source language vectors, built as described in Section 4.3.1, to the ones of the candidate translations. This comparison serves to quantify the similarity of the source and target words represented by the vectors and the highest ranked pairs are retained.

For the comparison to take place, the source vectors have to be translated in the target language. In most previous work, the vectors were translated using external seed dictionaries: the first translation proposed for a word in the dictionary was used to translate all instances of the word in the vectors irrespective of their sense. Here, we replace the external dictionary with the output of a data-driven cross-lingual WSD method (Apidianaki, 2009) which renders the method knowledge light and adaptable to other language pairs.

The translation clusters obtained during WSI (cf. Section 4.2) describe the senses of the English words in the parallel corpus. We exploit this sense inventory for disambiguating the features in the English vectors extracted from the comparable corpus. More precisely, we ask the WSD method to select among the available clusters the one that correctly translates in Slovene the sense of the English features in the vectors built from the comparable corpus. The selection is performed by comparing information from the context of a feature, which corresponds to the rest of the vector where the feature appears, to the source language vectors of the translations which served to their clustering. Inside the vectors, the features are ordered according to their score, calculated as described in Section 4.3.1. Feature weights filter out the *weak* features, i.e. features with a score below the experimentally set threshold of 0.01. The retained features are then considered as a bag of words.

On the clusters' side, the information used for disambiguation is found in the source language vectors that revealed the similarity of the translations. If common features (CFs) exist between the context of a feature and the vectors of the translations in a cluster, a score is calculated corresponding to the mean of the weights of the CFs with the clustered translations, where weights correspond to the total weights (*tw*'s) computed between features and translations during WSI. In formula 5, CF_j is the set of CFs and N_{CF} is the number of translations T_i characterized by a CF.

$$wsd\_score = \frac{\sum_{i=1}^{N_{CF}} \sum_j w(T_i, CF_j)}{N_{CF} \cdot |CF_j|} \quad (5)$$

PoS	Feature	Assigned Cluster	MFT
Nouns	party	{oseba, stran, pogodbenica, stranka}	stranka
	matter	{zadeva, vprašanje}	zadeva
Verbs	settle	{urediti, rešiti, reševati}	rešiti
	follow	{upoštevati, spremljati, slediti}	slediti
Adjs	alternative	{nadomesten, alternativen}	alternativen
	involved	{vključen, vpleten}	vključen

Table 2: Disambiguation results.

The cluster that receives the highest score is selected and assigned to the feature as a sense tag. The features are also tagged with their most frequent translation (MFT) in the parallel corpus, which sometimes already exists in the cluster selected during WSD.

In Table 2, we present examples of disambiguated features of different PoS from the vector of the word *transition*. The context used for disambiguation consists of the other strong features in the vector and the cluster that best describes the sense of the features in this context is selected. In the last column, we provide the MFT of the feature in the parallel corpus. In the examples shown here the MFT translation already exists in the cluster selected by the WSD method but this is not always the case. As we will show in the Evaluation section, the configuration where the MFT from the cluster assigned during disambiguation is selected (called CLMFT) gives better results than MFT, which shows that the MFT in the selected cluster is not always the most frequent alignment for the word in the parallel corpus. Furthermore, the clusters provide supplementary material (i.e. multiple semantically correct translations) for comparing the vectors in the target language and improving the baseline results. Still, MFT remains a very powerful heuristic due to the skewed distribution of word senses and translations.

4.4 Vector comparison

The translation clusters proposed during WSD for the features in the vectors built from the source side of the comparable corpus serve to translate the vectors in the target language. In our experiments, we compare three different ways of translating the source language features.

1. by keeping the most frequent translation/alignment of the feature in the parallel corpus (MFT);
2. by keeping the most frequent translation from the cluster assigned to the feature during disambiguation (CLMFT); and
3. by using the same cluster as in the second approach, but producing features for all translations in the cluster with the same weight (CL).

The first approach (MFT) serves as the baseline since, instead of the sense clustering and WSD results, it just uses the most frequent sense/alignment heuristic. In the first batch of experiments, we noticed that the results of the CL and CLMFT approaches heavily depend on the part-of-speech of the features. So, we divided the CL and CLMFT approaches into three sub-approaches:

1. translate only nouns, verbs or adjectives with the clusters and other features with the MFT approach (CLMFT_N, CLMFT_V, CLMFT_A);
2. translate nouns and adjectives with the clusters and verbs with the MFT approach (CLMFT_NA); and
3. translate nouns and verbs with the clusters and adjectives with the MFT approach (CLMFT_NV).

The distance between the translated source and the target-language vectors is computed by the Dice metric. By comparing the translated source vectors to the target language ones, we obtain a ranked list of candidate translations for each gold standard entry.

5 Evaluation

5.1 Metrics

The final result of our method consists in ranked lists of translation candidates for gold standard entries. We evaluate this output by the mean reciprocal rank (MRR) measure which takes into account the rank of the first good translation found for each entry. Formally, MRR is defined as

$$MRR = \frac{1}{|Q|}\sum_{i=1}^{|Q|}\frac{1}{rank_i} \quad (6)$$

where $|Q|$ is the length of the query, i.e. the number of gold standard entries we compute translation candidates for, and $rank_i$ is the position of the first correct translation in the candidate list.

5.2 Results

Table 4 shows the translation extraction results for different configurations. The MFT score is used as the baseline. We observe that disambiguating all features in the vectors (CL) yields lower results than the baseline compared to selecting only the most frequent translation from the cluster which slightly outperforms the MFT baseline. In the CLMFT_N, CLMFT_NA, CLMFT_NV configurations we disambiguate noun features, nouns and adjectives, and nouns and verbs, respectively, and translate words of other PoS using the MFT. In CLMFT_N, for instance, nouns are disambiguated while verbs and adjectives are translated by the word to which they were most frequently aligned in the parallel corpus. The three configurations where nouns are disambiguated (CLMFT_N, CLMFT_NA, CLMFT_NV) give better results compared to those addressing verbs or adjectives alone. Interestingly, disambiguating only adjectives gives worse results than disambiguating only verbs, but the combination of nouns and adjectives outperforms the combination of nouns and verbs.

In CLMFT, features of all PoS are disambiguated but we only keep the most frequent translation in the cluster and ignore the other translations. This setting gives much better results than CL, where the whole cluster is used, which highlights two facts: first, that disambiguation is beneficial for translation extraction and, second, that the noise present in the automatically built clusters harms the quality of the translations extracted from the comparable corpus. The better score obtained for CLMFT compared to MFT also shows that, in many cases, the most frequent translation in the cluster does not coincide with the most frequent alignment of the word in the parallel corpus. So, disambiguation helps to select a more appropriate translation than the MFT approach. This improvement compared to the baseline shows again that WSD is useful in this setting.

	MRR
MFT	0.0685
CLMFT	0.0807
CL	0.0434
CLMFT_N	0.0817
CLMFT_A	0.07
CLMFT_V	0.0714
CLMFT_NA	0.0842
CLMFT_NV	0.08048

Table 3: Results of the experiment.

		MRR diff	p-value
MFT	CLMFT	0.0122	0.1830
MFT	CL	0.0251	0.0410
CLMFT	CL	0.0373	0.0120
MFT	CLMFT_NA	0.0157	0.4296
MFT	CLMFT_NV	0.0120	0.5195

Table 4: Comparison of different configurations.

In Table 4, the results for different configurations are compared. The statistical significance of the difference in the results was calculated by approximate randomization (1,000 repetitions). We observe that the differences between the CL and MFT configurations and the CL and CLMFT ones, are statistically significant. This confirms that taking most frequent translations, disambiguated or not, works better than exploiting all the information in the clusters. The remainder of the differences in the results are not statistically significant. One could wonder why the p-values are that high in case of the MFT setting on one side and CLMFT_NA and CLMFT_NV settings on the other side although the differences in the results are not that high. The most probable explanation is that there is a low intersection in correct results and errors. Because of that, flipping the results between the two systems – as performed in approximate randomization – often generates differences higher than the initial difference on the original results.

5.3 Qualitative analysis

Manual evaluation of the results shows that the procedure can deal with concrete words much better than with abstract ones. For example, the correct translation of the headword *enquiry* is the third highest-ranked translation. The results are also much better with monosemous and domain-specific terms (e.g. the correct translation for *cataclysm* is the top-ranking candidate). On the other hand, general and polysemous expressions that can appear in a wide range of contexts are a much tougher nut to crack. For example, the correct translation candidate for word *role*, which can be used in a variety of contexts as well as metaphorically, is in the tenth position, whereas no correct translation was found for *transition*. However, it must be noted that even if the correct translation is not found in the results, the output of our method is in most cases a very coherent and solid description of the semantic field of the headword in question. This means that the list can still be useful for lexicographers to illicit the correct translation that is missing, or organize the vocabulary in terms of their relational-semantic principles.

We have also performed an error analysis in cases where the correct translation could not be found among the candidates, which consisted of checking the 30 strongest disambiguated features of an erroneously translated headword. We observed cases where the strongest features in the vectors are either very abstract and generic or too heterogeneous for our method to be able to perform well. This was the case with the headwords *characterisation*, *antecedent* and *thread*. In cases where the strongest features represented the concept clearly but the correct translation was not found, we examined cluster, WSD and MFT quality, as suggested by the parallel corpus. The main source of errors in these cases is the noise in the clusters which is often due to pre-processing errors, especially in the event of multi-word expressions. It seems that clustering is also problematic for abstract or generic words, where senses might be lumped together. The WSD step, on the other hand, does not seem to introduce noise to the procedure as it is correct in almost all the cases we have examined.

6 Discussion and conclusion

We have shown how cross-lingual WSD can be applied to bilingual lexicon extraction from comparable corpora. The disambiguation of source language features using translation clusters constitutes the main contribution of this work and presents several advantages. First, the method performs disambiguation by using sense descriptions derived from the data, which clearly differentiates our method from the approaches based on external lexicons and extends its applicability to resource-poor languages. The translation clusters acquired through WSI serve to disambiguate the features in the source language context vectors and to produce less noisy translated vectors. An additional advantage is that the sense clusters often contain more than one translation and, therefore, provide supplementary material for the comparison of the vectors in the target language.

The results show that data-driven semantic analysis can help to circumvent the need for an external seed dictionary, traditionally considered as a prerequisite for translation extraction from parallel corpora. Moreover, it is clear that disambiguating the vectors improves the quality of the extracted lexicons and manages to beat the simpler, but yet powerful, most frequent translation heuristic. These encouraging results pave the way towards pure data-driven methods for bilingual lexicon extraction. This knowledge-light approach can be applied to languages and domains that do not dispose of large-scale seed dictionaries but for which parallel corpora are available.

An avenue that we intend to explore in future work is to extract translations corresponding to different senses of the headwords. Up to now, research on translation extraction has most often aimed the identification of one good translation for a source word in the comparable corpus. This has also been the case because most works have focused on identifying translations for specialized terms that do not convey different senses. However, words in a general language corpus like Wikipedia can be polysemous and it is important to identify translations corresponding to their different senses. Moreover, polysemy makes the translation extraction procedure more difficult, as features corresponding to different senses are mingled in the same vector. A way to discover translations corresponding to different word senses would be to apply a monolingual WSI method on the source side of the comparable corpus which would group the closely related usages of the headwords together, and to then build vectors for each usage group hopefully describing a distinct sense. Using the generated sets of vectors separately will allow to extract translations corresponding to different senses of the source words.

References

Marianna Apidianaki, Nikola Ljubešić, and Darja Fišer. 2012. Disambiguating vectors for bilingual lexicon extraction from comparable corpora. In *Eighth Language Technologies Conference*, pages 10–15, Ljubljana, Slovenia.

Marianna Apidianaki. 2008. Translation-oriented sense induction based on parallel corpora. In *Proceedings of the 6th International Conference on Language Resources and Evaluation (LREC-08)*, pages 3269–3275, Marrakech, Morocco.

Marianna Apidianaki. 2009. Data-driven Semantic Analysis for Multilingual WSD and Lexical Selection in Translation. In *Proceedings of the 12th Conference of the European Chapter of the Association for Computational Linguistics (EACL-09)*, pages 77–85, Athens, Greece.

Thorsten Brants. 2000. TnT - A Statistical Part-of-Speech Tagger. In *Proceedings of the Sixth Applied Natural Language Processing (ANLP-2000)*, Seattle, WA.

Hervé Déjean, Eric Gaussier, Jean-Michel Renders, and Fatiha Sadat. 2005. Automatic processing of multilingual medical terminology: applications to thesaurus enrichment and cross-language information retrieval. *Artificial Intelligence in Medicine*, 33(2):111–124, February.

Tomaž Erjavec, Darja Fišer, Simon Krek, and Nina Ledinek. 2010. The JOS Linguistically Tagged Corpus of Slovene. In *Proceedings of the Seventh International Conference on Language Resources and Evaluation (LREC'10)*, Valletta, Malta.

Christiane Fellbaum, editor. 1998. *WordNet: An Electronic Lexical Database*. MIT Press, Cambridge, MA.

Darja Fišer and Nikola Ljubešić. 2011. Bilingual lexicon extraction from comparable corpora for closely related languages. In *Proceedings of the International Conference Recent Advances in Natural Language Processing 2011*, pages 125–131, Hissar, Bulgaria. RANLP 2011 Organising Committee.

Darja Fišer and Benoît Sagot. 2008. Combining multiple resources to build reliable wordnets. In *TSD 2008 - Text Speech and Dialogue*, Lecture Notes in Computer Science, Brno, Czech Republic. Springer.

Pascale Fung. 1998. Machine translation and the information soup, third conference of the association for machine translation in the americas, amta '98, langhorne, pa, usa, october 28-31, 1998, proceedings. In *AMTA*, volume 1529 of *Lecture Notes in Computer Science*. Springer.

Gregory Grefenstette. 1994. *Explorations in Automatic Thesaurus Discovery*. Kluwer Academic Publishers, Norwell, MA.

Amir Hazem and Emmanuel Morin. 2012. Ica for bilingual lexicon extraction from comparable corpora. In *Proceedings of the 5th Workshop on Building and Using Comparable Corpora (BUCC)*, Istanbul, Turkey.

Hiroyuki Kaji. 2003. Word sense acquisition from bilingual comparable corpora. In *HLT-NAACL*.

Philipp Koehn and Kevin Knight. 2002. Learning a translation lexicon from monolingual corpora. In *In Proceedings of ACL Workshop on Unsupervised Lexical Acquisition*, pages 9–16.

Philipp Koehn. 2005. Europarl: A Parallel Corpus for Statistical Machine Translation. In *Proceedings of MT Summit X*, pages 79–86, Phuket, Thailand.

Erwin Marsi and Emiel Krahmer. 2010. Automatic analysis of semantic similarity in comparable text through syntactic tree matching. In *Proceedings of the 23rd International Conference on Computational Linguistics (Coling 2010)*, pages 752–760, Beijing, China, August. Coling 2010 Organizing Committee.

Dragos Stefan Munteanu and Daniel Marcu. 2005. Improving Machine Translation Performance by Exploiting Non-Parallel Corpora. *Computational Linguistics*, 31(4):477–504.

Franz Josef Och and Hermann Ney. 2003. A Systematic Comparison of Various Statistical Alignment Models. *Computational Linguistics*, 29(1):19–51.

Pablo Gamallo Otero. 2007. Learning bilingual lexicons from comparable english and spanish corpora. In *Proceedings of MT Summit XI*, pages 191–198.

Emmanuel Prochasson, Emmanuel Morin, and Kyo Kageura. 2009. Anchor points for bilingual lexicon extraction from small comparable corpora. In *Machine Translation Summit 2009*, page 8.

Reinhard Rapp. 1999. Automatic identification of word translations from unrelated english and german corpora. In *Proceedings of the 37th Annual Meeting of the Association for Computational Linguistics*, pages 519–526, College Park, Maryland, USA, June. Association for Computational Linguistics.

Xabier Saralegi, Iñaki San Vicente, and Antton Gurrutxaga. 2008. Automatic extraction of bilingual terms from comparable corpora in a popular science domain. In *Proceedings of the Building and using Comparable Corpora workshop, 6th International Conference on Language Resources and Evaluations (LREC)*, Marrakech, Morocco.

Helmut Schmid. 1994. Probabilistic Part-of-Speech Tagging Using Decision Trees. In *Proceedings of the International Conference on New Methods in Language Processing*, pages 44–49, Manchester, UK.

Li Shao and Hwee Tou Ng. 2004. Mining new word translations from comparable corpora. In *Proceedings of Coling 2004*, pages 618–624, Geneva, Switzerland, Aug 23–Aug 27. COLING.

Matthew G. Snover, Bonnie J. Dorr, and Richard M. Schwartz. 2008. Language and translation model adaptation using comparable corpora. In *EMNLP*, pages 857–866.

Ralf Steinberger, Bruno Pouliquen, Anna Widiger, Camelia Ignat, Toma Erjavec, and Dan Tufi. 2006. The jrc-acquis: A multilingual aligned parallel corpus with 20+ languages. In *In Proceedings of the 5th International Conference on Language Resources and Evaluation (LREC'2006)*, pages 2142–2147.

Kun Yu and Junichi Tsujii. 2009. Extracting bilingual dictionary from comparable corpora with dependency heterogeneity. In *Proceedings of Human Language Technologies: The 2009 Annual Conference of the North American Chapter of the Association for Computational Linguistics, Companion Volume: Short Papers*, pages 121–124, Boulder, Colorado, June. Association for Computational Linguistics.

Bilingual Lexicon Extraction via Pivot Language and Word Alignment Tool

Hong-Seok Kwon Hyeong-Won Seo Jae-Hoon Kim
Korea Maritime University,
Dongsam-Dong, Yeongdo-Gu, Busan, South Korea
hong8c@naver.com, wonn24@gmail.com, jhoon@hhu.ac.kr

Abstract

This paper presents a simple and effective method for automatic bilingual lexicon extraction from less-known language pairs. To do this, we bring in a bridge language named the pivot language and adopt information retrieval techniques combined with natural language processing techniques. Moreover, we use a freely available word aligner: Anymalign (Lardilleux et al., 2011) for constructing context vectors. Unlike the previous works, we obtain context vectors via a pivot language. Therefore, we do not require to translate context vectors by using a seed dictionary and improve the accuracy of low frequency word alignments that is weakness of statistical model by using Anymalign. In this paper, experiments have been conducted on two different language pairs that are bi-directional Korean-Spanish and Korean-French, respectively. The experimental results have demonstrated that our method for high-frequency words shows at least 76.3 and up to 87.2% and for the low-frequency words at least 43.3% and up to 48.9% within the top 20 ranking candidates, respectively.

1 Introduction

Bilingual lexicons are an important resource in many domains, for example, machine translation, cross-language information retrieval, and so on. The direct way of bilingual lexicon extraction is to align words from a parallel corpus (Wu and Xia, 1994), which contains source texts and their translations. For some language pairs, however, collecting the parallel corpus is not easy and are restricted to specific domains. For these reasons, many researchers in bilingual lexicon extraction have focused on comparable corpora (Fung, 1995; Yu and Tsujii, 2009; Ismail and Manandhar, 2010). These corpora are also hard to build on less-known language pairs, for instances, Korean and Spanish, Korean and French, and so on. Therefore, some researchers have studied the use of pivot languages as an intermediary language to extract bilingual lexicons (Tanaka and Ummemura, 1994; Wu and Wang, 2007; Tsunakawa et al., 2008).

On the other hand, some researchers adopt information retrieval (IR) techniques to extract bilingual lexicons (Fung, 1998; Gaussier et al., 2004; Hazem et al., 2012). The techniques are collecting all the lexical units from each of two languages, L_1 and L_2, respectively, and then are generating context vectors S and T for the collected lexical units in $L_1$and L_2, respectively. The context vector, S and T are translated using seed dictionaries, which are manually constructed by hand and of which the size is huge for accurate translation. Finally, the context vectors, S and T are compared with each other in order to get their translation candidates.

In this paper, we propose a simple and effective method for bilingual lexicons between two less-known language pairs using a pivot language and IR techniques. The pivot language is used for representing both of context vectors of a source language and a target language and IR techniques for calculating the similarity between the source context vector and the target context vector represented by the pivot language. Unlike the previous studies, therefore, we use two parallel corpora, Korean (KR)-English (EN) and English (EN) and English (EN)-Spanish (ES). Here English is the pivot language. We also use a free available word aligner, called Anymalign to generate the context vectors easily.

The proposed method has many advantages such as easy adaptation to less-known language pairs through a pivot language like English, easy extension to multi-word expression, and dramatic reduction in labor-intensive words to get a large scale seed dictionary.

The remainder of this paper is organized as follows: we describe the proposed approach in Section 2. The experimental results are presented in Section 3. Finally Section 4 draws conclusions and discusses the future works.

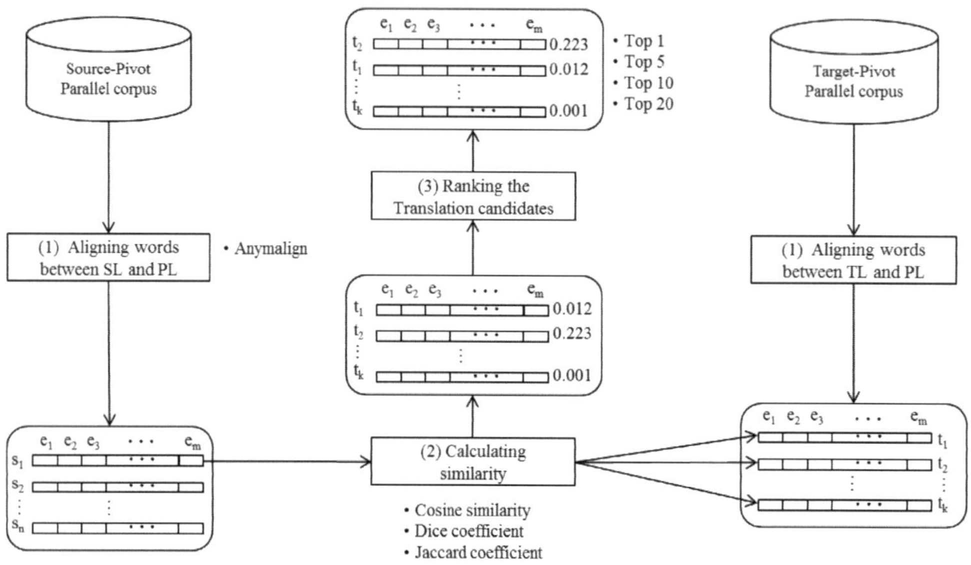

Figure 1. Overall structure of the proposed method.

2 Proposed Approach

In this paper, a simple and effective method for bilingual lexicons between two less-known language pairs using a pivot language and IR techniques. We use parallel corpora with more accurate alignment information instead of comparable corpora. It, however, is difficult to obtain parallel corpora for less-known language pairs. For such reasons, we use a pivot language which is well-known like English.

The pivot language is used for representing both of context vectors of a source language and a target language. Unlike the previous studies using comparable corpora, therefore, we use two parallel corpora through the pivot language like Korean (KR)-English (EN) and English (EN)-Spanish (ES) and IR techniques for calculating the similarity between the source context vector and the target context vector represented by the pivot language.

In the previous works, translating context-vectors is required using a seed dictionary, but in this paper, translating them is not needed anymore. Therefore, any bilingual dictionaries are not expected. Besides, we use a free available word aligner, called Anymalign, to construct context-vectors. Anymalign shows high accuracy for low-frequency words to extract translation candidates (Lardilleux et al., 2011). Overall structure of the proposed method is depicted in Figure 1. The proposed method can be summarized in the following three steps:

i. To build source context vectors and target source context vectors for each word in the source language (eg. KR) and the target language (eg. ES) using two sets of independent parallel corpora that are KR-EN and EN-ES, respectively. All words in context vectors are weighted by Anymalign.

ii. To calculate the similarity between each word in source context vector and all words in the target context vectors on the basis of the cosine measure

iii. To sort the top *k* word pairs based on their similarity scores

Two parallel corpora share a pivot language, English, in our case, and are used to build context vectors because Korean-Spanish bilingual corpora are publicly unavailable. Anymalign is used to weight all words in the context vectors.

As mentioned before, in the previous work, a seed dictionary is required to translate context vectors at this time, but we do not carry out them. After context vectors are built once, all source and target context vectors are compared each other to get its similarity between them by using the cosine measure. Finally, top *k* word pairs are extracted as a result.

3 Experiments and Results

In this paper, we extract translation candidates from two different language pairs that are bidirectional KR-ES and KR-FR.

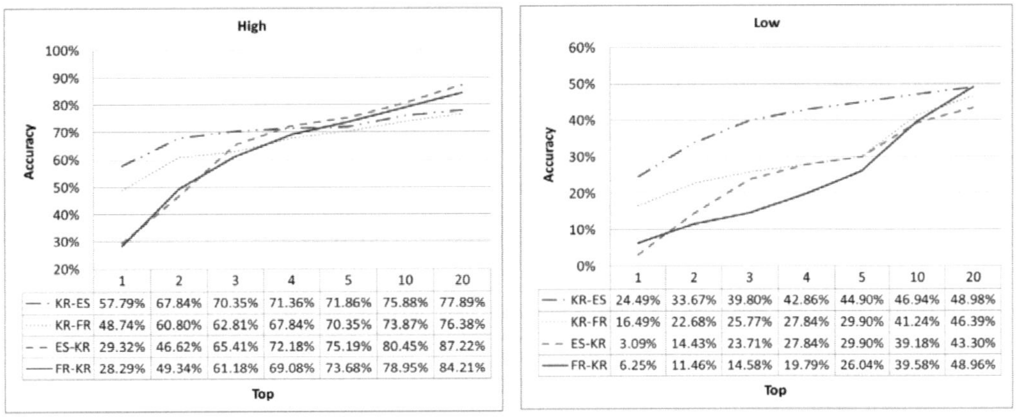

Figure 2. Accuracies of the proposed method for HIGH and LOW words.

3.1 Experimental setting

3.1.1 Parallel corpora

We used the KR-EN parallel corpora compiled by Seo et al. (2006) (433,151 sentence pairs), and two sets of sub-corpora (500,000 sentence pairs each) that are randomly selected from ES-EN and FR-EN in the Europarl parallel corpus (Koehn, 2005). The average number of words per sentence is described in Table 1 below. The number of words in ES-EN and FR-EN parallel corpora is nearly similar, but the number of KR words (called eojeol in Korean) in KR-EN parallel corpus is lower than that of EN words. In fact, KR words are a little bit different from EN words and others. Korean words consist of one morpheme or more. Therefore, the number of KR words can be similar to that of EN words if morphemes instead of words are counted.

KR-EN		ES-EN		FR-EN	
KR	**EN**	**ES**	**EN**	**FR**	**EN**
19.2	**31**	26.4	**25.4**	29.7	**27.1**

Table 1. The average number of words per sentence.

3.1.2 Data preprocessing

All words are tokenized by the following tools: Hannanum[1] (Lee et al., 1999) for Korean, TreeTagger[2] (Schmid, 1994) for English, Spanish and French. All words in English, Spanish, and French are converted to lower case, and those in Korean are morphologically analyzed into morphemes and pos-tagged by Hannanum.

[1] http://kldp.net/projects/hannanum

[2] http://www.ims.uni-stuttgart.de/projekte/corplex/TreeTagger/

3.1.3 Building evaluation dictionary

To evaluate the performance of the proposed method, we build two sets of bilingual lexicons (KR-ES and KR-FR) manually using the Web dictionary[3]. Each lexicon is unidirectional, meaning that they list the meanings of words of one language in another, and contains 100 high frequent words (denoted by HIGH hereafter) and 100 low rare words (denoted by LOW hereafter), respectively. The frequent words are randomly selected from 50% in high rank and the rare words from 20% in low rank. Table 2 shows the average number of the translations per source word in each lexicon. The number means the degree of ambiguity and is same as the number of polysemous words.

Evaluation dictionary	HIGH	LOW
KR-FR	5.79	2.26
KR-ES	7.36	3.12
ES-KR	10.31	5.49
FR-KR	10.42	6.32

Table 2. The average number of the translations per source word in the evaluation dictionaries.

3.1.4 Evaluation metrics

We evaluate the quality of translation candidates extracted by the proposed systems. Similar to the evaluation in information retrieval, the accuracy, the recall, and the mean reciprocal rank (MRR) (Voorhees, 1999) are used as evaluation metrics. The accuracy is the fraction of its translation candidates that are correct. The recall is the ratio of the suggested translation candidates that agree with the marked answer to the total number of translations in the evaluation words. The MRR is

[3] http://dic.naver.com/

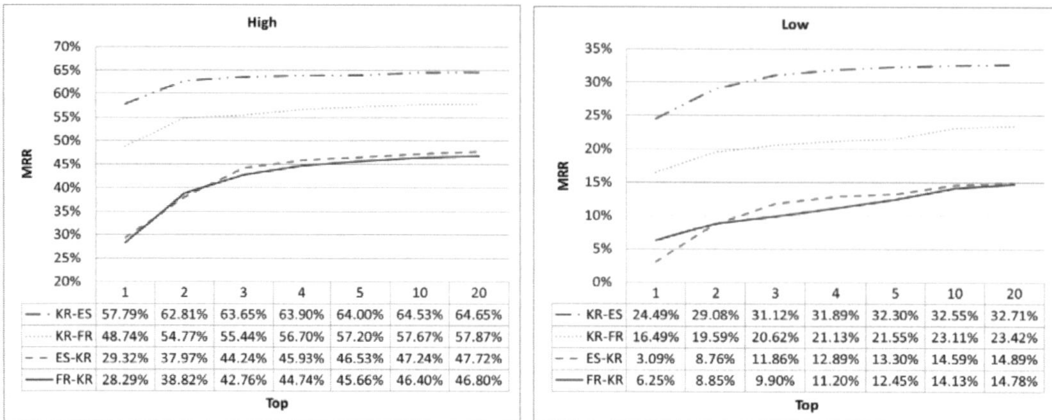

Figure 3. MRR of the proposed method for HIGH and LOW words.

the average of the reciprocal ranks of translation candidates that are correct translations for a sample of evaluation words.

3.2 Results

The accuracies of the HIGH and LOW words are shown in Figure 2. As seen in the figure, at the top 4 below, the accuracies of ES-KR and FR-KR are lower than the others. The difference can be attributed to stopwords such cardinal, ordinal, etc. The stopwords is normalized by Tree-Tagger for ES and FR, but not normalized by Korean POS-tagger (Hannanum). KR stopwords can badly affect the accuracies of ES-KR and FR-KR. In Table 3 below, '300' and '4' are stopwords and examples of the mistranslation of atención (attention)' in Spanish. Accordingly, '주목 (attention)' can be extracted as the first translation candidate if '300' and '4' are removed as stopwords.

Rank	Source language	Target language	Similarity score
1	atención	300	0.999
2	atención	주목 (attention)	0.993
3	atención	4	0.894
4	atención	눈(eye)	0.838
5	atención	모으(gather)	0.802

Table 3. Top 5 translation candidates of 'atención (attention)'.

The MRR results of the proposed method are shown in Figure 3. As shown in Figure 3, the MRR of the HIGH words is rapidly increased until the top 5, after then the MRR is steadily increased. This means that correct translation candidates tend to appear within the top 5. In the same experiments, the correct translation candidates for the LOW words tend to appear within top 10.

Lastly, the recalls of HIGH and LOW words are calculated in Table 4 below. As seen in the figure, the best recall is 32.7% on the KR-FR for HIGH words. One of reasons can be why words usually have one sense per corpus in parallel corpus (Fung, 1998). Another reason can be why words do not belong to various domains and our data sets only come from European Parliament proceedings and news article.

	Top20 Recall	
Language pairs	High 100	Low 100
KR-FR	32.73%	24.20%
KR-ES	27.49%	26.20%
ES-KR	29.55%	20.64%
FR-KR	27.30%	20.52%

Table 4. Recalls for HIGH and LOW words.

Our experimental results show that the proposed method is encouraging results because we do not use any linguistic resources such as a seed dictionary, and that the proposed method is sufficiently valuable where parallel corpus is unavailable between source and target languages.

4 Conclusion

We have presented an IR based approach for extracting bilingual lexicons from parallel corpus via pivot languages. We showed that the proposed method overcomes some of the problems of previous works that need a seed dictionary and use comparable corpora instead of parallel corpora in terms of lack of linguistic resources.

In future work, we will remove stopwords, and some words that have similar meaning could be clustered to improve the performance. Furthermore, we will handle multi word expression. Lastly, we plan to resolve a domain-constraint.

Acknowledgments

This work was supported by the Korea Ministry of Knowledge Economy (MKE) under Grant No.10041807

References

P. Fung. 1995. Compiling bilingual lexicon entries from a non-parallel English-Chinese corpus. In *Proceedings of the Third Workshop on Very Large Corpora (VLC'95)*, pages 173-183.

P. Fung. 1998. A statistical view on bilingual lexicon extraction: from parallel corpora to non-parallel corpora. In *Proceedings of the Parallel Text Processing*, pages 1-16.

E. Gaussier, J.-M. Renders, I. Matveeva, C. Goutte and H. Dejean. 2004. A geometric view on bilingual lexcion extraction from comparable corpora. In *Proceedings of the 42th Annual Meeting of the Association for Computational Linguistics*, Barcelona, Spain, pages 527-534.

A. Hazem and E. Morin. 2012. Adaptive dictionary for bilingual lexicon extraction from comparable corpora. In *Proceedings of the 8th International Conference on Language Resources and Evaluation (LREC'12)*, pages 288-292.

A. Ismail and S. Manandhar. 2010. Bilingual lexicon extraction from comparable corpora using in-domain terms. In *Proceedings of the International Conference on Computational Linguistics*, pages 481-489.

P. Koehn. 2005. EuroParl: A parallel corpus for statistical machine translation. In *proceedings of the Conference on the* 10th *Machine Translation Summit*, page 79-86.

W. Lee, S. Kim, G. Kim and K. Choi. 1999. Implementation of modularized morphological analyzer. In *Proceedings of The 11th Annual Conference on Human and Cognitive Language Technology*, pages 123-136.

A. Lardilleux, Y. Lepage, and F. Yvon. 2011. The contribution of low frequencies to multilingual sub-sentential alignment: a differential associative approach. *International Journal of Advanced Intelligence*, 3(2):189-217.

H Schmid. 1994. Probabilistic part-of-speech tagging using decision trees. In *Proceedings of International Conference on New Methods in Language Processing*, Manchester, UK, pages 44-49.

H. Seo, H. Kim, H. Cho, J. Kim and S. Yang, 2006. Automatically constructing English-Korean parallel corpus from web documents. *Korea Information Proceedings Society*, 13(2):161-164.

K. Tanaka and K. Umemura. 1994. Construction of a Bilingual Dictionary Intermediated by a Third Language. In *Proceedings of the 15th International Conference on Computational Linguistics (Coling' 94)*, Kyoto, Japan, August, pages 297-303.

T. Tsunakawa, N. Okazaki, and J. Tsujii. 2008. Building Bilingual Lexicons Using Lexical Translation Probabilities via Pivot Languages. In *Proceedings of the* 22nd *International Conference on Computational Linguistics,* Posters Proceedings, pages 18-22.

E. Voorhees. 1999. The TREC-8 Question Answering Track Report. In *8th Text Retrieval Conference (TREC-8)*, pages 77-82.

D. Wu and X. Xia. 1994. Learning an English-Chinese lexicon from a parallel corpus. In *Proceedings of the First Conference of the Association for Machine Translation in the Americas (AMTA 1994, Columbia, Maryland, USA, October)*, pages 206-213.

H. Wu and H. Wang. 2007. Pivot Language Approach for Phrase-Based Statistical Machine Translation. In *Proceedings of 45th Annual Meeting of the Association for Computational Linguistics*, pages 856-863.

K. Yu and J. Tsujii. 2009. Bilingual dictionary extraction from Wikipedia. In *Proceedings of the 12th Machine Translation Summit (MTS 2009)*, Ottawa, Ontario, Canada.

Using WordNet and Semantic Similarity for Bilingual Terminology Mining from Comparable Corpora

Dhouha Bouamor
CEA, LIST, Vision and Content Engineering Laboratory, 91191 Gif-sur-Yvette CEDEX France
dhouha.bouamor@cea.fr

Nasredine Semmar
CEA, LIST, Vision and Content Engineering Laboratory, 91191 Gif-sur-Yvette CEDEX France
nasredine.semmar@cea.fr

Pierre Zweigenbaum
LIMSI-CNRS, F-91403 Orsay CEDEX France
pz@limsi.fr

Abstract

This paper presents an extension of the standard approach used for bilingual lexicon extraction from comparable corpora. We study of the ambiguity problem revealed by the seed bilingual dictionary used to translate context vectors. For this purpose, we augment the standard approach by a Word Sense Disambiguation process relying on a WordNet-based semantic similarity measure. The aim of this process is to identify the translations that are more likely to give the best representation of words in the target language. On two specialized French-English comparable corpora, empirical experimental results show that the proposed method consistently outperforms the standard approach.

1 Introduction

Bilingual lexicons play a vital role in many Natural Language Processing applications such as Machine Translation (Och and Ney, 2003) or Cross-Language Information Retrieval (Shi, 2009). Research on lexical extraction from multilingual corpora have largely focused on parallel corpora. The scarcity of such corpora in particular for specialized domains and for language pairs not involving English pushed researchers to investigate the use of comparable corpora (Fung, 1998; Chiao and Zweigenbaum, 2003). These corpora are comprised of texts which are not exact translation of each other but share common features such as domain, genre, sampling period, etc.

The main work in this research area could be seen as an extension of Harris's *distributional hypothesis* (Harris, 1954). It is based on the simple observation that a word and its translation are likely to appear in similar contexts across languages (Rapp, 1995). Based on this assumption, the alignment method, known as the *standard approach* builds and compares context vectors for each word of the source and target languages.

A particularity of this approach is that, to enable the comparison of context vectors, it requires the existence of a seed bilingual dictionary to translate source context vectors. The use of the bilingual dictionary is problematic when a word has several translations, whether they are synonymous or polysemous. For instance, the French word *action* can be translated into English as *share, stock, lawsuit* or *deed*. In such cases, it is difficult to identify in flat resources like bilingual dictionaries, wherein entries are usually unweighted and unordered, which translations are most relevant. The standard approach considers all available translations and gives them the same importance in the resulting translated context vectors independently of the domain of interest and word ambiguity. Thus, in the financial domain, translating *action* into *deed* or *lawsuit* would probably introduce noise in context vectors.

In this paper, we present a novel approach which addresses the word ambiguity problem neglected in the standard approach. We introduce a use of a WordNet-based semantic similarity measure permitting the disambiguation of translated context vectors. The basic intuition behind this method is that instead of taking all translations of each seed word to translate a context vector, we only use the translations that are more likely to give the best representation of the context vector in the target language. We test the method on two specialized French-English comparable corpora *(financial and medical)* and report improved results, especially when many of the words in the corpus are ambiguous.

The remainder of the paper is organized as follows: Section 2 presents the standard approach and recalls in some details previous work addressing the task of bilingual lexicon extraction from comparable corpora. In section 3 we present our context disambiguation process. Before concluding and presenting directions for future work, we describe in section 4 the experimental protocol we followed and discuss the obtained results.

2 Bilingual lexicon extraction

2.1 Standard Approach

Most previous works addressing the task of bilingual lexicon extraction from comparable corpora are based on the standard approach (Fung, 1998; Chiao and Zweigenbaum, 2002; Laroche and Langlais, 2010). Formally, this approach is composed of the following three steps:

1. **Building context vectors**: Vectors are first extracted by identifying the words that appear around the term to be translated S in a window of N words. Generally, an association measure like the mutual information (Morin and Daille, 2006), the log-likelihood (Morin and Prochasson, 2011) or the Discounted Odds-Ratio (Laroche and Langlais, 2010) are employed to shape the context vectors.

2. **Translation of context vectors**: To enable the comparison of source and target vectors, source terms vectors are translated in the target language by using a seed bilingual dictionary. Whenever it provides several translations for an element, all proposed translations are considered. Words not included in the bilingual dictionary are simply ignored.

3. **Comparison of source and target vectors**: Translated vectors are compared to target ones using a similarity measure. The most widely used is the cosine similarity, but many authors have studied alternative metrics such as the Weighted Jaccard index (Prochasson et al., 2009) or the City-Block distance (Rapp, 1999). According to similarity values, a ranked list of translations for S is obtained.

2.2 Related Work

Recent improvements of the standard approach are based on the assumption that the more the context vectors are representative, the better the bilingual lexicon extraction is. Prochasson et al. (2009) used transliterated words and scientific compound words as 'anchor points'. Giving these words higher priority when comparing target vectors improved bilingual lexicon extraction. In addition to transliteration, Rubino and Linarès (2011) combined the contextual representation within a thematic one. The basic intuition of their work is that a term and its translation share thematic similarities. Hazem and Morin (2012) recently proposed a method that filters the entries of the bilingual dictionary based upon POS-tagging and domain relevance criteria, but no improvements was demonstrated.

Gaussier et al. (2004) attempted to solve the problem of different word ambiguities in the source and target languages. They investigated a number of techniques including canonical correlation analysis and multilingual probabilistic latent semantic analysis. The best results, with a very small improvement were reported for a mixed method. One important difference with Gaussier et al. (2004) is that they focus on words ambiguities on source and target languages, whereas we consider that it is sufficient to disambiguate only translated source context vectors.

A large number of Word Sense Disambiguation WSD techniques were previously proposed in the literature. The most popular ones are those that compute semantic similarity with the help of existing thesauri such as WordNet (Fellbaum, 1998). This resource groups English words into sets of synonyms called *synsets*, provides short, general definitions and records various semantic relations (hypernymy, meronymy, etc.) between these synonym sets. This thesaurus has been applied to many tasks relying on word-based similarity, including document (Hwang et al., 2011) and image (Cho et al., 2007; Choi et al., 2012) retrieval systems. In this work, we use this resource to derive a semantic similarity between lexical units within the same context vector. To the best of our knowledge, this is the first application of WordNet to the task of bilingual lexicon extraction from comparable corpora.

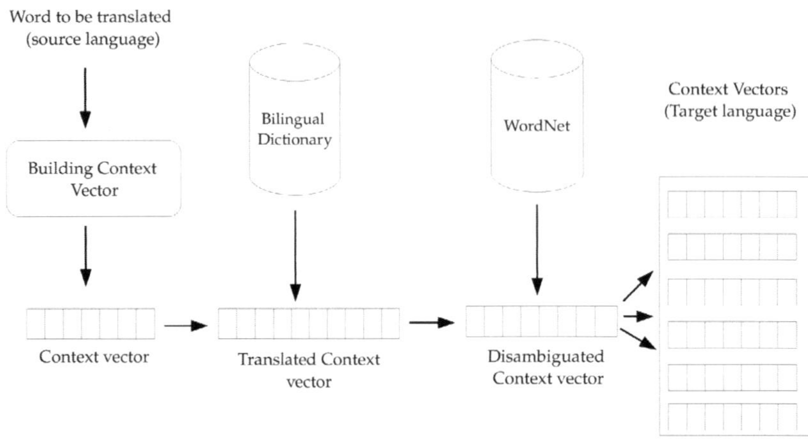

Figure 1: Overall architecture of the lexical extraction approach

3 Context Vector Disambiguation

The approach we propose includes the three steps of the standard approach. As it was mentioned in section 1, when lexical extraction applies to a specific domain, not all translations in the bilingual dictionary are relevant for the target context vector representation. For this reason, we introduce a WordNet-based WSD process that aims at improving the adequacy of context vectors and therefore improve the results of the standard approach. Figure 1 shows the overall architecture of the lexical extraction process. Once translated into the target language, the context vectors disambiguation process intervenes. This process operates *locally* on each context vector and aims at finding the most prominent translations of polysemous words. For this purpose, we use monosemic words as a seed set of disambiguated words to infer the polysemous word's translations senses. We hypothesize that a word is monosemic if it is associated to only one entry in the bilingual dictionary. We checked this assumption by probing monosemic entries of the bilingual dictionary against WordNet and found that 95% of the entries are monosemic in both resources.

Formally, we derive a semantic similarity value between all the translations provided for each polysemous word by the bilingual dictionary and all monosemic words appearing whithin the same context vector. There is a relatively large number of word-to-word similarity metrics that were previously proposed in the literature, ranging from path-length measures computed on semantic networks, to metrics based on models of distributional similarity learned from large text collections. For simplicity, we use in this work, the Wu and Palmer (1994) (WUP) path-length-based semantic similarity measure. It was demonstrated by (Lin, 1998) that this metric achieves good performances among other measures. WUP computes a score (equation 1) denoting how similar two word senses are, based on the depth of the two synsets (s_1 and s_2) in the WordNet taxonomy and that of their Least Common Subsumer (LCS), i.e., the most specific word that they share as an ancestor.

$$Wup_{Sim}(s_1, s_2) = \frac{2 \times depth(LCS)}{depth(s_1) + depth(s_2)} \quad (1)$$

In practice, since a word can belong to more than one synset in WordNet, we determine the semantic similarity between two words w_1 and w_2 as the maximum Wup_{Sim} between the synset or the synsets that include the $synsets(w_1)$ and $synsets(w_2)$ according to the following equation:

$$Sem_{Sim}(w_1, w_2) = \max\{Wup_{Sim}(s_1, s_2); (s_1, s_2) \in synsets(w_1) \times synsets(w_2)\} \quad (2)$$

Context Vector	Translations	Comparison	Ave_Sim
liquidité	liquidity	–	–
action	act	Sem_{Sim}(act,liquidity), Sem_{Sim}(act,dividend)	0.2139
	action	Sem_{Sim}(action,liquidity), Sem_{Sim}(action,dividend)	0.4256
	stock	Sem_{Sim}(stock,liquidity), Sem_{Sim}(stock,dividend)	***0.5236***
	deed	Sem_{Sim}(deed,liquidity), Sem_{Sim}(deed,dividend)	0.1594
	lawsuit	Sem_{Sim}(lawsuit,liquidity), Sem_{Sim}(lawsuit,dividend)	0.1212
	fact	Sem_{Sim}(fact,liquidity), Sem_{Sim}(fact,dividend)	0.1934
	operation	Sem_{Sim}(operation,liquidity), Sem_{Sim}(operation,dividend)	0.2045
	share	Sem_{Sim}(share,liquidity), Sem_{Sim}(share,dividend)	***0.5236***
	plot	Sem_{Sim}(plot,liquidity), Sem_{Sim}(plot,dividend)	0.2011
dividende	dividend	–	–

Table 1: Disambiguation of the context vector of the French term *bénéfice [income]* in the *corporate finance* domain. *liquidité* and *dividende* are monosemic and are used to infer the most similar translations of the term *action*.

Then, to identify the most prominent translations of each polysemous unit w_p, an *average similarity* is computed for each translation w_p^j of w_p:

$$Ave\_Sim(w_p^j) = \frac{\sum_{i=1}^{N} Sem_{Sim}(w_i, w_p^j)}{N} \quad (3)$$

where N is the total number of monosemic words and Sem_{Sim} is the similarity value of w_p^j and the ith monosemic word. Hence, according to average relatedness values $Ave\_Sim(w_p^j)$, we obtain for each polysemous word w_p an ordered list of translations $w_p^1 \dots w_p^n$. This allows us to select translations of words which are more salient than the others to represent the word to be translated.

In Table 1, we present the results of the disambiguation process for the context vector of the French term *bénéfice* in the *corporate finance* corpus. This vector contains the words *action*, *dividende*, *liquidité* and others. The bilingual dictionary provides the following translations {*act, stock, action, deed, lawsuit, fact, operation, plot, share*} for the French polysemous word *action*. We use the monosemic words *dividende* and *liquidité* to disambiguate the word *action*. From observing average similariy values (Ave_Sim), we notice that the words *share* and *stock* are on the top of the list and therefore are most likely to represent the source word *action* in this context.

Corpus	French	English
Corporate finance	$402,486$	$756,840$
Breast cancer	$396,524$	$524,805$

Table 2: Comparable corpora sizes in term of words.

4 Experiments and Results

4.1 Resources

4.1.1 Comparable corpora

We conducted our experiments on two French-English comparable corpora specialized on the *corporate finance* and the *breast cancer* domains. Both corpora were extracted from Wikipedia[1]. We consider the topic in the source language (for instance *finance des entreprises* [corporate finance]) as a query to Wikipedia and extract all its sub-topics (i.e., sub-categories in Wikipedia) to construct a domain-specific *category tree*. A sample of the *corporate finance* sub-domain's category tree is shown in Figure 2. Then, based on the constructed tree, we collect all Wikipedia pages belonging to one of these categories and use *inter-language links* to build the comparable corpus. Both corpora were normalized through the following linguistic preprocessing steps: tokenisation, part-of-speech tagging, lemmatisation, and function word removal. The resulting corpora[2] sizes are given in Table 2.

[1] `http://dumps.wikimedia.org/`
[2] Comparable corpora will be shared publicly

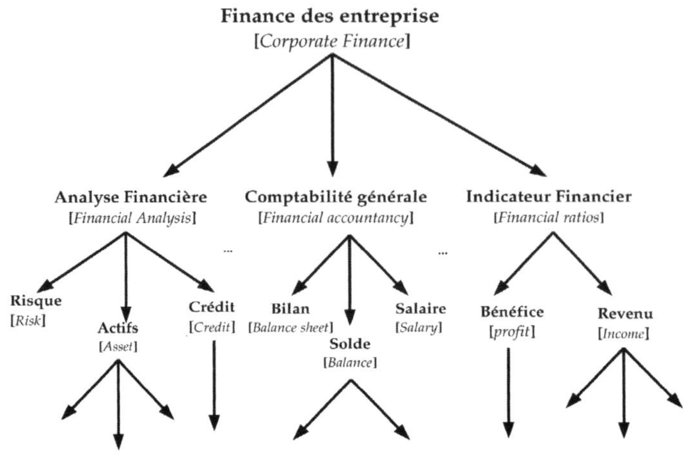

Figure 2: Wikipedia categories tree of the *corporate finance* sub-domain.

4.1.2 Bilingual dictionary

The bilingual dictionary used to translate context vectors consists of an in-house manually revised bilingual dictionary which contains about 120,000 entries belonging to the general domain. It is important to note that words on both corpora has on average, 7 translations in the bilingual dictionary.

4.1.3 Evaluation list

In bilingual terminology extraction from comparable corpora, a reference list is required to evaluate the performance of the alignment. Such lists are usually composed of about 100 single terms (Hazem and Morin, 2012; Chiao and Zweigenbaum, 2002). Here, we created two reference lists[3] for the *corporate finance* and the *breast cancer* domains. The first list is composed of 125 single terms extracted from the glossary of bilingual micro-finance terms[4]. The second list contains 96 terms extracted from the French-English MESH and the UMLS thesauri[5]. Note that reference terms pairs appear at least five times in each part of both comparable corpora.

4.2 Experimental setup

Three other parameters need to be set up: (1) the window size, (2) the association measure and the (3) similarity measure. To define context vectors, we use a seven-word window as it approximates syntactic dependencies. Concerning the rest of the parameters, we followed Laroche and Langlais (2010) for their definition. The authors carried out a complete study of the influence of these parameters on the bilingual alignment and showed that the most effective configuration is to combine the Discounted Log-Odds ratio (equation 4) with the cosine similarity. The Discounted Log-Odds ratio is defined as follows:

$$\textit{Odds-Ratio}_{disc} = \log \frac{(O_{11} + \frac{1}{2})(O_{22} + \frac{1}{2})}{(O_{12} + \frac{1}{2})(O_{21} + \frac{1}{2})} \quad (4)$$

where O_{ij} are the cells of the 2×2 contingency matrix of a token s co-occurring with the term S within a given window size.

4.3 Results and discussion

It is difficult to compare results between different studies published on bilingual lexicon extraction from comparable corpora, because of difference between (1) used corpora (in particular their construction constraints and volume), (2) target domains, and also (3) the coverage and relevance of linguistic resources used for translation. To the best of our knowledge, there is no common benchmark that can serve as a reference. For this reason, we use the results of the standard approach (SA) described in section 2.1 as a reference. We evaluate the performance of both the SA and ours with respect to Top$N$ precision (P_N), recall (R_N) and Mean Reciprocal Rank (MRR) (Voorhees, 1999). Precision is the total number of correct translations divided by the number of terms for which the system gave at least one answer. Recall is equal to

[3]Reference lists will be shared publicly
[4]`http://www.microfinance.lu/en/`
[5]`http://www.nlm.nih.gov/`

a) Corporate Finance

Method	P1	P10	P20	R1	R10	R20	MRR
Standard Approach (SA)	0.046	0.140	0.186	0.040	0.120	0.160	0.064
WN-T_1	0.065	0.196	0.261	0.056	0.168	0.224	0.089
WN-T_2	0.102	**0.252**	0.308	0.080	**0.216**	0.264	0.122
WN-T_3	0.102	0.242	**0.327**	0.088	0.208	**0.280**	0.122
WN-T_4	**0.112**	0.224	0.299	**0.090**	0.190	0.250	**0.124**
WN-T_5	0.093	0.205	0.280	0.080	0.176	0.240	0.110
WN-T_6	0.084	0.205	0.233	0.072	0.176	0.200	0.094
WN-T_7	0.074	0.177	0.242	0.064	0.152	0.208	0.090

b) Breast Cancer

Method	P1	P10	P20	R1	R10	R20	MRR
Standard Approach (SA)	0.342	0.542	0.585	0.250	0.395	0.427	0.314
WN-T_1	0.257	0.500	0.571	0.187	0.364	0.416	0.257
WN-T_2	0.314	0.614	**0.671**	0.229	0.447	**0.489**	0.313
WN-T_3	0.342	**0.628**	**0.671**	0.250	**0.458**	**0.489**	0.342
WN-T_4	0.342	0.571	0.642	0.250	0.416	0.468	0.332
WN-T_5	**0.357**	0.571	0.657	**0.260**	0.416	0.479	**0.348**
WN-T_6	0.357	0.571	0.652	0.260	0.416	0.468	0.347
WN-T_7	0.357	0.585	0.657	0.260	0.427	0.479	0.339

Table 3: Precision, Recall at Top$N$ (N=1,10,20) and MRR at Top20 for the two domains. In each column, bold show best results. Underline show best results overall.

the ratio of correct translation to the total number of terms. The MRR takes into account the rank of the first good translation found for each entry. Formally, it is defined as:

$$MRR = \frac{1}{Q} \sum_{|Q|}^{i=1} \frac{1}{rank_i} \tag{5}$$

where Q is the total number of terms to be translated and $rank_i$ is the position of the first correct translation in the translations candidates.

Our method provides a ranked list of translations for each polysemous word. A question that arises here is whether we should introduce only the best ranked translation in the context vector or consider a larger number of words, especially when a translations list contain synonyms (*share* and *stock* in Table 1). For this reason, we take into account in our experiments different number of translations, noted WN-T_i, ranging from the pivot translation ($i = 1$) to the seventh word in the translations list. This choice is motivated by the fact that words in both corpora have on average 7 translations in the bilingual dictionary. The baseline (SA) uses all translations associated to each entry in the bilingual dictionary. Table 3a displays the results obtained for the *corporate finance* corpus. The first substantial observation is that our method which consists in disambiguating polysemous words within context vectors consistently outperforms the standard approach (SA) for all configurations. The best MRR is reported when for each polysemous word, we keep the most similar four translations (WN-T_4) in the context vector of the term to be translated. However, the highest Top20 precision and recall are obtained by WN-T_3. Using the top three word translations in the vector boosts the Top20 precision from 0.186 to 0.327 and the Top20 recall from 0.160 to 0.280. Concerning the Breast Cancer corpus, slightly different results were obtained. As Table 3b show, when the context vectors are totally disambiguated (i.e. each source unit is translated by at most one word in context vectors), all Top$N$ precision, recall and MRR decrease. However, we report improvements against the SA in most other cases. For WN-T_5, we obtain the maximum MRR score with an improvement of $+0.034$ over the SA. But, as for the *corporate finance* corpus, the best Top20 precision and recall are reached by the WN-T_3 method, with a gain of $+0.082$ in both Top10 and Top20 precision and of about $+0.06$ in Top10 and Top20 recall.

From observing result tables of both *corporate finance* and *breast cancer* domains, we notice that our approach performs better than the SA but with different degrees. The improvements achieved in

Corpus	Corpus P_R	Vectors P_R
Corporate finance	41%	$91,6\%$
Breast cancer	47%	$85,1\%$

Table 4: Comparable corpora's and context vector's Polysemy Rates P_R.

the *corporate finance* domain are higher than those reported in the *breast cancer* domain. The reason being that the vocabulary used in the *breast cancer* corpus is more specific and therefore less ambiguous than that used in *corporate finance* texts. The results given in table 4 validate this assumption. In this table, we give the polysemy rates of the comparable corpora (Corpus P_R) and that of context vectors (Vectors P_R). P_R indicates the percentage of words that are associated to more than one translation in the bilingual dictionary. The results show that *breast cancer* corpus is more polysemic than that of the *corporate finance*. Nevertheless, even if in both corpora, the candidates' context vectors are highly polysemous, *breast cancer*'s context vectors are less polysemous than those of the *corporate finance* texts. In this corpus, $91,6\%$ of the words used as entries to define context vectors are polysemous. This shows that the ambiguity present in specialized comparable corpora hampers bilingual lexicon extraction, and that disambiguation positively affects the overall results. Even though the two corpora are fairly different (subject and polysemy rate), the optimal Top20 precision and recall results are obtained when considering up to three most similar translations in context vectors. This behavior shows that the disambiguation method is relatively robust to domain change. We notice also that the addition of supplementary translations, which are probably noisy in the given domain, degrades the overall results but remains greater than the SA.

5 Conclusion

We presented in this paper a novel method that extends the standard approach used for bilingual lexicon extraction from comparable corpora. The proposed method disambiguates polysemous words in context vectors and selects only the translations that are most relevant to the general context of the corpus. Conducted experiments on two highly polysemous specialized comparable corpora show that integrating such process leads to a better performance than the standard approach. Although our initial experiments are positive, we believe that they could be improved in a number of ways. In addition to the metric defined by (Wu and Palmer, 1994), we plan to apply other semantic similarity and relatedness measures and compare their performance. It would also be interesting to mine much more larger comparable corpora and focus on their quality as presented in (Li and Gaussier, 2010). We want also to test our method on bilingual lexicon extraction for a larger panel of specialized corpora, where disambiguation methods are needed to prune translations that are irrelevant to the domain.

References

Yun-Chuang Chiao and Pierre Zweigenbaum. 2002. Looking for candidate translational equivalents in specialized, comparable corpora. In *Proceedings of the 19th international conference on Computational linguistics - Volume 2*, COLING '02, pages 1–5. Association for Computational Linguistics.

Yun-Chuang Chiao and Pierre Zweigenbaum. 2003. The effect of a general lexicon in corpus-based identification of french-english medical word translations. In *Proceedings Medical Informatics Europe, volume 95 of Studies in Health Technology and Informatics*, pages 397–402, Amsterdam.

Miyoung Cho, Chang Choi, Hanil Kim, Jungpil Shin, and PanKoo Kim. 2007. Efficient image retrieval using conceptualization of annotated images. Lecture Notes in Computer Science, pages 426–433. Springer.

Dongjin Choi, Jungin Kim, Hayoung Kim, Myunggwon Hwang, and Pankoo Kim. 2012. A method for enhancing image retrieval based on annotation using modified wup similarity in wordnet. In *Proceedings of the 11th WSEAS international conference on Artificial Intelligence, Knowledge Engineering and Data Bases*, AIKED'12, pages 83–87, Stevens Point, Wisconsin, USA. World Scientific and Engineering Academy and Society (WSEAS).

Christiane Fellbaum. 1998. *WordNet: An Electronic Lexical Database*. Bradford Books.

Pascale Fung. 1998. A statistical view on bilingual lexicon extraction: From parallel corpora to non-parallel corpora. In *Parallel Text Processing*, pages 1–17. Springer.

Éric Gaussier, Jean-Michel Renders, Irina Matveeva, Cyril Goutte, and Hervé Déjean. 2004. A geometric view on bilingual lexicon extraction from comparable corpora. In *ACL*, pages 526–533.

Z.S. Harris. 1954. Distributional structure. *Word*.

Amir Hazem and Emmanuel Morin. 2012. Adaptive dictionary for bilingual lexicon extraction from comparable corpora. In *Proceedings, 8th international conference on Language Resources and Evaluation (LREC)*, Istanbul, Turkey, May.

Myunggwon Hwang, Chang Choi, and Pankoo Kim. 2011. Automatic enrichment of semantic relation network and its application to word sense disambiguation. *IEEE Transactions on Knowledge and Data Engineering*, 23:845–858.

Audrey Laroche and Philippe Langlais. 2010. Revisiting context-based projection methods for term-translation spotting in comparable corpora. In *23rd International Conference on Computational Linguistics (Coling 2010)*, pages 617–625, Beijing, China, Aug.

Bo Li and Ëric Gaussier. 2010. Improving corpus comparability for bilingual lexicon extraction from comparable corpora. In *23rd International Conference on Computational Linguistics (Coling 2010)*, Beijing, China, Aug.

Dekang Lin. 1998. An information-theoretic definition of similarity. In *Proceedings of the Fifteenth International Conference on Machine Learning*, ICML '98, pages 296–304, San Francisco, CA, USA. Morgan Kaufmann Publishers Inc.

Emmanuel Morin and Béatrice Daille. 2006. Comparabilité de corpus et fouille terminologique multilingue. In *Traitement Automatique des Langues (TAL)*.

Emmanuel Morin and Emmanuel Prochasson. 2011. Bilingual lexicon extraction from comparable corpora enhanced with parallel corpora. In *Proceedings, 4th Workshop on Building and Using Comparable Corpora (BUCC)*, page 27–34, Portland, Oregon, USA.

Franz Josef Och and Hermann Ney. 2003. A systematic comparison of various statistical alignment models. *Comput. Linguist.*, 29(1):19–51, March.

Emmanuel Prochasson, Emmanuel Morin, and Kyo Kageura. 2009. Anchor points for bilingual lexicon extraction from small comparable corpora. In *Proceedings, 12th Conference on Machine Translation Summit (MT Summit XII)*, page 284–291, Ottawa, Ontario, Canada.

Reinhard Rapp. 1995. Identifying word translations in non-parallel texts. In *Proceedings of the 33rd annual meeting on Association for Computational Linguistics*, ACL '95, pages 320–322. Association for Computational Linguistics.

Reinhard Rapp. 1999. Automatic identification of word translations from unrelated english and german corpora. In *Proceedings of the 37th annual meeting of the Association for Computational Linguistics on Computational Linguistics*, ACL '99, pages 519–526. Association for Computational Linguistics.

Raphaël Rubino and Georges Linarès. 2011. A multi-view approach for term translation spotting. In *Computational Linguistics and Intelligent Text Processing*, Lecture Notes in Computer Science, pages 29–40.

Lei Shi. 2009. Adaptive web mining of bilingual lexicons for cross language information retrieval. In *Proceedings of the 18th ACM conference on Information and knowledge management*, CIKM '09, pages 1561–1564, New York, NY, USA. ACM.

Ellen M. Voorhees. 1999. The trec-8 question answering track report. In *In Proceedings of TREC-8*, pages 77–82.

Zhibiao Wu and Martha Palmer. 1994. Verbs semantics and lexical selection. In *Proceedings of the 32nd annual meeting on Association for Computational Linguistics*, ACL '94, pages 133–138. Association for Computational Linguistics.

A Comparison of Smoothing Techniques for Bilingual Lexicon Extraction from Comparable Corpora

Amir Hazem and **Emmanuel Morin**
Laboratore d'Informatique de Nantes-Atlantique (LINA)
Université de Nantes, 44322 Nantes Cedex 3, France
{Amir.Hazem, Emmanuel.Morin}@univ-nantes.fr

Abstract

Smoothing is a central issue in language modeling and a prior step in different natural language processing (NLP) tasks. However, less attention has been given to it for bilingual lexicon extraction from comparable corpora. If a first work to improve the extraction of low frequency words showed significant improvement while using distance-based averaging (Pekar et al., 2006), no investigation of the many smoothing techniques has been carried out so far. In this paper, we present a study of some widely-used smoothing algorithms for language n-gram modeling (Laplace, Good-Turing, Kneser-Ney...). Our main contribution is to investigate how the different smoothing techniques affect the performance of the standard approach (Fung, 1998) traditionally used for bilingual lexicon extraction. We show that using smoothing as a pre-processing step of the standard approach increases its performance significantly.

1 Introduction

Cooccurrences play an important role in many corpus based approaches in the field of natural-language processing (Dagan et al., 1993). They represent the observable evidence that can be distilled from a corpus and are employed for a variety of applications such as machine translation (Brown et al., 1992), information retrieval (Maarek and Smadja, 1989), word sense disambiguation (Brown et al., 1991), etc. In bilingual lexicon extraction from comparable corpora, frequency counts for word pairs often serve as a basis for distributional methods, such as the standard approach (Fung, 1998) which compares the cooccurrence profile of a given source word, a vector of association scores for its translated cooccurrences (Fano, 1961; Dunning, 1993), with the profiles of all words of the target language. The distance between two such vectors is interpreted as an indicator of their semantic similarity and their translational relation. If using association measures to extract word translation equivalents has shown a better performance than using a raw cooccurrence model, the latter remains the core of any statistical generalisation (Evert, 2005).

As has been known, words and other type-rich linguistic populations do not contain instances of all types in the population, even the largest samples (Zipf, 1949; Evert and Baroni, 2007). Therefore, the number and distribution of types in the available sample are not reliable estimators (Evert and Baroni, 2007), especially for small comparable corpora. The literature suggests two major approaches for solving the data sparseness problem: smoothing and class-based methods. Smoothing techniques (Good, 1953) are often used to better estimate probabilities when there is insufficient data to estimate probabilities accurately. They tend to make distributions more uniform, by adjusting low probabilities such as zero probabilities upward, and high probabilities downward. Generally, smoothing methods not only prevent zero probabilities, but they also attempt to improve the accuracy of the model as a whole (Chen and Goodman, 1999). Class-based models (Pereira et al., 1993) use classes of similar words to distinguish between unseen cooccurrences. The relationship between given words is modeled by analogy with other words that are in some sense similar to the given ones. Hence, class-based models provide an alternative to the independence assumption on the cooccurrence of given words w_1 and w_2: the more frequent w_2 is, the higher estimate of $P(w_2|w_1)$ will be, regardless of w_1.

Starting from the observation that smoothing estimates ignore the expected degree of association between words (assign the same estimate for all unseen cooccurrences) and that class-based models may not structure and generalize word cooccurrence to class cooccurrence patterns without losing too much information, (Dagan et al., 1993) proposed an alternative to these latter approaches to estimate the probabilities of unseen cooccurrences. They presented a method that makes analogies between each specific unseen cooccurrence and other cooccurrences that contain similar words. The analogies are based on the assumption that similar word cooccurrences have similar values of mutual information. Their method has shown significant improvement for both: word sense disambiguation in machine translation and data recovery tasks. (Pekar et al., 2006) employed the nearest neighbor variety of the previous approach to extract translation equivalents for low frequency words from comparable corpora. They used a distance-based averaging technique for smoothing (Dagan et al., 1999). Their method yielded a significant improvement in relation to low frequency words.

Starting from the assumption that smoothing improves the accuracy of the model as a whole (Chen and Goodman, 1999), we believe that smoothed context vectors should lead to better performance for bilingual terminology extraction from comparable corpora. In this work we carry out an empirical comparison of the most widely-used smoothing techniques, including additive smoothing (Lidstone, 1920), Good-Turing estimate (Good, 1953), Jelinek-Mercer (Mercer, 1980), Katz (Katz, 1987) and kneser-Ney smoothing (Kneser and Ney, 1995). Unlike (Pekar et al., 2006), the present work does not investigate unseen words. We only concentrate on observed cooccurrences. We believe it constitutes the most systematic comparison made so far with different smoothing techniques for aligning translation equivalents from comparable corpora. We show that using smoothing as a pre-processing step of the standard approach, leads to significant improvement even without considering unseen cooccurrences.

In the remainder of this paper, we present in Section 2, the different smoothing techniques. The steps of the standard approach and our extended method are then described in Section 3. Section 4 describes the experimental setup and our resources. Section 5 presents the experiments and comments on several results. We finally discuss the results in Section 6 and conclude in Section 7.

2 Smoothing Techniques

Smoothing describes techniques for adjusting the maximum likelihood estimate of probabilities to reduce more accurate probabilities. The smoothing techniques tend to make distributions more uniform. In this section we present the most widely used techniques.

2.1 Additive Smoothing

The Laplace estimator or the additive smoothing (Lidstone, 1920; Johnson, 1932; Jeffreys, 1948) is one of the simplest types of smoothing. Its principle is to estimate probabilities P assuming that each unseen word type actually occurred once. Then, if we have N events and V possible words instead of :

$$\mathrm{P(w)} = \frac{\mathrm{occ(w)}}{\mathrm{N}} \tag{1}$$

We estimate:

$$\mathrm{P_{addone}(w)} = \frac{\mathrm{occ(w)} + 1}{\mathrm{N} + \mathrm{V}} \tag{2}$$

Applying Laplace estimation to word's cooccurrence suppose that : if two words cooccur together n times in a corpus, they can cooccur together $(n+1)$ times. According to the maximum likelihood estimation (MLE):

$$\mathrm{P(w_{i+1}|w_i)} = \frac{\mathrm{C(w_i, w_{i+1})}}{\mathrm{C(w_i)}} \tag{3}$$

Laplace smoothing:

$$\mathrm{P^*(w_{i+1}|w_i)} = \frac{\mathrm{C(w_i, w_{i+1})} + 1}{\mathrm{C(w_i)} + \mathrm{V}} \tag{4}$$

Several disadvantages emanate from this method:

1. The probability of frequent n-grams is underestimated.
2. The probability of rare or unseen n-grams is overestimated.

3. All the unseen n-grams are smoothed in the same way.

4. Too much probability mass is shifted towards unseen n-grams.

One improvement is to use smaller added count following the equation below:

$$P^*(w_{i+1}|w_i) = \frac{\delta + C(w_i, w_{i+1})}{\delta|V| + C(w_i)} \quad (5)$$

with $\delta \in]0, 1]$.

2.2 Good-Turing Estimator

The Good-Turing estimator (Good, 1953) provides another way to smooth probabilities. It states that for any n-gram that occurs r times, we should pretend that it occurs r^* times. The Good-Turing estimators use the count of things you have seen once to help estimate the count of things you have never seen. In order to compute the frequency of words, we need to compute N_c, the number of events that occur c times (assuming that all items are binomially distributed). Let N_r be the number of items that occur r times. N_r can be used to provide a better estimate of r, given the binomial distribution. The adjusted frequency r^* is then:

$$r^* = (r+1)\frac{N_{r+1}}{N_r} \quad (6)$$

2.3 Jelinek-Mercer Smoothing

As one alternative to missing n-grams, useful information can be provided by the corresponding (n-1)-gram probability estimate. A simple method for combining the information from lower-order n-gram in estimating higher-order probabilities is linear interpolation (Mercer, 1980). The equation of linear interpolation is given below:

$$P_{int}(w_{i+1}|w_i) = \lambda P(w_{i+1}|w_i) + (1-\lambda)P(w_i) \quad (7)$$

λ is the confidence weight for the longer n-gram. In general, λ is learned from a held-out corpus. It is useful to interpolate higher-order n-gram models with lower-order n-gram models, because when there is insufficient data to estimate a probability in the higher order model, the lower-order model can often provide useful information. Instead of the cooccurrence counts, we used the Good-Turing estimator in the linear interpolation as follows:

$$c^*_{int}(w_{i+1}|w_i) = \lambda c^*(w_{i+1}|w_i) + (1-\lambda)P(w_i) \quad (8)$$

2.4 Katz Smoothing

(Katz, 1987) extends the intuitions of Good-Turing estimate by adding the combination of higher-order models with lower-order models. For a bigram w^i_{i-1} with count $r = c(w^i_{i-1})$, its corrected count is given by the equation:

$$c_{katz}(w^i_{i-1}) = \begin{cases} r^* & \text{if } r > 0 \\ \alpha(w_{i-1})PML(w_i) & \text{if } r = 0 \end{cases} \quad (9)$$

and:

$$\alpha(w_{i-1}) = \frac{1 - \sum_{w_i:c(w^i_{i-1})>0} P_{katz}(w^i_{i-1})}{1 - \sum_{w_i:c(w^i_{i-1})>0} PML(w_{i-1})} \quad (10)$$

According to (Katz, 1987), the general discounted estimate c^* of Good-Turing is not used for all counts c. Large counts where $c > k$ for some threshold k are assumed to be reliable. (Katz, 1987) suggests $k = 5$. Thus, we define $c^* = c$ for $c > k$, and:

$$c^* = \frac{(c+1)\frac{N_{c+1}}{N_c} - c\frac{(k+1)N_{k+1}}{N_1}}{1 - \frac{(k+1)N_{k+1}}{N_1}} \quad (11)$$

2.5 Kneser-Ney Smoothing

Kneser-Ney have introduced an extension of absolute discounting (Kneser and Ney, 1995). The estimate of the higher-order distribution is created by subtracting a fixed discount D from each non-zero count. The difference with the absolute discounting smoothing resides in the estimate of the lower-order distribution as shown in the following equation:

$$r = \begin{cases} \frac{Max(c(w^i_{i-n+1})-D,0)}{\sum_{w_i} c(w^i_{i-n+1})} & \text{if } c(w^i_{i-n+1}) > 0 \\ \alpha(w^{i-1}_{i-n+1})P_{kn}(w_i|w^{i-1}_{i-n+2}) & \text{if } c(w^i_{i-n+1}) = 0 \end{cases} \quad (12)$$

where $r = P_{kn}(w_i|w^{i-1}_{i-n+1})$ and $\alpha(w^{i-1}_{i-n+1})$ is chosen to make the distribution sum to 1 (Chen and Goodman, 1999).

3 Methods

In this section we first introduce the different steps of the standard approach, then we present our extended approach that makes use of smoothing as a new step in the process of the standard approach.

3.1 Standard Approach

The main idea for identifying translations of terms in comparable corpora relies on the distributional hypothesis [1] that has been extended to the bilingual scenario (Fung, 1998; Rapp, 1999). If many variants of the standard approach have been proposed (Chiao and Zweigenbaum, 2002; Hervé Déjean and Gaussier, 2002; Morin et al., 2007; Gamallo, 2008)[among others], they mainly differ in the way they implement each step and define its parameters. The standard approach can be carried out as follows:

Step 1 For a source word to translate w_i^s, we first build its context vector $v_{w_i^s}$. The vector $v_{w_i^s}$ contains all the words that cooccur with w_i^s within windows of n words. Lets denote by $cooc(w_i^s, w_j^s)$ the cooccurrence value of w_i^s and a given word of its context w_j^s. The process of building context vectors is repeated for all the words of the target language.

Step 2 An association measure such as the pointwise mutual information (Fano, 1961), the log-likelihood (Dunning, 1993) or the discounted odds-ratio (Laroche and Langlais, 2010) is used to score the strength of correlation between a word and all the words of its context vector.

Step 3 The context vector $v_{w_i^s}$ is projected into the target language $v_{w_i^s}^t$. Each word w_j^s of $v_{w_i^s}$ is translated with the help of a bilingual dictionary D. If w_j^s is not present in D, w_j^s is discarded. Whenever the bilingual dictionary provides several translations for a word, all the entries are considered but weighted according to their frequency in the target language (Morin et al., 2007).

Step 4 A similarity measure is used to score each target word w_i^t, in the target language with respect to the translated context vector, $v_{w_i^s}^t$. Usual measures of vector similarity include the cosine similarity (Salton and Lesk, 1968) or the weighted Jaccard index (WJ) (Grefenstette, 1994) for instance. The candidate translations of the word w_i^s are the target words ranked following the similarity score.

[1] words with similar meaning tend to occur in similar contexts

3.2 Extended Approach

We aim at investigating the impact of different smoothing techniques for the task of bilingual terminology extraction from comparable corpora. Starting from the assumption that word cooccurrences are not reliable especially for small corpora (Zipf, 1949; Evert and Baroni, 2007) and that smoothing is usually used to counteract this problem, we apply smoothing as a preprocessing step of the standard approach. Each $cooc(w_i^s, w_j^s)$ is smoothed according to the techniques described in Section 2. The smoothed cooccurrence $cooc^*(w_i^s, w_j^s)$ is then used for calculating the association measure between w_i^s and w_j^s and so on (steps 2, 3 and 4 of the standard approach are unchanged). We chose not to study the prediction of unseen cooccurrences. The latter has been carried out successfully by (Pekar et al., 2006). We concentrate on the evaluation of smoothing techniques of known cooccurrences and their effect according to different association and similarity measures.

4 Experimental Setup

In order to evaluate the smoothing techniques, several resources and parameters are needed. We present hereafter the experiment data and the parameters of the standard approach.

4.1 Corpus Data

The experiments have been carried out on two English-French comparable corpora. A specialized corpus of 530,000 words from the medical domain within the sub-domain of 'breast cancer' and a specialize corpus from the domain of 'wind-energy' of 300,000 words. The two bilingual corpora have been normalized through the following linguistic pre-processing steps: tokenization, part-of-speech tagging, and lemmatization. The function words have been removed and the words occurring once (i.e. hapax) in the French and the English parts have been discarded. For the breast cancer corpus, we have selected the documents from the Elsevier website[2] in order to obtain an English-French specialized comparable corpora. We have automatically selected the documents published between 2001 and 2008 where the title or the keywords contain the term 'cancer du sein' in French and 'breast cancer' in English. We collected 130 documents in French and 118 in

[2] www.elsevier.com

English. As summarised in Table 1, The comparable corpora comprised about 6631 distinct words in French and 8221 in English. For the wind energy corpus, we used the *Babook* crawler (Groc, 2011) to collect documents in French and English from the web. We could only obtain 50 documents in French and 65 in English. As the documents were collected from different websites according to some keywords of the domain, this corpus is more noisy and not well structured compared to the breast cancer corpus. The wind-energy corpus comprised about 5606 distinct words in French and 6081 in English.

	Breast cancer	Wind energy
$Tokens_S$	527,705	307,996
$Tokens_T$	531,626	314,551
$\|S\|$	8,221	6,081
$\|T\|$	6,631	5,606

Table 1: Corpus size

4.2 Dictionary

In our experiments we used the French-English bilingual dictionary ELRA-M0033 of about 200,000 entries[3]. It contains, after linguistic preprocessing steps and projection on both corpora fewer than 4000 single words. The details are given in Table 2.

	Breast cancer	Wind energy
$\|ELRA_S\|$	3,573	3,459
$\|ELRA_T\|$	3,670	3,326

Table 2: Dictionary coverage

4.3 Reference Lists

In bilingual terminology extraction from specialized comparable corpora, the terminology reference list required to evaluate the performance of the alignment programs is often composed of 100 single-word terms (SWTs) (180 SWTs in (Hervé Déjean and Gaussier, 2002), 95 SWTs in (Chiao and Zweigenbaum, 2002), and 100 SWTs in (Daille and Morin, 2005)). To build our reference lists, we selected only the French/English pair of SWTs which occur more than five times in each part of the comparable corpus. As a result of filtering, 321 French/English SWTs were extracted (from the UMLS[4] meta-thesaurus.) for the breast cancer corpus, and 100 pairs for the wind-energy corpus.

4.4 Evaluation Measure

Three major parameters need to be set to the standard approach, namely the similarity measure, the association measure defining the entry vectors and the size of the window used to build the context vectors. (Laroche and Langlais, 2010) carried out a complete study of the influence of these parameters on the quality of bilingual alignment. As a similarity measure, we chose to use Weighted Jaccard Index (Grefenstette, 1994) and Cosine similarity (Salton and Lesk, 1968). The entries of the context vectors were determined by the log-likelihood (Dunning, 1993), mutual information (Fano, 1961) and the discounted Odds-ratio (Laroche and Langlais, 2010). We also chose a 7-window size. Other combinations of parameters were assessed but the previous parameters turned out to give the best performance. We note that 'Top k' means that the correct translation of a given word is present in the k first candidates of the list returned by the standard approach. We use also the mean average precision *MAP* (Manning et al., 2008) which represents the quality of the system.

$$MAP(Q) = \frac{1}{|Q|}\sum_{i=1}^{|Q|}\frac{1}{m_i}\sum_{m_i=1}^{k}P(R_{ik}) \quad (13)$$

where $|Q|$ is the number of terms to be translated, m_i is the number of reference translations for the ith term (always 1 in our case), and $P(R_{ik})$ is 0 if the reference translation is not found for the ith term or $1/r$ if it is (r is the rank of the reference translation in the translation candidates).

4.5 Baseline

The baseline in our experiments is the standard approach (Fung, 1998) without any smoothing of the data. The standard approach is often used for comparison (Pekar et al., 2006; Gamallo, 2008; Prochasson and Morin, 2009), etc.

4.6 Training Data Set

Some smoothing techniques such as the Good-Turing estimators need a large training corpus to

[3]ELRA dictionary has been created by Sciper in the Technolangue/Euradic project

[4]http://www.nlm.nih.gov/research/umls

estimate the adjusted cooccurrences. For that purpose, we chose a training general corpus of 10 million words. We selected the documents published in 1994 from the 'Los Angeles Times/Le Monde' newspapers.

5 Experiments and Results

We conducted a set of three experiments on two specialized comparable corpora. We carried out a comparison between the standard approach (SA) and the smoothing techniques presented in Section 2 namely : additive smoothing (Add1), Good-Turing smoothing (GT), the Jelinek-Mercer technique (JM), the Katz-Backoff (Katz) and kneser-Ney smoothing (Kney). Experiment 1 shows the results for the breast cancer corpus. Experiment 2 shows the results for the wind energy corpus and finally experiment 3 presents a comparison of the best configurations on both corpora.

5.1 Experiment 1

Table 3 shows the results of the experiments on the breast cancer corpus. The first observation concerns the standard approach (SA). The best results are obtained using the Log-Jac parameters with a MAP = 27.9%. We can also notice that for this configuration, only the Additive smoothing significantly improves the performance of the standard approach with a MAP = 30.6%. The other smoothing techniques even degrade the results. The second observation concerns the Odds-Cos parameters where none of the smoothing techniques significantly improved the performance of the baseline (SA). Although Good-Turing and Katz-Backoff smoothing give slightly better results with respectively a MAP = 25.2 % and MAP = 25.3 %, these results are not significant. The most notable result concerns the PMI-COS parameters. We can notice that four of the five smoothing techniques improve the performance of the baseline. The best smoothing is the Jelinek-Mercer technique which reaches a MAP = 29.5% and improves the Top1 precision of 6% and the Top10 precision of 10.3%.

5.2 Experiment 2

Table 4 shows the results of the experiments on the wind energy corpus. Generally the results exhibit the same behaviour as the previous experiment. The best results of the standard approach are obtained using the Log-Jac parameters with a MAP = 25.7%. Here also, only the Additive smoothing significantly improves the performance of the standard approach with a MAP = 39.7%. The other smoothing techniques also degrade the results. About the Odds-Cos parameters, except the additive smoothing, here again none of the smoothing techniques significantly improved the performance of the baseline. Finally the most remarkable result still concerns the PMI-COS parameters where the same four of the five smoothing techniques improve the performance of the baseline. The best smoothing is the Jelinek-Mercer technique which reaches a MAP = 30.1% and improves the Top1 and and the Top10 precisions by 14.0%.

	SA	Add1	GT	JM	Katz	Kney	Config
P1	15.5	17.1	18.7	**21.5**	18.7	05.3	PMI-Cos
P5	31.1	32.7	32.0	**38.3**	33.9	13.4	PMI-Cos
P10	34.5	37.0	37.0	**44.8**	38.0	15.2	PMI-Cos
MAP	22.6	24.8	25.6	**29.5**	25.9	09.1	PMI-Cos
P1	15.8	16.1	16.8	14.6	**17.1**	09.0	Odds-Cos
P5	**34.8**	33.6	34.2	33.0	33.9	19.6	Odds-Cos
P10	40.4	**41.7**	39.8	38.3	40.1	25.2	Odds-Cos
MAP	24.8	24.4	25.2	23.3	**25.3**	14.1	Odds-Cos
P1	20.2	**22.4**	14.6	14.6	14.6	16.2	Log-Jac
P5	35.8	**40.5**	27.7	26.7	26.7	29.9	Log-Jac
P10	42.6	**44.2**	34.2	33.3	33.0	33.9	Log-Jac
MAP	27.9	**30.6**	21.4	21.2	21.2	22.9	Log-Jac

Table 3: Results of the experiments on the "Breast cancer" corpus (except the Odds-Cos configuration, the improvements indicate a significance at the 0.05 level using the Student t-test).

	SA	Add1	GT	JM	Katz	Kney	Config
P1	07.0	14.0	14.0	**21.0**	16.0	09.0	PMI-Cos
P5	27.0	32.0	31.0	**37.0**	30.0	17.0	PMI-Cos
P10	37.0	42.0	43.0	**51.0**	44.0	28.0	PMI-Cos
MAP	17.8	23.6	22.9	**30.1**	24.2	14.1	PMI-Cos
P1	12.0	**17.0**	12.0	12.0	12.0	06.0	Odds-Cos
P5	31.0	**35.0**	31.0	32.0	28.0	16.0	Odds-Cos
P10	38.0	**44.0**	36.0	39.0	35.0	21.0	Odds-Cos
MAP	21.8	**26.5**	19.8	20.8	19.7	11.1	Odds-Cos
P1	17.0	**22.0**	13.0	13.0	13.0	14.0	Log-Jac
P5	36.0	**38.0**	27.0	27.0	27.0	29.0	Log-Jac
P10	42.0	**50.0**	37.0	38.0	38.0	39.0	Log-Jac
MAP	25.7	**29.7**	20.5	21.3	21.3	22.9	Log-Jac

Table 4: Results of the experiments on the "Wind Energy" corpus (except the Odds-Cos configuration, the improvements indicate a significance at the 0.05 level using the Student t-test).

5.3 Experiment 3

In this experiment, we would like to investigate whether the smoothing techniques are more efficient for frequent translation equivalents or less frequent ones. For that purpose, we split the breast cancer reference list of 321 entries into two sets of translation pairs. A set of 133 frequent pairs named : *High-test set* and a set of 188 less frequent pairs called *Low-test set*. The initial reference list of 321 pairs is the *Full-test set*. We consider frequent pairs those of a frequency higher than 100. We chose to analyse the two configurations that provided the best performance that is : Log-Jac and Pmi-Cos parameters according to the *Full-test*, *High-test* and *Low-test* sets.

Figure 1 shows the results using the Log-Jac configuration. We can see that the additive smoothing always outperforms the standard approach for all the test sets. The other smoothing techniques are always under the baseline and behave approximately the same way. Figure 2 shows the results using the PMI-COS configuration. We can see that except the Kneser-Ney smoothing, all the smoothing techniques outperform the standard approach for all the test sets. We can also notice that the Jelinek-Mercer smoothing improves more notably the *High-test* set.

6 Discussion

Smoothing techniques are often evaluated on their ability to predict unseen n-grams. In our experiments we only focused on smoothing observed cooccurrences of context vectors. Hence, the previous evaluations of smoothing techniques may not always be consistent with our findings. This is for example the case for the additive smoothing technique. The latter which is described as a poor estimator in statistical NLP, turns out to perform well when associated with the Log-Jac parameters. This is because we did not consider unseen cooccurences which are over estimated by the Add-one smoothing. Obviously, we can imagine that adding one to all unobserved cooccurrences would not make sense and would certainly degrade the results. Except the add-one smoothing, none of the other algorithms reached good results when associated to the Log-Jac configuration. This is certainly related to the properties of the log-likelihood association measure. Additive smoothing has been used to address the problem of rare words aligning to too many words (Moore, 2004). At each iteration of the standard Expectation-Maximization (EM) procedure all the translation probability estimates are smoothed by adding virtual counts to uniform probability distribution over all target words. Here also additive smoothing has shown interesting results. According to these findings, we can consider the additive smoothing as an appropriate technique for our task.

Concerning the Odds-Cos parameters, although there have been slight improvements in the add-one algorithm, smoothing techniques have shown disappointing results. Here again the Odds-ratio association measure seems to be incompatible with re-estimating small cooccurrences. More investigations are certainly needed to highlight the reasons for this poor performance. It seems that smoothing techniques based on discounting does not fit well with association measures based on contingency table. The most noticeable improvement concerns the PMI-Cos configurations. Except Kneser-Ney smoothing, all the other techniques showed better performance than the standard approach. According to the results, point-wise mutual information performs better with smoothing techniques especially with the linear interpolation of Jelinek-Mercer method that combines high-order (cooccurrences) and low-order (unigrams) counts of the Good-Turing estimations. Jelinek-Mercer smoothing counteracts the disadvantage of the point-wise mutual information which consists of over estimating less frequent words. This latter weakness is corrected first by the Good-Turing estimators and then by considering the low order counts. The best performance was obtained with $\lambda = 0.5$.

Smoothing techniques attempt to improve the accuracy of the model as a whole. This particularity has been confirmed by the third experiment where we noticed the smoothing improvements for both reference lists, that is the *High-test* and *Low-test* sets. This latter experiment has shown that smoothing observed cooccurrences is useful for all frequency ranges. The difference of precision between the two test lists can be explained by the fact that less frequent words are harder to translate.

In statistical NLP, smoothing techniques for n-gram models have been addressed in a number of studies (Chen and Goodman, 1999). The ad-

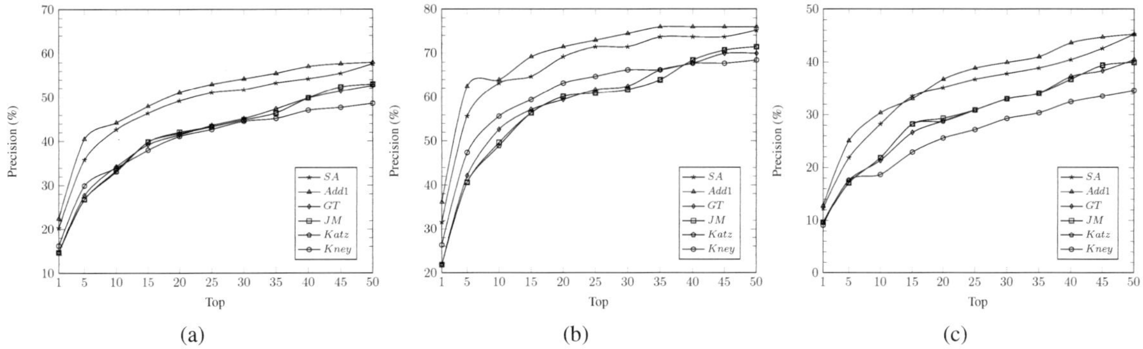

Figure 1: A set of three figures on the breast cancer corpus for the Log-Jac configuration : (a) Full-test set ; (b) High-test set; and (c) Low-test set.

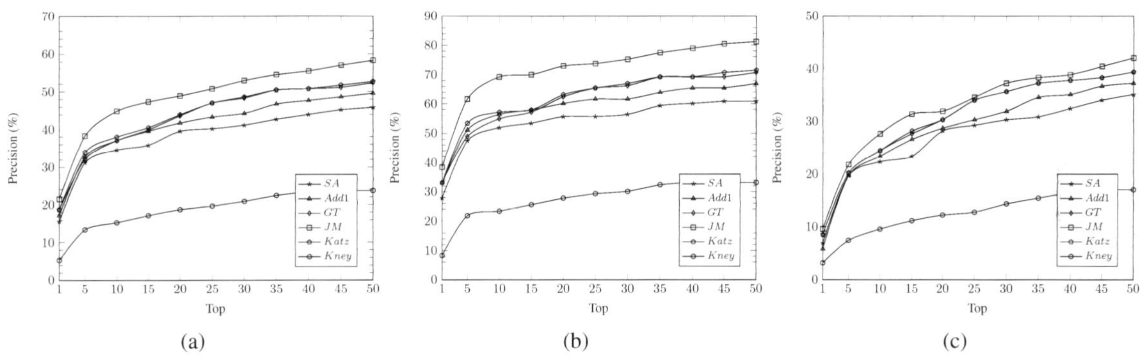

Figure 2: A set of three figures on the breast cancer corpus for the PMI-COS configuration : (a) Full-test set ; (b) High-test set; and (c) Low-test set.

ditive smoothing that performs rather poorly has shown good results in our evaluation. The Good-Turing estimate which is not used in isolation forms the basis of later techniques such as Back-off or Jelinek-Mercer smoothing, two techniques that generally work well. The good performance of $Katz$ and JM on the PMI-Cos configuration was expected. The reason is that these two methods have used the Good-Turing estimators which also achieved good performances in our experiments. Concerning the Kneser-Ney algorithm, surprisingly this performed poorly in our experiments while it is known to be one of the best smoothing techniques. Discounting a fixed amount in all counts of observed cooccurrences degrades the results in our data set. We also implemented the modified Knener-ney method (not presented in this paper) but this also performed poorly. We conclude that discounting is not an appropriate method for observed cooccurrences. Especially for point-wise mutual information that over-estimates low frequencies, hense, discounting low cooccurrences will increase this over-estimation.

7 Conclusion

In this paper, we have described and compared the most widely-used smoothing techniques for the task of bilingual lexicon extraction from comparable corpora. Regarding the empirical results of our proposition, performance of smoothing on our dataset was better than the baseline for the Add-One smoothing combined with the Log-Jac parameters and all smoothing techniques except the Kneser-ney for the Pmi-Cos parameters. Our findings thus lend support to the hypothesis that a re-estimation process of word cooccurrence in a small specialized comparable corpora is an appropriate way to improve the accuracy of the standard approach.

Acknowledgments

The research leading to these results has received funding from the French National Research Agency under grant ANR-12-CORD-0020.

References

Brown, P. F., Pietra, S. D., Pietra, V. J. D., and Mercer, R. L. (1991). Word-sense disambiguation using statistical methods. In *Proceedings of the 29th Annual Meeting of the Association for Computational Linguistics (ACL'91)*, pages 264–270, California, USA.

Brown, P. F., Pietra, V. J. D., de Souza, P. V., Lai, J. C., and Mercer, R. L. (1992). Class-based n-gram models of natural language. *Computational Linguistics*, 18(4):467–479.

Chen, S. F. and Goodman, J. (1999). An empirical study of smoothing techniques for language modeling. *Computer Speech & Language*, 13(4):359–393.

Chiao, Y.-C. and Zweigenbaum, P. (2002). Looking for candidate translational equivalents in specialized, comparable corpora. In *Proceedings of the 19th International Conference on Computational Linguistics (COLING'02)*, pages 1208–1212, Tapei, Taiwan.

Dagan, I., Lee, L., and Pereira, F. C. N. (1999). Similarity-based models of word cooccurrence probabilities. *Machine Learning*, 34(1-3):43–69.

Dagan, I., Marcus, S., and Markovitch, S. (1993). Contextual word similarity and estimation from sparse data. In *Proceedings of the 31ST Annual Meeting of the Association for Computational Linguistics (ACL'93)*, pages 164–171, Ohio, USA.

Daille, B. and Morin, E. (2005). French-English Terminology Extraction from Comparable Corpora. In *Proceedings of the 2nd International Joint Conference on Natural Language Processing (IJCLNP'05)*, pages 707–718, Jeju Island, Korea.

Dunning, T. (1993). Accurate Methods for the Statistics of Surprise and Coincidence. *Computational Linguistics*, 19(1):61–74.

Evert, S. (2005). *The statistics of word cooccurrences : word pairs and collocations*. PhD thesis, University of Stuttgart, Holzgartenstr. 16, 70174 Stuttgart.

Evert, S. and Baroni, M. (2007). zipfr: Word frequency modeling in r. In *Proceedings of the 45th Annual Meeting of the Association for Computational Linguistics (ACL'07)*, Prague, Czech Republic.

Fano, R. M. (1961). *Transmission of Information: A Statistical Theory of Communications*. MIT Press, Cambridge, MA, USA.

Fung, P. (1998). A Statistical View on Bilingual Lexicon Extraction: From Parallel Corpora to Non-parallel Corpora. In *Proceedings of the 3rd Conference of the Association for Machine Translation in the Americas (AMTA'98)*, pages 1–16, Langhorne, PA, USA.

Gamallo, O. (2008). Evaluating two different methods for the task of extracting bilingual lexicons from comparable corpora. In *Proceedings of LREC 2008 Workshop on Comparable Corpora (LREC'08)*, pages 19–26, Marrakech, Marroco.

Good, I. J. (1953). The population frequencies of species and the estimation of population parameters. *Biometrika*, 40:16–264.

Grefenstette, G. (1994). *Explorations in Automatic Thesaurus Discovery*. Kluwer Academic Publisher, Boston, MA, USA.

Groc, C. D. (2011). Babouk : Focused Web Crawling for Corpus Compilation and Automatic Terminology Extraction. In *Proceedings of The IEEE-WICACM International Conferences on Web Intelligence*, pages 497–498, Lyon, France.

Hervé Déjean and Gaussier, É. (2002). Une nouvelle approche à l'extraction de lexiques bilingues à partir de corpus comparables. *Lexicometrica, Alignement lexical dans les corpus multilingues*, pages 1–22.

Jeffreys, H. (1948). *Theory of Probability*. Clarendon Press, Oxford. 2nd edn Section 3.23.

Johnson, W. (1932). Probability: the deductive and inductive problems. *Mind*, 41(164):409–423.

Katz, S. M. (1987). Estimation of probabilities from sparse data for the language model component of a speech recognizer. *IEEE Transactions on Acoustics, Speech and Signal Processing*, 35(3):400–401.

Kneser, R. and Ney, H. (1995). Improved backing-off for M-gram language modeling. In *Proceedings of the 20th International Conference on Acoustics, Speech, and Signal Processing (ICASSP'95)*, pages 181–184, Michigan, USA.

Laroche, A. and Langlais, P. (2010). Revisiting Context-based Projection Methods for Term-Translation Spotting in Comparable Corpora. In *Proceedings of the 23rd International Conference on Computational Linguistics (COLING'10)*, pages 617–625, Beijing, China.

Lidstone, G. J. (1920). Note on the general case of the bayes-laplace formula for inductive or a posteriori probabilities. *Transactions of the Faculty of Actuaries*, 8:182–192.

Maarek, Y. S. and Smadja, F. A. (1989). Full text indexing based on lexical relations an application: Software libraries. In *SIGIR*, pages 198–206, Massachusetts, USA.

Manning, D. C., Raghavan, P., and Schütze, H. (2008). Introduction to information retrieval. Cambridge University Press.

Mercer, L. ; Jelinek, F. (1980). Interpolated estimation of markov source parameters from sparse data. In *Workshop on pattern recognition in Practice*, Amsterdam, The Netherlands.

Moore, R. C. (2004). Improving ibm word alignment model 1. In *Proceedings of the 42nd Annual Meeting of the Association for Computational Linguistics (ACL'04)*, pages 518–525, Barcelona, Spain.

Morin, E., Daille, B., Takeuchi, K., and Kageura, K. (2007). Bilingual Terminology Mining – Using Brain, not brawn comparable corpora. In *Proceedings of the 45th Annual Meeting of the Association for Computational Linguistics (ACL'07)*, pages 664–671, Prague, Czech Republic.

Pekar, V., Mitkov, R., Blagoev, D., and Mulloni, A. (2006). Finding translations for low-frequency words in comparable corpora. *Machine Translation*, 20(4):247–266.

Pereira, F. C. N., Tishby, N., and Lee, L. (1993). Distributional clustering of english words. In *Proceedings of the 31ST Annual Meeting of the Association for Computational Linguistics (ACL'93)*, pages 183–190, Ohio, USA.

Prochasson, E. and Morin, E. (2009). Anchor points for bilingual extraction from small specialized comparable corpora. *TAL*, 50(1):283–304.

Rapp, R. (1999). Automatic Identification of Word Translations from Unrelated English and German Corpora. In *Proceedings of the 37th Annual Meeting of the Association for Computational Linguistics (ACL'99)*, pages 519–526, College Park, MD, USA.

Salton, G. and Lesk, M. E. (1968). Computer evaluation of indexing and text processing. *Journal of the Association for Computational Machinery*, 15(1):8–36.

Zipf, G. K. (1949). *Human Behaviour and the Principle of Least Effort: an Introduction to Human Ecology*. Addison-Wesley.

Chinese–Japanese Parallel Sentence Extraction from Quasi–Comparable Corpora

Chenhui Chu, Toshiaki Nakazawa, Sadao Kurohashi
Graduate School of Informatics, Kyoto University
Yoshida-honmachi, Sakyo-ku
Kyoto, 606-8501, Japan
{chu,nakazawa}@nlp.ist.i.kyoto-u.ac.jp kuro@i.kyoto-u.ac.jp

Abstract

Parallel sentences are crucial for statistical machine translation (SMT). However, they are quite scarce for most language pairs, such as Chinese–Japanese. Many studies have been conducted on extracting parallel sentences from noisy parallel or comparable corpora. We extract Chinese–Japanese parallel sentences from quasi–comparable corpora, which are available in far larger quantities. The task is significantly more difficult than the extraction from noisy parallel or comparable corpora. We extend a previous study that treats parallel sentence identification as a binary classification problem. Previous method of classifier training by the Cartesian product is not practical, because it differs from the real process of parallel sentence extraction. We propose a novel classifier training method that simulates the real sentence extraction process. Furthermore, we use linguistic knowledge of Chinese character features. Experimental results on quasi–comparable corpora indicate that our proposed approach performs significantly better than the previous study.

1 Introduction

In statistical machine translation (SMT) (Brown et al., 1993; Koehn et al., 2007), the quality and quantity of the parallel sentences are crucial, because translation knowledge is acquired from a sentence–level aligned parallel corpus. However, except for a few language pairs, such as English–French, English–Arabic and English–Chinese, parallel corpora remain a scarce resource. The cost of manual construction for parallel corpora is high. As non–parallel corpora are far more available, constructing parallel corpora from non–parallel corpora is an attractive research field.

Non–parallel corpora include various levels of comparability: noisy parallel, comparable and quasi–comparable. Noisy parallel corpora contain non–aligned sentences that are nevertheless mostly bilingual translations of the same document, comparable corpora contain non–sentence–aligned, non–translated bilingual documents that are topic–aligned, while quasi–comparable corpora contain far more disparate very–non–parallel bilingual documents that could either be on the same topic (in–topic) or not (out–topic) (Fung and Cheung, 2004). Most studies focus on extracting parallel sentences from noisy parallel corpora or comparable corpora, such as bilingual news articles (Zhao and Vogel, 2002; Utiyama and Isahara, 2003; Munteanu and Marcu, 2005; Tillmann, 2009; Abdul-Rauf and Schwenk, 2011), patent data (Utiyama and Isahara, 2007; Lu et al., 2010) and Wikipedia (Adafre and de Rijke, 2006; Smith et al., 2010). Few studies have been conducted on quasi–comparable corpora. Quasi–comparable corpora are available in far larger quantities than noisy parallel or comparable corpora, while the parallel sentence extraction task is significantly more difficult.

While most studies are interested in language pairs between English and other languages, we focus on Chinese–Japanese, where parallel corpora are very scarce. This study extracts Chinese–Japanese parallel sentences from quasi–comparable corpora. We adopt a system proposed by Munteanu and Marcu (2005), which is for parallel sentence extraction from comparable corpora. We extend the system in several aspects to make it even suitable for quasi–comparable corpora. The core component of the system is a classifier which can identify parallel sentences from non–parallel sentences. Previous method of classifier training by the Cartesian product is not practical, because it differs from the real process of parallel sentence extraction. We propose a novel

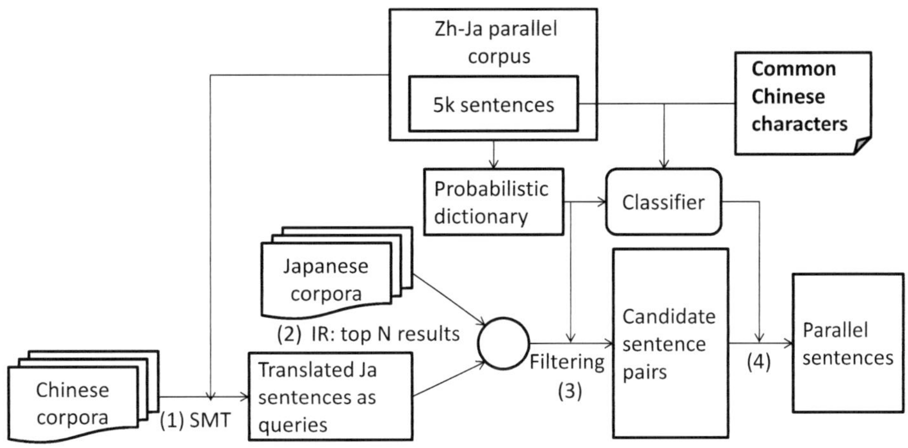

Figure 1: Parallel sentence extraction system.

method of classifier training and testing that simulates the real sentence extraction process, which guarantees the quality of the extracted sentences. Since Chinese characters are used both in Chinese and Japanese, they can be powerful linguistic clues to identify parallel sentences. Therefore, we use Chinese character features, which significantly improve the accuracy of the classifier. We conduct parallel sentence extraction experiments on quasi–comparable corpora, and evaluate the quality of the extracted sentences from the perspective of MT performance. Experimental results show that our proposed system performs significantly better than the previous study.

2 Parallel Sentence Extraction System

The overview of our parallel sentence extraction system is presented in Figure 1. Source sentences are translated to target language using a SMT system (1). We retrieve the top N documents from target language corpora with a information retrieval (IR) framework, using the translated sentences as queries (2). For each source sentence, we treat all target sentences in the retrieved documents as candidates. Then, we pass the candidate sentence pairs through a sentence ratio filter and a word–overlap–based filter based on a probabilistic dictionary, to reduce the candidates keeping more reliable sentences (3). Finally, a classifier trained on a small number of parallel sentences, is used to identify the parallel sentences from the candidates (4). A parallel corpus is needed to train the SMT system, generate the probabilistic dictionary and train the classifier.

Our system is inspired by Munteanu and Marcu (2005), however, there are several differences. The first difference is query generation. Munteanu and Marcu (2005) generate queries by taking the top N translations of each source word according to the probabilistic dictionary. This method is imprecise due to the noise in the dictionary. Instead, we adopt a method proposed by Abdul–Rauf and Schwenk (2011). We translate the source sentences to target language with a SMT system trained on the parallel corpus. Then use the translated sentences as queries. This method can generate more precise queries, because phrase–based MT is better than word–based translation.

Another difference is that we do not conduct document matching. The reason is that documents on the same topic may not exist in quasi–comparable corpora. Instead, we retrieve the top N documents for each source sentence. In comparable corpora, it is reasonable to only use the best target sentence in the retrieved documents as candidates (Abdul-Rauf and Schwenk, 2011). In quasi–comparable corpora, it is important to further guarantee the recall. Therefore, we keep all target sentences in the retrieved documents as candidates.

Our system also differs by the way of classifier training and testing, which is described in Section 3 in detail.

3 Binary Classification of Parallel Sentence Identification

Parallel sentence identification from non–parallel sentences can be seen as a binary classification problem (Munteanu and Marcu, 2005; Tillmann, 2009; Smith et al., 2010; Ştefănescu et al., 2012).

Since the quality of the extracted sentences is determined by the accuracy of the classifier, the classifier becomes the core component of the extraction system. In this section, we first describe the training and testing process, then introduce the features we use for the classifier.

3.1 Training and Testing

Munteanu and Marcu (2005) propose a method of creating training and test instances for the classifier. They use a small number of parallel sentences as positive instances, and generate non–parallel sentences from the parallel sentences as negative instances. They generate all the sentence pairs except the original parallel sentence pairs in the Cartesian product, and discard the pairs that do not fulfill the condition of a sentence ratio filter and a word–overlap–based filter. Furthermore, they randomly discard some of the non–parallel sentences when necessary, to guarantee the ratio of negative to positive instances smaller than five for the performance of the classifier.

Creating instances by using the Cartesian product is not practical, because it differs from the real process of parallel sentence extraction. Here, we propose a novel method of classifier training and testing that simulates the real parallel sentence extraction process. For training, we first select 5k parallel sentences from a parallel corpus. Then translate the source side of the selected sentences to target language with a SMT system trained on the parallel corpus excluding the selected parallel sentences. We retrieve the top N documents from the target language side of the parallel corpus, using the translated sentences as queries. For each source sentence, we consider all target sentences in the retrieved documents as candidates. Finally, we pass the candidate sentence pairs through a sentence ratio filter and a word–overlap–based filter, and get the training instances. We treat the sentence pairs that exist in the original 5k parallel sentences as positive instances, while the remainder as negative instances. Note that positive instances may be less than 5k, because some of the parallel sentences do not pass the IR framework and the filters. For the negative instances, we also randomly discard some of them when necessary, to guarantee the ratio of negative to positive instances smaller than five. Test instances are generated by another 5k parallel sentences from the parallel corpus using the same method.

There are several merits of the proposed method. It can guarantee the quality of the extracted sentences, because of the similarity between the real sentence extraction process. Also, features from the IR results can be used to further improve the accuracy of the classifier. The proposed method can be evaluated not only on the test sentences that passed the IR framework and the filters, but also on all the test sentences, which is similar to the evaluation for the real extraction process. However, there is a limitation of our method that a both sentence–level and document–level aligned parallel corpus is needed.

3.2 Features

3.2.1 Basic Features

The following features are the basic features we use for the classifier, which are proposed by Munteanu and Marcu (2005):

- Sentence length, length difference and length ratio.
- Percentage of words on each side that have a translation on the other side (according to the probabilistic dictionary).
- Alignment features:
  - Percentage and number of words that have no connection.
  - The top three largest fertilities.
  - Length of the longest contiguous connected span.
  - Length of the longest unconnected substring.

Alignment features are extracted from the alignment results of the parallel and non–parallel sentences used as instances for the classifier. Note that alignment features may be unreliable when the quantity of non–parallel sentences is significantly larger than parallel sentences.

3.2.2 Chinese Character Features

Different from other language pairs, Chinese and Japanese share Chinese characters. In Chinese the Chinese characters are called Hanzi, while in Japanese they are called Kanji. Hanzi can be divided into two groups, Simplified Chinese (used in mainland China and Singapore) and Traditional Chinese (used in Taiwan, Hong Kong and Macau). The number of strokes needed to write characters

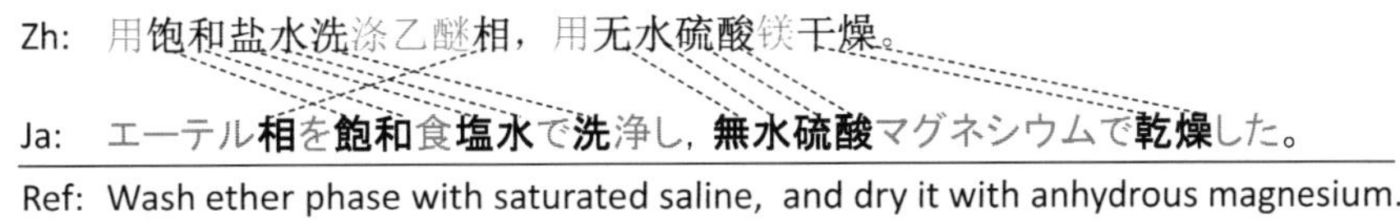

Figure 2: Example of common Chinese characters in a Chinese–Japanese parallel sentence pair.

Meaning	snow	love	begin
TC	雪 (U+96EA)	愛 (U+611B)	發 (U+767C)
SC	雪 (U+96EA)	爱(U+7231)	发(U+53D1)
Kanji	雪 (U+96EA)	愛 (U+611B)	発 (U+767A)

Table 1: Examples of common Chinese characters (TC denotes Traditional Chinese and SC denotes Simplified Chinese).

has been largely reduced in Simplified Chinese, and the shapes may be different from those in Traditional Chinese. Because Kanji characters originated from ancient China, many common Chinese characters exist between Hanzi and Kanji. Table 1 gives some examples of common Chinese characters in Traditional Chinese, Simplified Chinese and Japanese with their Unicode.

Since Chinese characters contain significant semantic information, and common Chinese characters share the same meaning, they can be valuable linguistic clues for many Chinese–Japanese NLP tasks. Many studies have exploited common Chinese characters. Tan et al. (1995) used the occurrence of identical common Chinese characters in Chinese and Japanese (e.g. "snow" in Table 1) in automatic sentence alignment task for document–level aligned text. Goh et al. (2005) detected common Chinese characters where Kanji are identical to Traditional Chinese, but different from Simplified Chinese (e.g. "love" in Table 1). Using a Chinese encoding converter[1] that can convert Traditional Chinese into Simplified Chinese, they built a Japanese–Simplified Chinese dictionary partly using direct conversion of Japanese into Chinese for Japanese Kanji words. Chu et al. (2011) made use of the Unihan database[2] to detect common Chinese characters which are visual variants of each other (e.g. "begin" in Table 1), and proved the effectiveness of common Chinese characters in Chinese–Japanese phrase alignment. Chu et al. (2012a) exploited common Chinese characters in Chinese word segmentation optimization, which improved the translation performance.

In this study, we exploit common Chinese characters in parallel sentence extraction. Chu et al. (2011) investigated the coverage of common Chinese characters on a scientific paper abstract parallel corpus, and showed that over 45% Chinese Hanzi and 75% Japanese Kanji are common Chinese characters. Therefore, common Chinese characters can be powerful linguistic clues to identify parallel sentences.

We make use of the Chinese character mapping table created by Chu et al. (2012b) to detect common Chinese characters. Following features are used. We use an example of Chinese–Japanese parallel sentence presented in Figure 2 to explain the features in detail, where common Chinese characters are in bold and linked with dotted lines.

- Number of Chinese characters on each side (Zh: 18, Ja: 14).
- Percentage of Chinese characters out of all characters on each side (Zh: 18/20=90%, Ja: 14/32=43%).
- Ratio of Chinese character numbers on both sides (18/14=128%).
- Number of n–gram common Chinese characters (1–gram: 12, 2–gram: 6, 3–gram: 2, 4–gram: 1).
- Percentage of n–gram common Chinese characters out of all n–gram Chinese characters on each side (Zh: 1–gram: 12/18=66%, 2–gram: 6/16=37%, 3–gram: 2/14=14%, 4–gram: 1/12=8%; Ja: 1–gram: 12/14=85%, 2–gram: 6/9=66%, 3–gram=: 2/5=40%, 4–gram: 1/3=33%).

Note that Chinese character features are only applicable to Chinese–Japanese. However, since Chinese and Japanese character information is a kind of cognates (words or languages which have the same origin), the similar idea can be applied to other language pairs by using cognates. Cognates among European languages have been shown effective in word alignments (Kondrak et al., 2003). We also can use cognates for parallel sentence extraction.

[1] http://www.mandarintools.com/zhcode.html
[2] http://unicode.org/charts/unihan.html

3.3 Rank Feature

One merit of our classifier training and testing method is that features from the IR results can be used. Here, we use the ranks of the retrieved documents returned by the IR framework as feature.

4 Experiments

We conducted classification and translation experiments to evaluate the effectiveness of our proposed parallel sentence extraction system.

4.1 Data

4.1.1 Parallel Corpus

The parallel corpus we used is a scientific paper abstract corpus provided by JST[3] and NICT[4]. This corpus was created by the Japanese project "Development and Research of Chinese–Japanese Natural Language Processing Technology", containing various domains such as chemistry, physics, biology and agriculture etc. This corpus is aligned in both sentence–level and document–level, containing 680k sentences and 100k articles.

4.1.2 Quasi–Comparable Corpora

The quasi–comparable corpora we used are scientific paper abstracts collected from academic websites. The Chinese corpora were collected from CNKI[5], containing 420k sentences and 90k articles. The Japanese corpora were collected from CiNii[6] web portal, containing 5M sentences and 880k articles. Note that since the paper abstracts in these two websites were written by Chinese and Japanese researchers respectively through different periods, documents on the same topic may not exist in the collected corpora. We investigated the domains of the Chinese and Japanese corpora in detail. We found that most documents in the Chinese corpora belong to the domain of chemistry. While the Japanese corpora contain various domains such as chemistry, physics, biology and computer science etc. However, the domain information is unannotated in both corpora.

4.2 Classification Experiments

We conducted experiments to evaluate the accuracy of the proposed method of classification, using different 5k parallel sentences from the parallel corpus as training and test data.

4.2.1 Settings

- Probabilistic dictionary: We took the top 5 translations with translation probability larger than 0.1 created from the parallel corpus.
- IR tool: Indri[7] with the top 10 results.
- Segmenter: For Chinese, we used a segmenter optimized for Chinese–Japanese SMT (Chu et al., 2012a). For Japanese, we used JUMAN (Kurohashi et al., 1994).
- Alignment: GIZA++[8].
- SMT: We used the state–of–the–art phrase–based SMT toolkit Moses (Koehn et al., 2007) with default options, except for the distortion limit (6→20).
- Classifier: LIBSVM[9] with 5–fold cross–validation and radial basis function (RBF) kernel.
- Sentence ratio filter threshold: 2.
- Word–overlap–based filter threshold: 0.25.
- Classifier probability threshold: 0.5.

4.2.2 Evaluation

We evaluate the performance of classification by computing precision, recall and F–value, defined as:

$$precision = 100 \times \frac{classified\_well}{classified\_parallel}, \quad (1)$$

$$recall = 100 \times \frac{classified\_well}{true\_parallel}, \quad (2)$$

$$F - value = 2 \times \frac{precision \times recall}{precision + recall}. \quad (3)$$

Where $classified\_well$ is the number of pairs that the classifier correctly identified as parallel, $classified\_parallel$ is the number of pairs that the classifier identified as parallel, $true\_parallel$ is the number of real parallel pairs in the test set. Note that we only use the top 1 result identified as parallel by the classifier for evaluation.

[3] http://www.jst.go.jp
[4] http://www.nict.go.jp
[5] http://www.cnki.net
[6] http://ci.nii.ac.jp
[7] http://www.lemurproject.org/indri
[8] http://code.google.com/p/giza-pp
[9] http://www.csie.ntu.edu.tw/~cjlin/libsvm

Features	Precision	Recall	F–value
Munteanu+ 2005	88.43	85.20/79.76	86.78/83.87
+Chinese character	91.62	93.63/87.66	92.61/89.60
+Rank	**92.15**	**94.53/88.50**	**93.32/90.29**

Table 2: Classification results for the filtered test sentences (before "/") and all the test sentences (after "/").

Classifier	# sentences
Munteanu+ 2005 (Cartesian)	27,077
Munteanu+ 2005 (Proposed)	5,994
+Chinese character (Proposed)	3,936
+Rank (Proposed)	3,516

Table 3: Number of extracted sentences.

4.2.3 Results

We conducted classification experiments, comparing the following three experimental settings:

- Munteanu+ 2005: Only using the features proposed by Munteanu and Marcu (2005).
- +Chinese character: Add the Chinese character features.
- +Rank: Further add the rank feature.

Results evaluated for the test sentences that passed the IR framework and the filters, and all the test sentences are shown in Table 2. We can see that the Chinese character features can significantly improve the accuracy. The accuracy can be further improved by the rank feature.

4.3 Translation Experiments

We extracted parallel sentences from the quasi–comparable corpora, and evaluated Chinese–to–Japanese MT performance by appending the extracted sentences to two baseline settings.

4.3.1 Settings

- Baseline: Using all the 680k parallel sentences in the parallel corpus as training data (containing 11k sentences of chemistry domain).
- Tuning: Using another 368 sentences of chemistry domain.
- Test: Using another 367 sentences of chemistry domain.
- Language model: 5–gram LM trained on the Japanese side of the parallel corpus (680k sentences) using SRILM toolkit[10].
- Classifier probability threshold: 0.6.

The reason we evaluate on chemistry domain is the one we described in Section 4.1.2 that most documents in the Chinese corpora belong to the domain of chemistry. We keep all the sentence pairs rather than the top 1 result (used in the classification evaluation) identified as parallel by the classifier. The other settings are the same as the ones used in the classification experiments.

4.3.2 Results

Numbers of extracted sentences using different classifiers are shown in Table 3, where

- Munteanu+ 2005 (Cartesian): Classifier trained using the Cartesian product, and only using the features proposed by Munteanu and Marcu (2005).
- Munteanu+ 2005 (Proposed): Classifier trained using the proposed method, and only using the features proposed by Munteanu and Marcu (2005).
- +Chinese character (Proposed): Add the Chinese character features.
- +Rank (Proposed): Further add the rank feature.

We can see that the extracted number is significantly decreased by the proposed method compared to the Cartesian product, which may indicate the quality improvement of the extracted sentences. Adding more features further decreases the number.

We conducted Chinese–to–Japanese translation experiments by appending the extracted sentences to the baseline. BLEU–4 scores for experiments are shown in Table 4. We can see that our proposed method of classifier training performs better than the Cartesian product. Adding the Chinese character features and rank feature further improves the translation performance significantly.

[10]http://www.speech.sri.com/projects/srilm

Example 1

Zh: **最后，**本文**说明了**光学算符**的物理意义。**

(**Finally,** this article **explains the physical meaning of** the optical operator.)

Ja: **最後に**化学ポテンシャル**の物理的意味について**簡単に**説明 した。**

(**Finally,** briefly **explain the physical meaning of** the chemical potential.)

Example 2

Zh: **发射光谱分析法的检出限**及其测量方法的探讨。

(Discussion of **detection limit** and measurement methods **of emission spectral analysis method**.)

Ja: 光電測光法による**発光分光分析方法の検出限界。**

(**Detection limit of emission spectral analysis method** by photoelectric photometry.)

Figure 3: Examples of extracted sentences (parallel subsentential fragments are in bold).

System	BLEU
Baseline	38.64
Munteanu+ 2005 (Cartesian)	38.10
Munteanu+ 2005 (Proposed)	38.54
+Chinese character (Proposed)	$38.87^{\dagger}$
+Rank (Proposed)	$\mathbf{39.47}^{\ddagger *}$

Table 4: BLEU scores for Chinese–to–Japanese translation experiments ("†" and "‡" denotes the result is better than "Munteanu+ 2005 (Cartesian)" significantly at $p < 0.05$ and $p < 0.01$ respectively, "*" denotes the result is better than "Baseline" significantly at $p < 0.01$).

4.3.3 Discussion

The translation results indicate that compared to the previous study, our proposed method can extract sentences with better qualities. However, when we investigated the extracted sentences, we found that most of the extracted sentences are not sentence–level parallel. Instead, they contain many parallel subsentential fragments. Figure 3 presents two examples of sentence pairs extracted by "+Rank (Proposed)", where parallel subsentential fragments are in bold. We investigated the alignment results of the extracted sentences. We found that most of the parallel subsentential fragments were correctly aligned with the help of the parallel sentences in the baseline system. Therefore, translation performance was improved by appending the extracted sentences. However, it also led to many wrong alignments among the non–parallel fragments which are harmful to translation. In the future, we plan to further extract these parallel subsentential fragments, which can be more effective for SMT (Munteanu and Marcu, 2006).

5 Related Work

As parallel sentences trend to appear in similar document pairs, many studies first conduct document matching, then identify the parallel sentences from the matched document pairs (Utiyama and Isahara, 2003; Fung and Cheung, 2004; Munteanu and Marcu, 2005). Approaches without document matching also have been proposed (Tillmann, 2009; Abdul-Rauf and Schwenk, 2011; Ştefănescu et al., 2012). These studies directly retrieve candidate sentence pairs, and select the parallel sentences using some filtering methods. We adopt a moderate strategy, which retrieves candidate documents for sentences.

The way of parallel sentence identification can be specified with two different approaches: binary classification (Munteanu and Marcu, 2005; Tillmann, 2009; Smith et al., 2010; Ştefănescu et al., 2012) and translation similarity measures (Utiyama and Isahara, 2003; Fung and Cheung, 2004; Abdul-Rauf and Schwenk, 2011). We adopt the binary classification approach with a novel classifier training and testing method and Chinese character features.

Few studies have been conducted for extracting parallel sentences from quasi–comparable corpora. We are aware of only two previous efforts. Fung and Cheung (2004) proposed a multi-level bootstrapping approach. Wu and Fung (2005) exploited generic bracketing Inversion Transduction Grammars (ITG) for this task. Our approach differs from the previous studies that we extend the approach for comparable corpora in several aspects to make it work well for quasi–comparable corpora.

6 Conclusion and Future Work

In this paper, we proposed a novel method of classifier training and testing that simulates the real parallel sentence extraction process. Furthermore, we used linguistic knowledge of Chinese character features. Experimental results of parallel sentence extraction from quasi–comparable corpora indicated that our proposed system performs significantly better than the previous study.

Our approach can be improved in several aspects. One is bootstrapping, which has been proven effective in some related works (Fung and Cheung, 2004; Munteanu and Marcu, 2005). In our system, bootstrapping can be done not only for extension of the probabilistic dictionary, but also for improvement of the SMT system used to translate the source language to target language for query generation. Moreover, as parallel sentences rarely exist in quasi–comparable corpora, we plan to extend our system to parallel subsentential fragment extraction. Our study showed that Chinese character features are helpful for Chinese–Japanese parallel sentence extraction. We plan to apply the similar idea to other language pairs by using cognates.

References

Sadaf Abdul-Rauf and Holger Schwenk. 2011. Parallel sentence generation from comparable corpora for improved smt. *Machine Translation*, 25(4):341–375.

Sisay Fissaha Adafre and Maarten de Rijke. 2006. Finding similar sentences across multiple languages in wikipedia. In *Proceedings of EACL*, pages 62–69.

Peter F. Brown, Stephen A. Della Pietra, Vincent J. Della Pietra, and Robert L. Mercer. 1993. The mathematics of statistical machine translation: Parameter estimation. *Association for Computational Linguistics*, 19(2):263–312.

Chenhui Chu, Toshiaki Nakazawa, and Sadao Kurohashi. 2011. Japanese-chinese phrase alignment using common chinese characters information. In *Proceedings of MT Summit XIII*, pages 475–482, Xiamen, China, September.

Chenhui Chu, Toshiaki Nakazawa, Daisuke Kawahara, and Sadao Kurohashi. 2012a. Exploiting shared Chinese characters in Chinese word segmentation optimization for Chinese-Japanese machine translation. In *Proceedings of the 16th Annual Conference of the European Association for Machine Translation (EAMT'12)*, Trento, Italy, May.

Chenhui Chu, Toshiaki Nakazawa, and Sadao Kurohashi. 2012b. Chinese characters mapping table of Japanese, Traditional Chinese and Simplified Chinese. In *Proceedings of the Eighth Conference on International Language Resources and Evaluation (LREC'12)*, Istanbul, Turkey, May.

Dan Ştefănescu, Radu Ion, and Sabine Hunsicker. 2012. Hybrid parallel sentence mining from comparable corpora. In *Proceedings of the 16th Annual Conference of the European Association for Machine Translation (EAMT'12)*, Trento, Italy, May.

Pascale Fung and Percy Cheung. 2004. Multi-level bootstrapping for extracting parallel sentences from a quasi-comparable corpus. In *Proceedings of Coling 2004*, pages 1051–1057, Geneva, Switzerland, Aug 23–Aug 27. COLING.

Chooi-Ling Goh, Masayuki Asahara, and Yuji Matsumoto. 2005. Building a Japanese-Chinese dictionary using kanji/hanzi conversion. In *Proceedings of the International Joint Conference on Natural Language Processing*, pages 670–681.

Philipp Koehn, Hieu Hoang, Alexandra Birch, Chris Callison-Burch, Marcello Federico, Nicola Bertoldi, Brooke Cowan, Wade Shen, Christine Moran, Richard Zens, Chris Dyer, Ondrej Bojar, Alexandra Constantin, and Evan Herbst. 2007. Moses: Open source toolkit for statistical machine translation. In *Proceedings of the 45th Annual Meeting of the Association for Computational Linguistics Companion Volume Proceedings of the Demo and Poster Sessions*, pages 177–180, Prague, Czech Republic, June. Association for Computational Linguistics.

Grzegorz Kondrak, Daniel Marcu, and Kevin Knight. 2003. Cognates can improve statistical translation models. In *Proceedings of the Human Language Technology Conference of the North American Chapter of the Association for Computational Linguistics*, pages 46–48.

Sadao Kurohashi, Toshihisa Nakamura, Yuji Matsumoto, and Makoto Nagao. 1994. Improvements of Japanese morphological analyzer JUMAN. In *Proceedings of the International Workshop on Sharable Natural Language*, pages 22–28.

Bin Lu, Tao Jiang, Kapo Chow, and Benjamin K. Tsou. 2010. Building a large english-chinese parallel corpus from comparable patents and its experimental application to smt. In *Proceedings of the 3rd Workshop on Building and Using Comparable Corpora, LREC 2010*, pages 42–49, Valletta, Malta, May.

Dragos Stefan Munteanu and Daniel Marcu. 2005. Improving machine translation performance by exploiting non-parallel corpora. *Computational Linguistics*, 31(4):477–504, December.

Dragos Stefan Munteanu and Daniel Marcu. 2006. Extracting parallel sub-sentential fragments from non-parallel corpora. In *Proceedings of the 21st International Conference on Computational Linguistics and 44th Annual Meeting of the Association for Computational Linguistics*, pages 81–88, Sydney, Australia, July. Association for Computational Linguistics.

Jason R. Smith, Chris Quirk, and Kristina Toutanova. 2010. Extracting parallel sentences from comparable corpora using document level alignment. In *Human Language Technologies: The 2010 Annual Conference of the North American Chapter of the Association for Computational Linguistics*, pages 403–411, Los Angeles, California, June. Association for Computational Linguistics.

Chew Lim Tan and Makoto Nagao. 1995. Automatic alignment of Japanese-Chinese bilingual texts. *IEICE Transactions on Information and Systems*, E78-D(1):68–76.

Christoph Tillmann. 2009. A beam-search extraction algorithm for comparable data. In *Proceedings of the ACL-IJCNLP 2009 Conference Short Papers*, pages 225–228, Suntec, Singapore, August. Association for Computational Linguistics.

Masao Utiyama and Hitoshi Isahara. 2003. Reliable measures for aligning japanese-english news articles and sentences. In *Proceedings of the 41st Annual Meeting of the Association for Computational Linguistics*, pages 72–79, Sapporo, Japan, July. Association for Computational Linguistics.

Masao Utiyama and Hitoshi Isahara. 2007. A japanese-english patent parallel corpus. In *Proceedings of MT summit XI*, pages 475–482.

Dekai Wu and Pascale Fung. 2005. Inversion transduction grammar constraints for mining parallel sentences from quasi-comparable corpora. In *IJCNLP*, pages 257–268.

Bing Zhao and Stephan Vogel. 2002. Adaptive parallel sentences mining from web abilingual news collections. In *Proceedings of the 2002 IEEE International Conference on Data Mining*, pages 745–748, Maebashi City, Japan. IEEE Computer Society.

A modular open-source focused crawler for mining monolingual and bilingual corpora from the web

Vassilis Papavassiliou **Prokopis Prokopidis**
Institute for Language and Speech Processing
Athena Research and Innovation Center
Athens, Greece
{vpapa, prokopis}@ilsp.gr

Gregor Thurmair
Linguatec
Gottfried-Keller-Str. 12, 81245
Munich, Germany
g.thurmair@linguatec.de

Abstract

This paper discusses a modular and open-source focused crawler (ILSP-FC) for the automatic acquisition of domain-specific monolingual and bilingual corpora from the Web. Besides describing the main modules integrated in the crawler (dealing with page fetching, normalization, cleaning, text classification, de-duplication and document pair detection), we evaluate several of the system functionalities in an experiment for the acquisition of pairs of parallel documents in German and Italian for the "Health & Safety at work" domain.

1 Introduction and motivation

There is a growing literature on using the Web for constructing various types of text collections, including monolingual, comparable, parallel and/or domain-specific corpora. Such resources can be used by linguists studying language use and change (Kilgarriff and Grefenstette, 2003), and at the same time they can be exploited in applied research fields like machine translation and multilingual information extraction. Moreover, these collections of raw data can be automatically annotated and used to produce, by means of induction tools, a second order or synthesized derivatives: rich lexica (with morphological, syntactic and lexico-semantic information), large bilingual dictionaries (word and multiword based) and transfer grammars.

To this end, several tools (i.e. web crawlers, HTML parsers, language identifiers, HTML cleaners, etc.) have been developed and combined in order to produce corpora useful for specific tasks. However, to the best of our knowledge, most of the available systems either omit some processing tasks or require access to the results of a search engine. For instance, the BootCaT toolkit (Baroni et al., 2006), a well-known suite of Perl scripts for bootstrapping specialized language corpora from the web, uses the Bing search engine and allows up to 5,000 queries per month.

In this paper, we present ILSP-FC, a modular system that includes components and methods for all the tasks required to acquire domain-specific corpora from the Web. The system is available as an open-source Java project[1] and due to its modular architecture, each of its components can be easily substituted by alternatives with the same functionalities. Depending on user-defined configuration, the crawler employs processing workflows for the creation of either monolingual or bilingual collections. For users wishing to try the system before downloading it, two web services[2] allow them to experiment with different configuration settings for the construction of monolingual and bilingual domain-specific corpora.

The organization of the rest of the paper is as follows. In Section 2, we refer to recent related work. In Section 3, we describe in detail the workflow of the proposed system. A solution for bootstrapping the focused crawler input is presented in Section 4. Then, an experiment on acquiring parallel documents in German and Italian for the "Health & Safety at work" domain (H&S) is described in Section 5, which also includes evaluation results on a set of criteria including parallelness and domain specificity. We conclude and mention future work in Section 6.

2 Related work

Web crawling for building domain-specific monolingual and/or parallel data involves several tasks (e.g. link ranking, cleaning, text classification, near-duplicates removal) that remain open issues. Even though there are several proposed methods

[1] http://nlp.ilsp.gr/redmine/projects/ilsp-fc

[2] http://nlp.ilsp.gr/ws/

for each of these tasks, in this section we refer only to a few indicative approaches.

Olston and Najork (2010) outline the fundamental challenges and describe the state-of-the-art models and solutions for web crawling. A general framework to fairly evaluate focused crawling algorithms under a number of performance metrics is proposed by Srinivasan et al. (2005). A short overview of cleaning methods is presented in Spousta et al. (2008) and the comparison of such methods is discussed in Baroni et al. (2008). Several algorithms (Qi and Davison, 2009) exploit the main content and the HTML tags of a web page in order to classify a page as relevant to a targeted domain or not. Methods for the detection and removal of near-duplicates (i.e. acquired web pages that have almost the same content) are reviewed and compared in Theobald et al. (2008).

Efficient focused web crawlers can be built by adapting existing open-source frameworks like Heritrix[3], Nutch[4] and Bixo[5]. For instance, Combine[6] is an open-source focused crawler that is based on a combination of a general web crawler and a text classifier. Other approaches make use of search engines APIs to identify in-domain web pages (Hong et al., 2010) or multilingual web sites (Resnik and Smith, 2003). Starting from these pages, Almeida and Simões (2010) try to detect which links point to translations, while Shi et al. (2006) harvest multilingual web sites and extract parallel content from them. Bitextor (Esplà-Gomis and Forcada, 2010) combines language identification with shallow features that represent HTML structures to mine parallel pages.

Besides structure similarity, systems like PT-Miner (Nie et al., 1999) and WeBiText (Désilets et al., 2008) filtered fetched web pages by keeping only those containing language markers in their URLs. Chen et al. (2004) proposed the Parallel Text Identification System, which incorporated a content analysis module using a predefined bilingual wordlist. Similarly, Zhang et al. (2006) and Utiyama et al. (2009) adopted the use of aligners in order to estimate the content similarity of candidate parallel web pages or mixed languages pages. Barbosa et al. (2012) proposed the use of bilingual dictionaries and generated translations (e.g. by Google Translate and Microsoft Bing) to extract parallel content from multilingual sites.

[3]http://crawler.archive.org/

[4]http://nutch.apache.org

[5]http://openbixo.org/

[6]http://combine.it.lth.se/

3 System architecture

In this section, we describe the main modules integrated in ILSP-FC. In general, the crawler initializes its frontier (i.e. the list of pages to be visited) from a seed URL list provided by the user (or constructed semi-automatically, see Section 4), classifies fetched pages as relevant to the targeted domain, extracts links from fetched web pages and adds them to the list of pages to be visited.

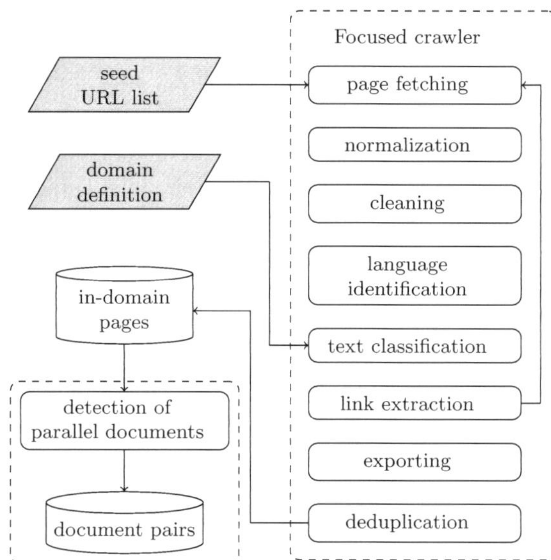

Figure 1: System architecture

In order to ensure modularity and scalability, the crawler is built using Bixo, an open source web mining toolkit that allows easy configuration of workflows and runs on top of the Hadoop[7] framework for distributed data processing.

3.1 Page Fetcher

The first module concerns page fetching. A multithreaded crawling implementation has been adopted in order to ensure concurrent visiting of multiple hosts. Users can configure several settings that determine the fetching process, including number of concurrent harvesters and filtering out specific document types. The crawler always respects standard robots.txt files, while politeness can also be affected with the use of settings regarding time intervals for revisiting URLs from the same website, maximum number of URLs from a specific host per iteration, maximum number of attempts to fetch a web page etc.

[7]http://hadoop.apache.org

3.2 Normalizer

The normalizer module uses the Apache Tika toolkit [8] to parse the structure of each fetched web page and extract its metadata. Extracted metadata are exported at a later stage (see Subsection 3.7) if the web document is considered relevant to the domain. The text encoding of the web page is also detected based on the HTTP Content-Encoding header and the charset part of the Content-Type header, and if needed, the content is converted into UTF-8. Besides default conversion, special care is taken for normalization of specific characters like no break space, narrow no-break space, three-per-em space, etc.

3.3 Cleaner

Apart from its textual content, a typical web page also contains boilerplate, i.e. "noisy" elements like navigation headers, advertisements, disclaimers, etc., which are of only limited or no use for the production of good-quality language resources. For removing boileplate, we use a modified version of Boilerpipe [9] (Kohlschütter et al, 2010) that also extracts structural information like *title*, *heading* and *list item*. At this stage, text is also segmented in paragraphs on the basis of specific HTML tags like *<p>*, *
* and *<li>*. Paragraphs judged to be boilerplate and/or detected as titles, etc. are properly annotated (see Subsection 3.7).

3.4 Language Identifier

The next processing module deals with language identification. We use the Cybozu[10] language identification library that considers n-grams as features and exploits a Naive Bayes classifier for language identification. If a web page is not in the targeted language, its only further use is in extraction of new links. Even though the main content of a web page is in the targeted language, it is likely that the web page includes a few paragraphs that are not in this language.Thus, the language identifier is also applied on each paragraph and marks them properly (see Subsection 3.7).

3.5 Text Classifier

The aim of this module is to identify if a page that is normalized and in the targeted language contains data relevant to the targeted domain. To this end, the content of the page is compared to a user-provided domain definition. Following the string-matching method adopted by the Combine web crawler, the definition consists of term triplets (<relevance weight, (multi-word) term, subdomain>) that describe a domain and, optionally, subcategories of this domain. Language-dependent stemmers from the Lucene[11] project are used to stem user-provided terms and document content. Based on the number of terms' occurrences, their location in the web page and the weights of found terms, a page relevance score p is calculated as follows:

$$p = \sum_{i=1}^{N} \sum_{j=1}^{4} n_{ij} \cdot w_i^t \cdot w_j^l,$$

where N is the amount of terms in the domain definition, w_i^t is the weight of term i, w_j^l is the weight of location j and n_{ij} denotes the number of occurrences of term i in location j. The four discrete locations in a web page are *title*, *metadata*, *keywords*, and plain text, with respective weights of 10, 4, 2, and 1.

Moreover, the amount of unique domain terms found in the main content of the page, m, is calculated. Then, the values p and m are compared with two predefined thresholds (t_1 and t_2) and if both values are higher than the thresholds, the web page is categorized as relevant to the domain and stored. It is worth mentioning that the user can affect the strictness of the classifier by setting the values of both thresholds in the crawler's configuration file.

3.6 Link Extractor

Even when a web page is not stored (because it was deemed irrelevant to the domain, or not in the targeted language), its links are extracted and added to the list of links scheduled to be visited. Since the crawling strategy is a critical issue for a focused crawler, the links should be ranked and the most promising links (i.e. links that point to "in-domain" web pages or candidate translations) should be followed first. To this end, a score s_l is calculated for each link l as follows:

$$s_l = c + p/L + \sum_{i=1}^{N} n_i \cdot w_i$$

where L is the amount of links originating from the source page, N is the amount of terms in the domain definition, n_i denotes the number of occurrences of the i-th term in the link's surrounding text and w_i is the weight of the i-th term. By using this

[8] http://tika.apache.org
[9] http://code.google.com/p/boilerpipe/
[10] http://code.google.com/p/language-detection/
[11] http://lucene.apache.org/

formulation, the score link is mainly influenced by the "domainess" of its surrounding text.

The parameter c is only added in case the crawler is used for building bilingual collections. It gets a high positive value if the link under consideration originates from a web page in L1 and "points" to a web page that is probably in L2. This is the case when, for example, L2 is German and the anchor text contains strings like "de", "Deutsch", etc. The insertion of this parameter forces the crawler to visit candidate translations before following other links.

3.7 Exporter

The Exporter module generates an XML file for each stored web document. Each file contains metadata (e.g. language, domain, URL, etc.) about the corresponding document inside a header element. Moreover, a *<body>* element contains the content of the document segmented in paragraphs. Apart from normalized text, each paragraph element *<p>* is enriched with attributes providing more information about the process outcome. Specifically, *<p>* elements in the XML files may contain the following attributes: i) *crawlinfo* with possible values *boilerplate*, meaning that the paragraph has been considered boilerplate (see Subsection 3.3), or *ooi-lang*, meaning that the paragraph is not in the targeted language; ii) *type* with possible values: *title, heading* and *listitem*; and iii) *topic* with a string value including all terms from the domain definition detected in this paragraph.

3.8 De-duplicator

Ignoring the fact[12] that the web contains many near-duplicate documents could have a negative effect in creating a representative corpus. Thus, the crawler includes a de-duplicator module that represents each document as a list containing the MD5 hashes of the main content's paragraphs, i.e. paragraphs without the *crawlinfo* attribute. Each document list is checked against all other document lists, and for each candidate pair, the intersection of the lists is calculated. If the ratio of the intersection cardinality to the cardinality of the shortest list is more than 0.8, the documents are considered near-duplicates and the shortest is discarded.

[12]Baroni et al. (2009) reported that during building of the Wacky corpora, the amount of collected documents was reduced by more than 50% after de-duplication.

3.9 Pair Detector

After in-domain pages are downloaded, the Pair Detector module uses two complementary methods to identify pairs of pages that could be considered parallel. The first method is based on co-occurrences, in two documents, of images with the same filename, while the second takes into account structural similarity.

In order to explain the workflow of the pair detection module, we will use the multilingual website `http://www.suva.ch` as a running example. Crawling this website using the processes described in previous subsections provides a pool of 707 HTML files (and their exported XML counterparts) that are found relevant to the H&S domain and in the targeted DE and IT languages (376 and 331 files, respectively).

Each XML file is parsed and the following features are extracted: i) the document *language*; ii) the *depth* of the original source page, (e.g. for `http://domain.org/d1/d2/d3/page.html`, depth is 4); iii) the *amount of paragraphs*; iv) the *length* (in terms of tokens) of the clean text; and v) the *fingerprint* of the main content, which is a sequence of integers that represent the structural information of the page, in a way similar to the approach described by Esplà-Gomis and Forcada (2010). For instance, the *fingerprint* of the extract in Figure 2 is [-2, 28, 145, -4, 9, -3, 48, -5, 740] with *boilerplate* paragraphs ignored; -2, -3 and -4 denote that the *type* attributes of corresponding *<p>* elements have *title*, *heading* and *listitem* values, respectively; -5 denotes the existence of the *topic* attribute in the last *<p>*; and positive integers are paragraph lengths in characters.

The *language* feature is used to filter out pairs of files that are in the same language. Pages that have a depth difference above 1 are also filtered out, on the assumption that it is very likely that translations are found at the same or neighbouring depths of the web site tree.

Next, we extract the filenames of the images from HTML source and each document is represented as a list of image filenames. Since it is very likely that some images appear in many web pages, we count the occurrence frequency of each image and discard relatively frequent images (i.e. Facebook and Twitter icons, logos etc.) from the lists.

In order to classify images into "critical" or "common" (see Figure 3) we need to calculate a threshold. In principle, one should ex-

```
<p type="title">Strategia degli investimenti</p> <!-- -2, 28-->
<p >I ricavi degli investimenti sono un elemento essenziale per finanziare le
   rendite e mantenere il potere d'acquisto dei beneficiari delle rendite.</p>
   <!--145-->
<p type="listitem">Document:</p> <!-- -4, 9 -->
<p crawlinfo="boilerplate" type="listitem">Factsheet "La strategia d'investimento
   della Suva in sintesi" (Il link viene aperto in una nuova finestra) </p> <!--
   ignored -->
<p type="heading">Perché la Suva effettua investimenti finanziari?</p> <!-- -3,
   48-->
<p topic="prevenzione degli infortuni;infortunio sul lavoro">Nonostante i molti
   sforzi compiuti nella prevenzione degli infortuni sul lavoro e nel tempo libero
   ogni anno accadono oltre 2500 infortuni con conseguenze invalidanti o mortali.
   In questi casi si versa una rendita per invalidità agli infortunati oppure una
   rendita per orfani o vedovile ai superstiti. Nello stesso anno in cui
   attribuisce una rendita, la Suva provvede ad accantonare i mezzi necessari a
   pagare le rendite future. La maggior parte del patrimonio investito dalla Suva è
    rappresentato proprio da questi mezzi, ossia dal capitale di copertura delle
   rendite. La restante parte del patrimonio è costituta da accantonamenti per
   prestazioni assicurative a breve termine come le spese di cura, le indennità
   giornaliere e le riserve.</p> <!-- -5, 740-->
```

Figure 2: An extract of an XML file for an Italian web page relevant to the H&S domain.

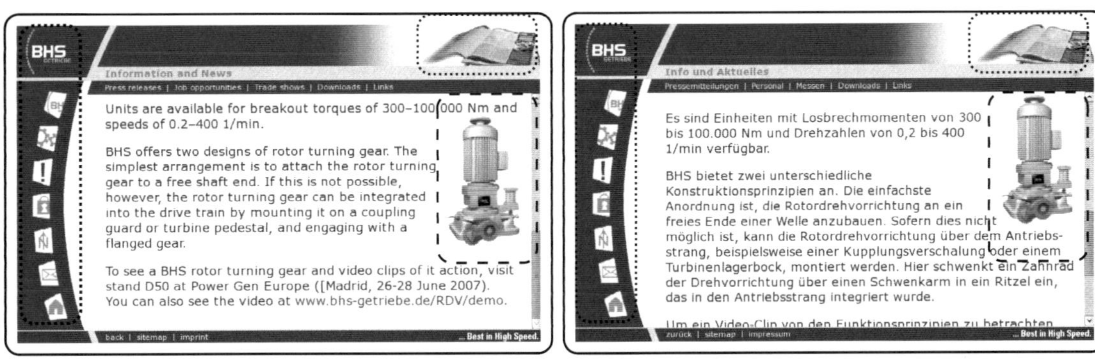

Figure 3: Critical (dashed) and common (dotted) images in a multilingual (EN/DE) site.

pect that low/high frequencies correspond to "critical"/"common" images. We employ a non-parametric approach for estimating the probability density function (Alpaydin, 2010) of the image frequencies using the following formula:

$$\hat{p}(x) = \frac{1}{Mh} \sum_{t=1}^{M} K\left(\frac{x-x^t}{h}\right)$$

where the random variable x defines the positions (i.e. images frequencies) at which the $\hat{p}(x)$ will be estimated, M is the amount of images, x^t denotes the values of data samples in the region of width h around the variable x, and $K(\cdot)$ is the normal kernel that defines the influence of values x^t in the estimation of $\hat{p}(x)$. The optimal value for h, the optimal bandwidth of the kernel smoothing window, was calculated as described in Bowman and Azzalini (1997).

Figure 4 illustrates the normalized histogram of image frequencies in the example collection and the estimated probability density function. One can identify a main lobe in the low values, which corresponds to "critical" images. Thus, the threshold is chosen to be equal to the minimum just after this lobe. The underlining assumption is that if a web page in L1 contains image(s) then the web page with its translation in L2 will contain more or less the same images. In case this assumption is not valid for a multilingual site (i.e. there are only images that appear in all pages, e.g. template icons), probably all images will be included. To eliminate this, we discard images that exist in more than 10% of the total HTML files.

Following this step, each document is examined against all others and two documents are considered parallel if a) the ratio of their paragraph amounts (the ratio of their lengths in terms of para-

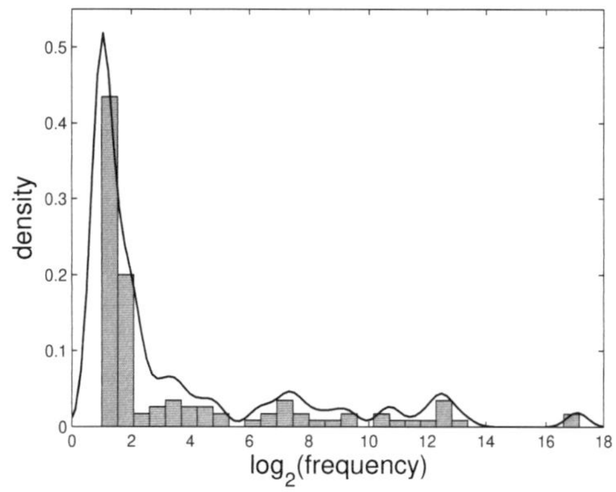

Figure 4: The normalized histogram and the estimated pdf of the image frequencies.

graphs), b) the ratio of their clean text lengths (in terms of tokens), and c) the Jaccard similarity coefficient of their image lists, are higher than empirically predefined thresholds.

More pairs are detected by examining structure similarity. Since the XML files contain information about structure, content (i.e. titles, headings, list items) and domain specificity (i.e. paragraphs with the *topic* attribute), we use these files instead of examining the similarity of the HTML source. A 3-dimensional feature vector is constructed for each candidate pair of parallel documents. The first element in this vector is the ratio of their fingerprint lengths, the second is the ratio of their sizes in paragraphs, and the third is the ratio of the edit distance of the fingerprints of the two documents to the maximum fingerprint length. Classification of a pair as parallel is achieved using a soft-margin polynomial Support Vector Machine trained with the positive and negative examples collected during our previous work (Pecina et al., 2012). Note that the dataset included only candidate pairs that met the criteria regarding the ratio of paragraphs amounts and the ratio of text lengths, mentioned above. As a result, negative instances (i.e. pairs of documents that have similar structure but are not real pairs) did not heavily outnumber positive ones and thus the training was not imbalanced (Akbani et al., 2004).

4 Bootstrapping the input of the focused crawler

In the work presented in previous sections, we assumed that users had access to already existing lists of seed terms and URLs for the initialization of the frontier and the classifier. But what if manually compiled resources for a particular domain/language(s) combination (e.g. ES/FR terminology for endocrinology or lists of EN/DE web sites related to floriculture) are impossible or difficult to find? Can we bootstrap such resources and provide them to users for post-editing? In this section, we present ongoing work towards this goal using the category graph and the external links of multilingual editions of Wikipedia.

We initialize the bootstrapping process by searching for a term defining the domain of interest (e.g. "ballet", "automotive accessories") in the category graph of the EN wikipedia. If a category is found, we recursively collect all pages in this category and its subcategories for a predefined depth. For each page we extract its title and we consider it a term that can participate in a list of domain-related seed terms. We use a set of pattern matching rules that exclude certain titles like those of disambiguation and redirect pages. Other rules exclude titles that refer to lists of related pages or titles that use upper case or title case and are probably abbreviations and named entities, respectively. Obviously, in a different setting where, for example, a user is interested in discovering named entities related to a domain, these titles should be handled differently.

The next step involves utilizing the links from each EN page to articles in wikipedias written in other languages. Based on which languages we are interested in, we again consider each title a seed term in language LANG, this time also storing the information that the term is also a LANG translation of the EN term.

During traversing the EN category graph and visiting corresponding articles in other languages, we also populate a list of seed URLs for the focused crawler, by keeping record of all links to URLs outside `wikipedia.org`. At this stage, we have all necessary resources to initiate monolingual focused crawls in each language we are interested in.

An optional last stage targets the automatic discovery of sites with multilingual content where parallel documents can be extracted from. During this stage, we visit each of the external links we collected and detect the language of the web page this link points to. From this web page, we extract its links and examine whether the anchor text of each link matches a set of patterns indicating that this link points to a translation (in a way similar to the process described in Subsection 3.6). If translation links are found, we store the site as a candidate for bilingual focused crawling. Also, since it is common that links to multilingual editions of a web site are not present in all of its pages, we repeat the same process for the home page of the site. Notice that it is a task for the FC to detect whether these sites (or one of their sections) also contain parallel documents in the targeted domain.

In a first set of experiments following this approach, we used September 2012 snapshots[13] for English, French, German, Greek, Portuguese and Spanish wikipedias (EN, FR, DE, EL, PT and ES, respectively). Although we leave detailed evaluation of created resources for future work, we present as example output a list of terms related to "Flowers" in Table 1. Notice that, since the number of articles of multilingual wikipedias varies considerably, the term list extracted for languages like EL is, as expected, smaller compared, for example, to the 547 and 293 terms collected for EN and ES, respectively. Finally, using the URLs extracted from the articles on the "Flowers" domain, Table 2 contains a sample of web sites detected for containing relevant multilingual content.

5 Evaluation Results

In order to assess the quality of the resources that ILSP-FC can produce, we evaluated it in a task of acquiring pairs of parallel documents in German and Italian for the "Health & Safety at work" (Arbeitsschutz/Sicurezza sul lavoro) domain. We assume that this task is relatively difficult, i.e. that the number of documents in this domain and pair of languages is relatively small in the web. Overall, our system delivered 807 document pairs for H&S, containing 1.40 and 1.21 million tokens for IT and DE, respectively. Numbers refer to tokens in the main content of the acquired web pages, i.e. to tokens in paragraphs without the attribute *crawlinfo* (see Subsection 3.7).

A sample of the acquired corpora were evaluated against a set of criteria discussed in the following subsections. We randomly selected 103 document pairs for manual inspection. The sample size was calculated according to a 95% confidence level and an at most 10% confidence interval.

[13] We use the Java Wikipedia Library (Zesch et al., 2008) to convert each snapshot into a database that allows structured access to several aspects of categories, articles, sections etc.

5.1 Parallelness

The number of the correctly identified parallel document pairs was obviously critical in this particular evaluation setting. We focused on the precision of the pair detector module, since it is not feasible to count how many pairs were missed. In the subset examined, 94 and 4 document pairs were judged as parallel and not parallel, respectively. The other 5 pairs were considered borderline cases, where more than 20% of the sentences in one document were translated in the other. Since about 95% of the crawled data are of good or sufficiently good quality, this shows that they are usable for further processing, e.g. for sentence alignment.

5.2 Domain specificity

We next evaluated how many documents in the selected data fit the targeted domain in both the IT and the DE partitions. The overall precision was about 77%, with 79 IT documents and 80 DE documents found relevant to the narrow domain chosen for evaluation.

Reported results on text-to-topic classification sometimes score higher; however they neglect a critical factor of influence, namely the distance between training and prediction datasets. In the "real world", scores between 75% and 85% are realistic to assume. It should be mentioned that the precision of the topic classifier strongly depends on the quality of the seed terms: by inspecting results, modifying the seed term list and re-crawling, results could easily be improved further.

5.3 Language identification

Since the language identifier is applied on every paragraph of the main content of each web page, we examined how many of the paragraphs have been marked correctly. Overall, 5223 and 4814 paragraphs of IT and DE documents were checked and only 13 and 65 wrong assignments were found, respectively.

Most errors (about 80%) were found in a single document with a lot of tokens denoting chemical substances that seem to confuse the language identifier. When excluding this document, figures rise to 99,67% and 99,95% for the DE and IT partitions, respectively. The rest of the errors mainly occurred in paragraphs containing sentences in different languages.

EN: 547	DE: 255	EL: 22	ES: 293	FR: 286	IT: 143	PT: 164
Gardenia	Gardenien	Γαρδένια	Gardenia	Gardénia	Gardenia	Gardenia
Calendula	Ringelblumen	Καλέντουλα	Calendula	Calendula	Calendula	Calendula
Lilium	Lilien	Κρίνο	Lilium	Lys	Lilium	Lírio
Peony	Pfingstrosen	Παιώνια	Paeoniaceae	Pivoine	Paeonia	Paeoniaceae
Tulip	Tulpen	Τουλίπα	Tulipa	Tulipe	Tulipa	Tulipa
Flower	Blüte	Άνθος	Flor	Fleur	Fiore	Flor
Crocus	Krokusse	Κρόκος	Crocus	Crocus	Crocus	Crocus
Anemone	Windröschen	Ανεμώνη	Anemone	Anémone	Anemone	Anemone

Table 1: Sample seed terms for the "Flowers" domain in 7 languages, collected automatically from multilingual editions of Wikipedia. The header of the table refers to the total terms collected for each language.

Wikipedia article	Seed URL	WebSite	Langs
EN: Omphalodes_verna	http://goo.gl/msylc	http://www.luontoportti.com	de,en,es,fr
ES: Tropaeolum	http://goo.gl/Ec5uK	http://www.chileflora.com	de,en,es
EN: Erythronium americanum	http://goo.gl/nEP2L	http://wildaboutgardening.org	en,fr
DE: Nickendes_Leimkraut	http://goo.gl/nuHNe	http://www.wildblumen.at	de,en,pt
DE: Titanenwurz	http://goo.gl/rLl9W	http://www.wilhelma.de	de,en

Table 2: Automatically detected web sites with multilingual content related to the "Flowers" domain. Column 1 presents the original LANG.wikipedia.org article from which the (shortened for readability purposes) seed URLs in column 2 were extracted. The seed URLs led to the 3rd column web sites, in which content in the languages of the 4th column was found.

5.4 Boilerplate removal

For this evaluation aspect, we evaluated how many "good" paragraphs were judged to be boilerplate, and how many "bad" paragraphs were missed. We examined 23178 and 23176 paragraphs of IT and DE documents and found 2326 and 2591 errors with an overall error rate around 10%. It should be noted that different strategies for boilerplate removal can be followed. One "classical" option is to remove everything that does not belong to the text, i.e. headers, advertisements etc. that "frame" real content. Another option is to attempt to remove everything which is irrelevant for MT sentence alignment; this goes beyond the first approach as it also removes short textual chunks, copyright disclaimers, etc. Most of the errors reported here were mainly due to this difference; i.e. they were paragraphs that were deemed not usable for MT alignment.

6 Conclusions and future work

In this paper we described and evaluated ILSP-FC, a system for mining domain-specific monolingual and bilingual corpora from the web. The system is available as open-source and is modular in the sense that each of its components can be easily substituted with similar software performing the same functionalities. The crawler can also be tested via web services that allow the user to perform experiments without the need to install it.

We have already used the crawler in producing monolingual and parallel corpora and other derivative resources. Evaluation has shown that the system can be used effectively in collecting resources of high quality, provided that the user can initialize it with lists of seed terms and URLs that can be easily found on the web. For domains for which no similar lists are available, we presented ongoing work for bootstrapping them from multilingual editions of Wikipedia. Future work includes evaluation and improvement of the bootstrapping component, more sophisticated methods for text classification, and grouping of collected data based on genre.

Acknowledgments

Work by the first two authors was partially funded by the European Union QTLaunchPad (FP7, Grant 296347) and Abu-MaTran (FP7-People-IAPP, Grant 324414) projects. An initial version of this work was produced during the EU Panacea project (FP7-ICT, Grant 248064).

References

Rehan Akbani, Stephen Kwek, and Nathalie Japkowicz. 2004. Applying support vector machines to imbalanced datasets. In *In Proceedings of the 15th European Conference on Machine Learning (ECML*, pages 39--50.

José João Almeida and Alberto Simões. 2010. Automatic parallel corpora and bilingual terminology extraction from parallel websites. In *3rd Workshop on Building and Using Comparable Corpora* .

Ethem Alpaydin. 2010. *Introduction to Machine Learning*. The MIT Press, 2nd edition.

Luciano Barbosa, Vivek Kumar Rangarajan Sridhar, Mahsa Yarmohammadi, and Srinivas Bangalore. 2012. Harvesting parallel text in multiple languages with limited supervision. In *COLING*, pages 201--214.

Marco Baroni, Adam Kilgarriff, Jan Pomikálek, and Pavel Rychlý. 2006. WebBootCaT: Instant Domain-Specific Corpora to Support Human Translators. In *Proceedings of the 11th Annual Conference of EAMT*, pages 47--252, Norway.

Marco Baroni, Francis Chantree, Adam Kilgarriff, and Serge Sharoff. 2008. Cleaneval: a competition for cleaning web pages. In *LREC'08*.

Marco Baroni, Silvia Bernardini, Adriano Ferraresi, and Eros Zanchetta. 2009. The WaCky Wide Web: a collection of very large linguistically processed web-crawled corpora. *Language Resources and Evaluation*, 43(3):209--226.

Adrian W. Bowman and Adelchi Azzalini. 1997. *Applied smoothing techniques for data analysis: the kernel approach with S-Plus illustrations*, volume 18. Oxford University Press.

Jisong Chen, Rowena Chau, and Chung-Hsing Yeh. 2004. Discovering parallel text from the World Wide Web. In *Proceedings of ACSW Frontiers '04*, volume 32, pages 157--161, Darlinghurst, Australia.

Alain Désilets, Benoit Farley, Marta Stojanovic, and Geneviève Patenaude. 2008. WeBiText: Building Large Heterogeneous Translation Memories from Parallel Web Content. In *Proceedings of Translating and the Computer (30)*, London, UK.

Miquel Esplà-Gomis and Mikel L. Forcada. 2010. Combining Content-Based and URL-Based Heuristics to Harvest Aligned Bitexts from Multilingual Sites with Bitextor. *The Prague Bulletin of Mathemathical Lingustics*, 93:77--86.

Gumwon Hong, Chi-Ho Li, Ming Zhou, and Hae-Chang Rim. 2010. An empirical study on web mining of parallel data. In *Proceedings of the 23rd COLING*, pages 474--482.

Adam Kilgarriff and Gregory Grefenstette. 2003. Introduction to the special issue on the web as corpus. *Computational Linguistics*, 29(3):333--348.

Jian-Yun Nie, Michel Simard, Pierre Isabelle, and Richard Durand. 1999. Cross-language information retrieval based on parallel texts and automatic mining of parallel texts from the Web. In *Proceedings of the 22nd annual international ACM SIGIR conference on research and development in information retrieval*, pages 74--81, New York.

Christopher Olston and Marc Najork. 2010. Web crawling. *Found. Trends Inf. Retr.*, 4(3):175--246.

Pavel Pecina, Antonio Toral, Vassilis Papavassiliou, Prokopis Prokopidis, and Josef van Genabith. 2012. Domain adaptation of statistical machine translation using web-crawled resources: a case study. In *Proceedings of the 16th Annual Conference of EAMT*, pages 145--152, Trento, Italy.

Xiaoguang Qi and Brian D. Davison. 2009. Web page classification: Features and algorithms. *ACM Computing Surveys*, 41:11--31.

Philip Resnik and Noah A. Smith. 2003. The Web as a parallel corpus. *Computational Linguistics*, 29:349--380.

Lei Shi, Cheng Niu, Ming Zhou, and Jianfeng Gao. 2006. A dom tree alignment model for mining parallel data from the web. In *COLING/ACL-2006*, pages 489--496.

Miroslav Spousta, Michal Marek, and Pavel Pecina. 2008. Victor: the Web-Page Cleaning Tool. In *Proceedings of the 4th Web as Corpus Workshop - Can we beat Google?*, pages 12--17, Marrakech.

Padmini Srinivasan, Filippo Menczer, and Gautam Pant. 2005. A General Evaluation Framework for Topical Crawlers. *Information Retrieval*, 8:417--447.

Martin Theobald, Jonathan Siddharth, and Andreas Paepcke. 2008. Spotsigs: robust and efficient near duplicate detection in large web collections. In *Proceedings of the 31st annual international ACM SIGIR conference on research and development in information retrieval*, pages 563--570.

Masao Utiyama, Daisuke Kawahara, Keiji Yasuda, and Eiichiro Sumita. 2009. Mining parallel texts from mixed-language web pages. In *MT Summit*.

Torsten Zesch, Christof Müller, and Iryna Gurevych. 2008. Extracting lexical semantic knowledge from wikipedia and wiktionary. In *Proceedings of the 6th International Conference on Language Resources and Evaluation*, Marrakech.

Ying Zhang, Ke Wu, Jianfeng Gao, and Phil Vines. 2006. Automatic Acquisition of Chinese-English Parallel Corpus from the Web. In *Proceedings of the 28th European Conference on Information Retrieval*, pages 420--431.

Building basic vocabulary across 40 languages

Judit Ács **Katalin Pajkossy** **András Kornai**
HAS Computer and Automation Research Institute
H-1111 Kende u 13-17, Budapest
{judit.acs,pajkossy,kornai}@sztaki.mta.hu

Abstract

The paper explores the options for building bilingual dictionaries by automated methods. We define the notion 'basic vocabulary' and investigate how well the conceptual units that make up this language-independent vocabulary are covered by language-specific bindings in 40 languages.

Introduction

Globalization increasingly brings languages in contact. At the time of the pioneering IBM work on the Hansard corpus (Brown et al., 1990), only two decades ago, there was no need for a Basque-Chinese dictionary, but today there is (Saralegi et al., 2012). While the methods for building dictionaries from parallel corpora are now mature (Melamed, 2000), there is a dearth of bilingual or even monolingual material (Zséder et al., 2012), hence the increased interest in comparable corpora.

Once we find bilingual speakers capable of carrying out a manual evaluation of representative samples, it is relatively easy to measure the precision of a dictionary built by automatic methods. But measuring recall remains a challenge, for if there existed a high quality machine-readable dictionary (MRD) to measure against, building a new one would largely be pointless, except perhaps as a means of engineering around copyright restrictions. We could measure recall against Wiktionary, but of course this is a moving target, and more importantly, the coverage across language pairs is extremely uneven.

What we need is a standardized vocabulary resource that is equally applicable to all language pairs. In this paper we describe our work toward creating such a resource by extending the *4lang* conceptual dictionary (Kornai and Makrai, 2013) to the top 40 languages (by Wikipedia size) using a variety of methods. Since some of the resources studied here are not available for the initial list of 40 languages, we extended the original list to 50 languages so as to guarantee at least 40 languages for every method. Throughout the paper, results are provided for all 50 languages, indicating missing data as needed.

Section 1 outlines the approach taken toward defining the basic vocabulary and translational equivalence. Section 2 describes how Wiktionary itself measures up against the 4lang resource directly and after triangulation across language pairs. Section 2.3 and Section 2.4 deals with extraction from multiply parallel and near-parallel corpora, and Section 3 offers some conclusions.

1 Basic vocabulary

The idea that there is a *basic* vocabulary composed of a few hundred or at most a few thousand elements has a long history going back to the Renaissance – for a summary, see Eco (1995). The first modern efforts in this direction are Thorndike's (1921) *Word Book,* based entirely on frequency counts (combining TF and DF measures), and Ogden's (1944) *Basic English,* based primarily on considerations of definability. Both had lasting impact, with Thorndike's approach forming the basis of much subsequent work on readability (Klare 1974, Kanungo and Orr 2009) and Ogden's forming the basis of the Simple English Wikipedia[1]. An important landmark is the Swadesh (1950) list, which puts special emphasis on cross-linguistic definability, as its primary goal is to support glottochronological studies.

Until the advent of large MRDs, the frequency-based method was much easier to follow, and Thorndike himself has extended his original list of ten thousand words to twenty thousand (Thorndike

[1] http://simple.wikipedia.org

1931) and thirty thousand (Thorndike and Lorge 1944). For a recent example see Davies and Gardner (2010), for a historical survey see McArthur (1998). The main problem with this approach is the lack of clear boundaries both at the top of the list, where function words dominate, and at the bottom, where it seems quite arbitrary to cut the list off after the top three hundred words (Diedrich 1938), the top thousand, as is common in foreign language learning, or the top five thousand, especially as the frequency curves are generally in good agreement with Zipf's law and thus show no obvious inflection point. The problem at the top is perhaps more significant, since any frequency-based listing will start with the function words of the language, characterizing more its grammar than its vocabulary. For this reason, the list is highly varied across languages, and what is a word (free form) in one language, like English *the*, often ends up as an affix (bound form) in another, like the Romanian suffix *-ul*. By choosing a frequency-based approach, we inevitably put the emphasis on comparing grammars and morphologies, instead of comparing vocabularies.

The definitional method is based on the assumption that dictionaries will attempt to define the more complex words by simpler ones. Therefore, starting with any word list L, the list $D(L)$ obtained by collecting the words appearing on the right-hand side of the dictionary definitions will be simpler, the list $D(D(L))$ obtained by repeating the method will be yet simpler, and so on, until we arrive at an irreducible list of basic words that can no longer be further simplified. Modern MRDs, starting with the Longman Dictionary of Contemporary English (LDOCE), generally enforce a strict list of words and word senses that can appear in definitions, which guarantees that the basic list will be a subset of this defining vocabulary. This method, while still open to charges of arbitrariness at the high end, in regards to the separation of function words from basic words, creates a bright line at the low end: no word, no matter how frequent, needs to be included as long as it is not necessary for defining other words.

In creating the 4lang conceptual dictionary (Kornai and Makrai, 2013), we took advantage of the fact that the definitional method is robust in terms of choosing the seed list L, and built a seed of approximately 3,500 entries composed of the Longman Defining Vocabulary (2,200 entries), the most frequent 2,000 words according to the Google unigram count (Brants and Franz 2006) and the BNC, as well as the most frequent 2,000 words from Polish (Halácsy et al 2004) and Hungarian (Kornai et al 2006). Since Latin is one of the four languages supported by 4lang (the other three being English, Polish, and Hungarian), we added the classic Diederich (1938) list and Whitney's (1885) *Roots*.

The basic list emerging from the iteration has 1104 elements (including two bound morphemes but excluding technical terms of the formal semantic model that have no obvious surface reflex). We will refer to this as the *basic* or *uroboros* set as it has the property that each of its members can be defined in terms of the others, and we reserve the name *4lang* for the larger set of 3,345 elements from which it was obtained. Since 4lang words can be defined using only the uroboros vocabulary, and every word in the Longman Dictionary of Contemporary English can be defined using the 4lang vocabulary (since this is a superset of LDV), we have full confidence that every sense of every non-technical word can be defined by the uroboros vocabulary. In fact, the Simple English Wikipedia is an attempt to do this (Yasseri et al., 2012) based on Ogden's Basic English, which overlaps with the uroboros set very significantly (Dice 0.527).

The lexicographic principles underlying 4lang have been discussed elsewhere (Kornai, 2012; Kornai and Makrai, 2013), here we just summarize the most salient points. First, the system is intended to capture everyday vocabulary. Once the boundaries of natural language are crossed, and goats are defined by their set of genes (rather than an old-fashioned taxonomic description involving cloven hooves and the like), or derivative is defined as $\lim_{\Delta \to 0}(f(x+\Delta) - f(x))/\Delta$, the uroboros vocabulary loses its grip. But for the non-technical vocabulary, and even the part of the technical vocabulary that rests on natural language (e.g. legal definitions or the definitions in philosophy and discursive prose in general), coverage of the uroboros set promises a strategy of gradually extending the vocabulary from the simple to the more complex. Thus, to define *Jupiter* as 'the largest planet of the Sun', we need to define *planet*, but not *large* as this item is already listed in the uroboros set. Since *planet* is defined 'as a large body in space that moves around a star', by substitution we will obtain for Jupiter the definition 'the largest body in space that moves around the Sun' where all the key items *large, body, space, move, around* are part of the uroboros set. Proper nouns like *Sun* are discussed further in (Kornai, 2010), but we note here that they constitute a very small proportion (less than 6%) of the basic vocabulary.

Second, the ultimate definitions of the uroboros elements are given in the formal language of machines (Eilenberg, 1974), and at that level the English words serve only a mnemonic purpose, and could in principle be replaced by any arbitrary names or even numbers. Because this would make debugging next to impossible, as in purposely obfuscated code, we resort to using English printnames for each concept, but it is important to keep in mind that these are only weakly reflective of the English word. For example, the system relies heavily on an element `has` that indicates the possessive relation both in the direct sense, as in *the Sun's planet, the planet of the Sun* and in its more indirect uses, as in *John's favorite actress* where there is no question of John being in possession of the actress. In other languages, `has` will generally be translated by morphemes (often bound morphemes) indicating possession, but there is no attempt to cross-link all relevant uses. The element *has* will appear in the definition of Latin *meus* and *noster* alike, but of course there is no claim that English *has* underlies the Latin senses. If we know how to express the basic vocabulary elements in a given language, which is the task we concentrate on here, and how to combine the expressions in that language, we are capable of defining all remaining words of the language.

In general, matching up function words cross-linguistically is an extremely hard task, especially as they are often expressed by inflectional morphology and our workflow, which includes stemming, just strips off the relevant elements. Even across languages where morphological analysis is a solved task, it will take a great deal of manual work to establish some form of translational equivalence, and we consider the issue out of scope here. But for content words, the use of language-independent concepts simplifies matters a great deal: instead of finding $\binom{40}{2}$ translation pairs for the 3,384 concepts that already have manual bindings in four languages (currently, Latin and Polish are only 90% complete), our goal is only to find reasonable printnames for the 1,104 basic concepts in all 40 languages. Translation pairs are only obtained indirectly, through the conceptual pivot, and thus do not amount to fully valid bilingual translation pairs. For example, *he-goat* in one language may just get mapped to the concept *goat*, and if *billy-goat* is present in another language, the strict translational equivalence between the gendered forms will be lost because of the poverty of the pivot. Nevertheless, rough equivalence at the conceptual level is already a useful notion, especially for filtering out candidate pairs produced by more standard bilingual dictionary building methods, to which we now turn.

2 Wiktionary

Wiktionary is a crowdsourced dictionary with many language editions that aim at eventually defining 'all words'. Although Wiktionary is primarily for human audience, since editors are expected to follow fairly strict formatting standards, we can automate the data extraction to a certain degree. While not a computational linguistic task par excellence, undoing the MediaWiki format, identifying the templates and simply detecting the translation pairs requires a great deal of scripting. Some Wiktionaries, among others the Bulgarian, Chinese, Danish, German, Hungarian, Korean, and Russian, are formatted so heterogeneously that automated extraction of translation pairs is very hard, and our results could be further improved.

Table 1 summarizes the coverage of Wiktionary on the basic vocabulary from the perspective of translation pairs with one manual member, English, Hungarian, Latin, and Polish respectively. The last column represents the overall coverage combining all four languages. As can be seen, the better resourced languages fare better in Wiktionary as well, with the most translations found using English as the source language (64.9% on the smaller basic set, and 64% on the larger 4lang vocabulary), Polish and Hungarian faring about

Table 1: 4lang coverage of Wiktionary data.

	Based on				
	en	hu	la	pl	all
4lang	59.43	22.09	7.9	19.6	64.01
uroboros	60.29	22.88	9.11	21.09	64.91

equally well, although the Polish list of 4lang has more missing bindings, and the least resourced Latin faring the worst.

Another measure of coverage is obtained by seeing how many language bindings are found on the average for each concept: 65% on 4lang and 64% for the basic set (32 out of the 50 languages considered here).

2.1 Triangulating

Next we used a simple triangulation method to expand the collection of translation pairs, which added new translation pairs if they had been linked with the same word in a third language. An example, the English:Romanian pair *guild:breaslă*, obtained through a Hungarian pivot, is shown in Figure 1.

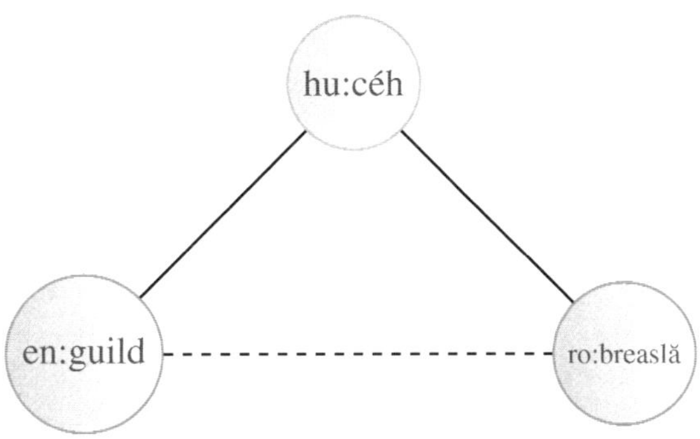

Figure 1: The non-dashed edge represents translation pairs extracted directly from the Wiktionaries. The pair *guild–breaslă* were found via triangulating.

While direct translation pairs come from the manually built Wiktionaries and can be considered gold (not entirely without reservations, but clearly over 90% correct in most language pairs we could manually spot-check), indirect pairs must be viewed with considerable suspicion, as multiple word senses bring in false positives quite often. Using 3,317,861 pairs extracted from 40 Wiktionaries, we obtained a total of 126,895,236 indirect pairs, but in the following table we consider only those that were obtained through at least two different third-language pivots with the pairs originating from different Wiktionaries, and discarded the vast majority, leaving 5,720,355 pairs that have double confirmation. Manual checking proved that the quality of these pairs is comparable to that of the original data (see Table 7). A similar method, within one dictionary rather than across several, was used in (Saralegi et al., 2012) to remove triangulation noise. Since recall would be considerably improved by some less aggressive filtering method, in the future we will also consider improving the similarity scores of our corpus-based methods using the single triangles we now discard.

Table 2: 4lang coverage of triangulating.

	Based on				
	en	hu	la	pl	all
4lang	76.09	64.91	43.25	53.74	85.81
basic	77.81	64.74	48.07	58.55	86.97

Table 3: 4lang coverage of Wiktionary data and triangulating.

	Based on				
	en	hu	la	pl	all
4lang	80.77	65.69	43.63	54.30	86.80
basic	82.07	65.47	48.41	59.13	87.81

Triangulating by itself improves coverage from 65% to 85.8% (4lang) and from 64% to 87% (basic), see Table 2. Table 3 shows the combined coverage which is not much different from Table 2 but considering that the triangulating used the Wiktionary data as input, we expected a very large intersection (it turned out to be more than 40% of the pairs acquired through triangulating). The average number of language bindings also improves significantly, to 43.5/50 (4lang) and 44/50 (basic).

2.2 Wikipedia titles

Another crowdsourced method that promises great precision is comparing Wikipedia article titles across languages: we extracted over 187m potential translation pairs this way. Yet the raw data is quite noisy, for example French *chambre* points to English *Câmara*, an article devoted to the fact that 'Câmara (meaning 'chamber') is a common surname in the Portuguese language' rather than to some article on *bedroom, room,* or *chamber*. We filtered this data in several ways. First, we discarded all pairs that contain words that appear five or fewer times in the frequency count generated from the language in question. This reduced the

Table 4: 4lang coverage of Wikipedia interwiki links (langlinks).

	Based on				
	en	hu	la	pl	all
4lang	21.51	14.4	9.54	12.26	31.74
basic	20.7	13.0	10.22	13.43	31.32

number of pairs to 15m. Most of these, unfortunately, are string-identical across languages, leaving us with a total of 6.15m nontrivial translation pairs. A large portion of these are named entities that do not always add meaningfully to a bilingual dictionary.

The average number of language bindings is 16.5 and 12.6 respectively. The combined results improve slightly as shown in Table 8.

2.3 Parallel texts

Using the Bible as a parallel text in dictionary building has a long tradition (Resnik et al., 1999). Somewhat surprisingly in the age of parallel corpora, the only secular text available in all our languages is the Universal Declaration of Human Rights, which is simply too short to add meaningfully to the coverage obtained on the Bible. In addition to downloading the collection at *http://homepages.inf.ed.ac.uk/s0787820/bible*, we used *http://www.jw.org* (for Dutch, Armenian and Korean), *www.gospelgo.com* (for Catalan, Kazakh, Macedonian, Malay and Persian), *http://www.biblegateway.com* (for Czech), *http://biblehub.com* (for English) and *http://www.mek.oszk.hu* (for Hungarian). To the extent feasible we tried to use modern Bible translations, resorting to more traditional translations only where we could not identify a more contemporary version.

The average number of languages with translations found is 19 (basic) and 17.8 (4lang). These

Table 5: 4lang coverage of the Bible data.

	Based on				
	en	hu	la	pl	all
4lang	19.64	15.17	13.78	14.13	35.49
basic	21.47	17.12	15.67	15.78	38.13

numbers are considerably weaker than the crowd-sourced results, suggesting that the dearth of multiply parallel texts, even in the best resourced group of 40 languages, needs to be addressed.

2.4 Comparable texts

Comparable corpora were built from Wikipedia articles in the following manner. For each language pair, we considered those articles that mutually linked each other, and took the first 50 words, excluding the title itself. Article pairs whose length differed drastically (more than a factor of five) were discarded.

Table 6: 4lang coverage of the dictionary extracted from Wikipedia as comparable corpora.

	Based on				
	en	hu	la	pl	all
4lang	5.58	5.66	4.30	4.96	16.00
basic	5.70	5.86	4.93	5.39	16.77

The 4lang coverage based solely on the translations acquired from comparable corpora is presented in Table 6. The average number of languages with translations found is 8 (basic) and 8.4 (4lang).

2.5 Evaluation

We used manual evaluation for a small subset of language pairs. Human annotators received a sample of 100 translation candidate-per-method. The samples were selected from translations that were found by only one method, as we suspect that translations found by several methods are more likely to be correct. Using this strict data selection

Table 7: Manual evaluation of extracted pairs that do not appear in more than one dictionary.

	Wikt	Tri	Title	Par	Comp
cs-hu	82	81	95	41	40
de-hu	92	87	96	46	68
fr-hu	76	80	89	43	54
fr-it	79	79	92	43	36
hu-en	87	75	92	28	63
hu-it	94	93	93	35	61
hu-ko	87	85	99	N/A	N/A
avg	85.3	82.9	93.7	39.3	53.7

criterion we evaluated the *added quality* of each method. Results are presented in Table 7. It is clear that set next to the crowdsourced methods, dictionary extraction from either parallel or comparable corpora cannot add new translations with high precision. When high quality input data is available, triangulating appears to be a powerful yet simple method.

3 Conclusions and future work

The major lesson emerging from this work is that currently, crowdsourced methods are considerably more powerful than the parallel and comparable corpora-based methods that we started with. The reason is simply the lack of sufficiently large parallel and near-parallel data sets, *even among the most commonly taught languages*. If one is actually interested in creating a resource, even a small resource such as our basic vocabulary set, with bindings for all 40 languages, one needs to engage the crowd.

Table 8: Summary of the increase in 4lang coverage achieved by each method. Wikt: Wiktionary, Tri: triangulating, WPT: Wikipedia titles, Par: the Bible as parallel corpora, WPC: Wikipedia articles as comparable corpora

Src	Set	Based on				
		en	hu	la	pl	all
Wikt	4lang	59.43	22.09	7.90	19.6	64.01
	basic	60.29	22.88	9.11	21.09	64.91
Tri	4lang	80.77	65.69	43.63	54.3	86.8
	basic	82.07	65.47	48.41	59.13	87.81
WPT	4lang	81.39	66.27	44.2	54.66	87.39
	basic	82.51	65.86	48.89	59.53	88.17
Par	4lang	82.22	67.35	45.99	55.4	88.22
	basic	83.27	67.04	50.62	60.25	88.91
WPC	4lang	81.56	66.49	44.42	54.77	87.58
	basic	82.66	66.06	49.14	59.62	88.33

The resulting *40lang* resource, currently about 88% complete, is available for download at *http://hlt.sztaki.hu*. The Wiktionary extraction tool is available at *https://github.com/juditacs/wikt2dict*. 40lang, while not 100% complete and verified, can already serve as an important addition to existing MRDs in several applications. In comparing corpora the extent vocabulary is shared across them is a critical measure, yet the task is not trivial even when these corpora are taken from the same language. We need to compare vocabularies at the conceptual level, and checking the shared 40lang content between two texts is a good first cut. Automated dictionary building itself can benefit from the resource, since both aligners and dictionary extractors benefit from known translation pairs.

Acknowledgments

The results presented here have improved since Ács (2013). Ács did the work on Wiktionary and Wikipedia titles, Pajkossy on parallel corpora, Kornai supplied the theory and advised. The statistics were created by Ács. We thank Attila Zséder, whose HunDict system (see *https://github.com/zseder/hundict*) was used on the (near)parallel data, for his constant support at every stage of the work. We also thank our annotators: Klára Szalay, Éva Novai, Angelika Sándor, and Gábor Recski.

The research reported in the paper was conducted with the support of the EFNILEX project *http://efnilex.efnil.org* of the European Federation of National Institutions for Language *http://www.efnil.org*, and OTKA grant #82333.

References

Judit Ács. 2013. Intelligent multilingual dictionary building. *MSc Thesis, Budapest University of Technology and Economics*.

Thorsten Brants and Alex Franz. 2006. Web 1T 5-gram version 1.

Peter Brown, John Cocke, Stephen Della Pietra, Vincent J. Della Pietra, Fredrick Jelinek, John D. Lafferty, Robert L. Mercer, and Paul S. Roossin. 1990. A statistical approach to machine translation. *Computational Linguistics*, 16:79–85.

M. Davies and D. Gardner. 2010. *A Frequency Dictionary of Contemporary American English: Word Sketches, Collocates, and Thematic Lists*. Routledge Frequency Dictionaries Series. Routledge.

Paul Bernard Diederich. 1939. *The frequency of Latin words and their endings*. The University of Chicago press.

Umberto Eco. 1995. *The Search for the Perfect Language*. Blackwell, Oxford.

Samuel Eilenberg. 1974. *Automata, Languages, and Machines*, volume A. Academic Press.

Péter Halácsy, András Kornai, László Németh, András Rung, István Szakadát, and Viktor Trón. 2004. Creating open language resources for Hungarian. In

Proceedings of the 4th international conference on Language Resources and Evaluation (LREC2004), pages 203–210.

Tapas Kanungo and David Orr. 2009. Predicting the readability of short web summaries. In *2nd ACM Int. Conf. on Web Search and Data Mining*.

George R. Klare. 1974. Assessing readability. *Reading Research Quarterly*, 10(1):62–102.

András Kornai and Márton Makrai. 2013. A 4lang fogalmi szótár [the 4lang concept dictionary]. In A. Tanács and V. Vincze, editors, *IX. Magyar Számitógépes Nyelvészeti Konferencia [Ninth Conference on Hungarian Computational Linguistics]*, pages 62–70.

A. Kornai, P. Halácsy, V. Nagy, Cs. Oravecz, V. Trón, and D. Varga. 2006. Web-based frequency dictionaries for medium density languages. In A. Kilgariff and M. Baroni, editors, *Proc. 2nd Web as Corpus Wkshp (EACL 2006 WS01)*, pages 1–8.

András Kornai. 2010. The algebra of lexical semantics. In Christian Ebert, Gerhard Jäger, and Jens Michaelis, editors, *Proceedings of the 11th Mathematics of Language Workshop*, LNAI 6149, pages 174–199. Springer.

András Kornai. 2012. Eliminating ditransitives. In Ph. de Groote and M-J Nederhof, editors, *Revised and Selected Papers from the 15th and 16th Formal Grammar Conferences*, LNCS 7395, pages 243–261. Springer.

Tom McArthur. 1998. *Living Words: Language, Lexicography, and the Knowledge Revolution*. Exeter Language and Lexicography Series. University of Exeter Press.

I Dan Melamed. 2000. Models of translational equivalence among words. *Computational Linguistics*, 26(2):221–249.

C.K. Ogden. 1944. *Basic English: A General Introduction with Rules and Grammar*. Psyche miniatures: General Series. Kegan Paul, Trench, Trubner.

Philip Resnik, Mari Broman Olsen, and Mona Diab. 1999. The bible as a parallel corpus: Annotating the ‘Book of 2000 Tongues’. *Computers and the Humanities*, 33(1-2):129–153.

Xabier Saralegi, Iker Manterola, and Iñaki San Vicente. 2012. Building a basque-chinese dictionary by using english as pivot. In Nicoletta Calzolari (Conference Chair), Khalid Choukri, Thierry Declerck, Mehmet Uğur Doğan, Bente Maegaard, Joseph Mariani, Jan Odijk, and Stelios Piperidis, editors, *Proceedings of the Eight International Conference on Language Resources and Evaluation (LREC'12)*, Istanbul, Turkey, may. European Language Resources Association (ELRA).

Morris Swadesh. 1950. Salish internal relationships. *International Journal of American Linguistics*, pages 157–167.

Edward L. Thorndike and Irving Lorge. 1944. *The teacher's word book of 30,000 words*. Teachers College Bureau of Publications.

Edward L. Thorndike. 1921. *The teacher's word book*. New York Teachers College, Columbia University.

E.L. Thorndike. 1931. *A teacher's word book*. New York Teachers College, Columbia University.

William Dwight Whitney. 1885. The roots of the Sanskrit language. *Transactions of the American Philological Association (1869-1896)*, 16:5–29.

Taha Yasseri, András Kornai, and János Kertész. 2012. A practical approach to language complexity: a wikipedia case study. *PLoS ONE*, 7(11):e48386. doi:10.1371/journal.pone.0048386.

Attila Zséder, Gábor Recski, Dániel Varga, and András Kornai. 2012. Rapid creation of large-scale corpora and frequency dictionaries. In *Proceedings to LREC 2012*.

Scientific registers and disciplinary diversification: a comparable corpus approach

Elke Teich
Universität des Saarlandes
e.teich@mx.uni-saarland.de

Stefania Degaetano-Ortlieb
Universität des Saarlandes
s.degaetano@mx.uni-saarland.de

Hannah Kermes
Universität des Saarlandes
h.kermes@mx.uni-saarland.de

Ekaterina Lapshinova-Koltunski
Universität des Saarlandes
e.lapshinova@mx.uni-saarland.de

Abstract

We present a study on linguistic contrast and commonality in English scientific discourse on the basis of a *monolingually comparable* corpus. The focus is on selected scientific disciplines at the boundaries to computer science (computational linguistics, bioinformatics, digital construction, microelectronics). The data basis is the English Scientific Text Corpus (SCITEX) which covers a time range of roughly thirty years (1970/80s to early 2000s). In particular, we investigate the disciplinary diversification/relatedness of scientific research articles in terms of register. Our results are relevant for research on *multilingually comparable* corpora as used in machine translation and related research, since they shed new light on the notion of 'comparablity'.

1 Introduction: Motivation and Goals

In the context of statistical machine translation, comparable corpora are typically bilingual, thematically similar corpora being utilized to extract translation equivalents to enrich translation models. These have proved to be useful, especially for technically specialized texts or for low resource languages where parallel corpora are rare (Chiao and Zweigenbaum (2002); Babych et al. (2007)).

The overarching goal of the paper is to provide evidence that the notion of comparability commonly used in that context is rather coarse and misses important aspects of linguistic variation. We report on a set of experiments in which a *monolingually* comparable corpus is studied. The corpus contains specialized, technical texts from nine scientific disciplines, related to each other by "interdisciplines" (such as computer science - linguistics - computational linguistics) (cf. Section 2 for details). Our study establishes the linguistic differences and commonalities between the disciplines considered on the basis of the concept of *register*, i.e., language variation according to situational context. Situational context is conventionally described in terms of field, tenor and mode of discourse (Quirk et al., 1985). It has been shown in numerous corpus-linguistic studies that particular situational settings have specific linguistic correlates at the level of lexico-grammar in the sense of clusters of lexico-grammatical features that occur non-randomly (see notably the work by Biber and colleagues, e.g., Biber (1988, 1993); Biber et al. (1999); Biber (2006, 2012)). Collectively, the linguistic features associated with field, tenor and mode then give rise to registers. More specifically, field of discourse relates to the topic of a discourse and is realized lexico-grammatically in functional verb classes (e.g., activity, communication, etc.) with corresponding arguments (e.g., Actor, Goal, Medium, etc.) and adjunct types (e.g., Time, Place, Manner, etc.). Tenor of discourse relates to the roles and attitudes of the participants in a discourse and is realized lexico-grammatically in mood, modality as well as stance expressions. Mode of discourse relates to the presentational function of language and is realized in Theme-Rheme and Given-New constellations. A register is then characterized by particular distributions of lexico-grammatical features according to a given contextual configuration.

Apart from exhibiting differences in field, tenor and mode, scientific texts are associated with particular discourse "styles" such as technicality, abstractness or informational density, which may again be linguistically realized in different ways and to different degrees across disciplines. Furthermore, in a highly dynamic social domain, such as the scientific one, both registers and discourse styles are relatively versatile and subject to change (cf. Ure (1971, 1982)). This may, for instance, affect conventional phraseology. Finally, register and stylistic features may be distributed unevenly across document parts, thus giving rise to variation according to document structure. In order to arrive at a comprehensive picture of the linguistic construal of disciplinarity, we thus need to consider the linguistic encodings according to register and the linguistic realization of discursive styles as well as take into account the inherently dynamic nature of scientific discourse.

Relating this back to the notion of comparability, the concept of register may thus provide the basis for a fine-grained description of comparability, as it acknowledges the multi-dimensional nature of linguistic variation.

Our methodology is informed by three sources: corpus linguistics, linguistic theory and data mining. Standard corpus methods are employed for the quantification of instances of linguistic features that are considered to be relevant indicators of variation across scientific disciplines and may be expected to significantly contribute to differences in language use across disciplines. The theoretical basis is provided by Systemic Functional Linguistics (SFL; Halliday (2004)). The reason for choosing SFL to inform analysis is its model of association of contextual variables with lexico-grammatical domains (cf. above on the notion of register).

In contrast to other corpus-based studies on register, our goal is not to uncover dimensions of variation or to discover text classes (as e.g. in Biber et al's work). The texts in our corpus are taken from 38 journals from nine disciplines (for details see Section 2) and the text classes are thus extrinsically defined. We can then think of analysis as a task of text classification, where we test whether the extrinsically defined classes have distinctive linguistic correlates and if so, how well the classes are distinguished linguistically and which features contribute most to their distinction. To this end, we employ data mining techniques, in particular automatic text classification (see Section 3 for details). A similar approach to the one developed here, also working on linguistic variation in the scientific domain, has been proposed earlier by Argamon et al. (2008). There is related work in translation studies by Baroni and Bernardini (2006) and Volansky et al. (2011), which uses automatic text classification to describe the specific properties of translations ('translationese'). The earliest work, to our knowledge, combining SFL with text classification is Whitelaw and Patrick's work on spam detection (Whitelaw and Patrick, 2004).

2 Corpus

2.1 Corpus Design and Pre-processing

We have built a corpus composed of English scientific research articles — the English Scientific Text Corpus (SCITEX; cf. Teich and Fankhauser (2010) and Degaetano-Ortlieb et al. (forthcoming)) — that covers nine scientific domains and amounts to approx. 34 million tokens, drawn from 38 sources. SCITEX contains full journal articles from two time periods, the 1970s/early 1980s (SASCITEX) and the early 2000s (DASCITEX). We selected at least two different journals for each discipline in both time slices. As our focus is on selected scientific domains at the boundaries to computer science and some other discipline, SCITEX has a three-way partition: (1) A-subcorpus: computer science, (2) B-subcorpus: computational linguistics, bioinformatics, digital construction and microelectronics, and (3) C-subcorpus: linguistics, biology, mechanical engineering and electrical engineering, as shown in Figure 1. In the present paper, we are mainly interested in the linguistic evolution of the inter-/transdisciplinary domains represented by the B-subcorpus, as these are the ones that have emerged in the given time frame (1970s/80s to present). We term these domains *contact disciplines*, since they have come about through contact between two existing dis-

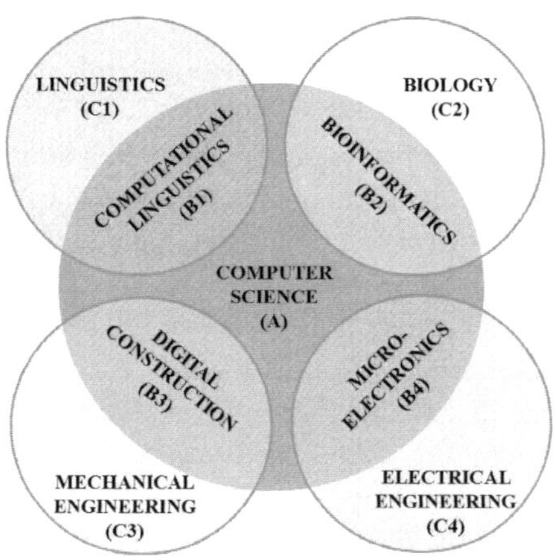

Figure 1: Scientific disciplines in the SCITEX corpus

ciplines (here: computer science and another established discipline represented in the A and C subcorpora, which we term *seed disciplines*). The main question we are interested in is whether the seed and contact disciplines have clearly distinguishable linguistic correlates in terms of register.

The text sources for SCITEX are full academic articles in the form of PDF files. These files were converted to plain text using an existing commercial software including optical character recognition (OCR).

In further processing we follow the common practices in corpus linguistics by (a) accounting for relevant metadata (e.g., *author, title, journal, year of publications*) and document structure (e.g., *abstract, conclusion*), and (b) using standard tools for preprocessing (e.g., tokenization, tagging, lemmatization, etc.). For corpus query, we employ the Corpus Query Processor (CQP) (CWB; Evert, 2004) which works on the basis of regular expressions. Utilities of CQP allow for the extraction of distributional information according to the annotated metadata and document structure.

3 Methods of Analysis

We carry out a diachronic analysis comparing the two time slices (1970s/80s vs. 2000s) represented in the SCITEX corpus, aiming to provide answers to the following questions:

1. How well are the individual disciplines distinguished?
2. How distinct are the contact disciplines from their seed disciplines?

Thus, analysis involves comparisons along the temporal and the disciplinary dimensions.

The hypothesis we have about the outcomes of our analysis is that disciplines will be better distinguished from one another over time, including the contact disciplines, reflecting a process of diversification within scientific writing over time.

3.1 Feature Selection

In the first step of analysis we need to determine which features to investigate. These should be features that bring out relevant and significant contrasts along the dimensions considered (time, discipline). For the choice of features potentially distinguishing individual (scientific) registers, we draw on SFL's model of register variation in which the contextual parameters of field, tenor and mode are associated with particular lexico-grammatical domains. Since we want to cover all three contextual parameters, we choose at least one feature for each. For field, we analyze functional verb classes as well as PoS-patterns that are potentially terminology-forming (e.g. noun-noun structures); for tenor, we analyze modal verbs and for mode we analyze theme type as well as conjunctive cohesive relations. As another feature, we analyze n-grams on the basis of PoS combinations (rather than words), since we have seen in a previous study that they may be involved in processes of conventionalization (Kermes and Teich, 2012).

Additionally, on an abstract level, scientific writing is a highly informational production that is characterized by technicality, information density and abstractness (cf. Halliday and Martin (1993)). Among the linguistic features realizing these properties are a relatively low type-token ratio (technicality), a relatively high lexical density and low grammatical intricacy (information density) and the frequent use of nominal categories (nouns, adjectives) (abstractness).

Table 1 displays the features considered in the analysis together with their associated contextual variables and/or abstract discourse properties they instantiate. Features are extracted from the corpus with CQP. For example, simple queries combine part-of-speech and concrete lemmas (e.g., *[pos="MD" & lemma="must|should"];* for modal verbs). More complex queries work with positional attributes, linguistic annotations and lists (e.g., < *s* >*[conj & lemma!=$modal-adverbs]...* as part of the extraction of textual Theme, which is realized in English as the first constituent in the clause).

3.2 Feature Evaluation

We employ statistical and machine learning methods to measure (a) how much individual features contribute to a possible distinction and (b) how well corpora are distinguished by these features. We employ classification techniques by using feature ranking (Information Gain) to determine the relative discriminatory force of features, and supervised machine learning (decision trees and support vector machines) to distinguish between the scientific registers in SCITEX. For these steps we use the WEKA data mining platform (Witten and Eibe, 2005).

contextual parameter/ abstract discourse property	**feature category**	**feature subcategory**
FIELD	term patterns	NN-of-NN, N-N, ADJ-N
	verb classes	activity (e.g., *make, show*) aspectual (e.g., *start, end*) causative (e.g., *let, allow*) communication (e.g., *note, describe*) existence (e.g., *exist, remain*) mental (e.g., *see, know*) occurrence (e.g., *change, grow*)
TENOR	modality	obligation/necessity (e.g., *must*) permission/possibility/ability (e.g., *can*) volition/prediction (e.g., *will*)
MODE	theme	experiential theme (e.g, *The algorithm...*) interpersonal theme (e.g., *Interestingly...*) textual theme (e.g., *But...*)
	conjunctive cohesive relations	additive (e.g., *and, furthermore*) adversative (e.g., *nonetheless, however*) causal (e.g., *thus, for this reason*) temporal (e.g., *then, at this point*)
TECHNICALITY	type-token ratio lexical vs. function words	STTR no. of lexical PoS categories
INFORMATION DENSITY	lexical density	lexical items per clause/sentence
	grammatical intricacy	clauses per sentence wh-words per sentence sentence length
ABSTRACTNESS	PoS distribution	no. of nominal vs. verbal categories
CONVENTIONALIZATION	n-grams on PoS basis length of sections	2-to-6-grams overall/per section tokens per section

Table 1: Features used in analysis

4 Results and Interpretation

Our analysis addresses the question of how distinctive the subcorpora in SCITEX are comparing the productions of the 1970/80s with those of the early 2000s. Considering the diachronic perspective, we expect to encounter a clearer separation of individual disciplines overall reflecting a process of diversification within scientific writing.

The analysis has two parts: First, we calculate Information Gain of the top twenty features, to see which features are the most discriminatory ones across disciplines. Second, we apply automatic classification, to see how well the subcorpora are distinguished on the basis of these features.

Table 2 shows the twenty most discriminatory features for the 70/80s across all subcorpora. The five highest ranking features are associated with field (NN: IGain 0.39, LEX: IGain 0.36, communication verbs: IGain 0.31) and mode (WL: IGain 0.33, LEX/C: IGain 0.32). In the mid range, we find some tenor features and in the lower range some other field features as well as document structure features.

When we compare these results with the ones for the early 2000s (see Table 3), three main observations can be made. First, features become much more pronounced, the IGain values rising substantially for the top 20 features (1970s/80s are in the range of 0.23 to 0.39, 2000s are in the range of 0.31 to 3.1). This includes the nine features that are identical across SASCITEX and DASCITEX: existence and communication verbs as well as adj-n term pattern for field, obligation modals for tenor, word and sentence length as well as lexical words per clause for mode, bi-grams for conventionalization, and length of main part for document structure, all become more pronounced in DASCITEX (higher IGains) and thus contribute more to the distinction between disciplines. The second observation is that while in SASCITEX only bi-grams ranges among the top 20 features, in DASCITEX we encounter an increase in the contribution of gram-based features to the DASCITEX-internal distinction.[1] This may point to the greater role of conventionalized language in the distinction between disciplines over time. Terminological studies based on n-grams might indicate a thematic comparability of disciplines. Consider one of the key concepts in computer science, ‘algorithm’. The distribution (per million) across the nine disciplines in DASCITEX varies greatly:

[1]Note again that in our analysis, n-grams are based on parts-of-speech, not words.

feature	IGain	contextual parameter	discourse property
NN	0.3931	field	technicality, abstractness
LEX	0.3647	field	technicality
communication	0.3119	field	
mental	0.2526	field	
existence	0.2372	field	
ADV	0.2282	field	abstractness
adj-n pattern	0.2253	field	technicality
volition	0.3184	tenor	
permission	0.2709	tenor	
MD	0.2679	tenor	
obligation	0.249	tenor	
WL	0.3326	mode	information density
LEX/C	0.3238	mode	information density
SL	0.2974	mode	information density
clauses/S	0.287	mode	information density
additive	0.2574	mode	
WH/S	0.2504	mode	information density
bi-grams	0.2382		conventionalization
main	0.2301		document structure
introduction	0.2257		document structure

Table 2: Feature ranking for the 70/80s (SASCITEX): Top 20 features

feature	IGain	contextual parameter	discourse property
existence	0.3987	field	
activity	0.3677	field	
communication	0.3636	field	
STTR	0.3582	field	technicality
adj-n pattern	0.3441	field	technicality
obligation	0.3548	tenor	
LEX/C	3.0803	mode	information density
SL	0.5567	mode	information density
WL	0.51	mode	information density
experiential-theme	0.344	mode	
causal	0.3302	mode	
main	0.5324		document structure
abstract	0.4981		document structure
n-grams_main	0.4925		conventionalization
bi-grams	0.3886		conventionalization
n-grams	0.3706		conventionalization
n-grams_abstr	0.3609		conventionalization
n-grams_4	0.3287		conventionalization
n-grams_3	0.3209		conventionalization
n-grams_intro	0.3115		conventionalization

Table 3: Feature ranking for the early 2000s (DASCITEX): Top 20 features

computer science (3427), microelectronics (1965), bioinformatics (1913), digital construction (1735), computational linguistics (1124), electrical engineering (955), mechanical engineering (129), biology (59) and linguistics (51). When we look at the top frequent token n-grams in which algorithm participates, we find, for example, 'approximation algorithm' which is mostly shared between computer science, the contact discipines and electrical engineering, 'learning algorithms' appears practically everywhere, and 'alignment algorithm' is almost only mentioned in computational linguistics and bioinformatics (with a few occurrences in computer science and one in biology). The stylistics across the disciplines is also noteworthy: pure stylistic tri-grams, such as the highly frequent 'in order to', 'the number of', 'based on the', 'as shown in', etc., are also good discriminators between different disciplines (cf. Kermes and Teich (2012)). Finally, at the levels of contextual and discourse properties, it can be noted that features associated with information density become better discriminators between disciplines in the 2000s having high IGain values, while tenor features step back decreasing in number, tending towards greater uniformity (only one tenor feature (obligation modals) in the top 20 features in the 2000s compared to four in the 70s/80s).

To see how these data are reflected according to disciplines, we perfom classification for both cor-

	A	B1	B2	B3	B4	C1	C2	C3	C4	total	accuracy in %
A	**108**	2	11	25	1	0	4	6	45	202	53.47
B1	3	**22**	22	19	7	26	4	9	13	125	**17.60**
B2	10	21	**142**	55	30	8	60	60	71	457	**31.07**
B3	16	24	52	**121**	32	7	17	37	55	361	**33.52**
B4	1	4	32	27	**91**	4	36	45	32	272	**33.46**
C1	2	24	16	8	1	**154**	4	6	4	219	70.32
C2	3	6	70	16	22	2	**358**	30	28	535	66.92
C3	10	10	60	45	44	6	37	**137**	39	388	35.31
C4	52	25	60	49	39	2	25	24	**248**	524	47.33

A: Computer Science, B1: Computational Linguistics, B2: Bioinformatics, B3: Digital Construction, B4: Microelectronics, C1: Linguistics, C2: Biology, C3: Mechanical Engineering, C4: Electrical Engineering

Table 4: Confusion matrix with decision tree for the 70/80s (SASCITEX)

	A	B1	B2	B3	B4	C1	C2	C3	C4	total	accuracy in %
A	**156**	0	3	4	0	1	1	0	37	202	77.23
B1	1	**26**	23	11	7	27	3	12	15	125	**20.80**
B2	2	2	**274**	47	13	4	32	37	46	457	**59.96**
B3	8	1	72	**156**	21	3	16	24	60	361	**43.21**
B4	0	1	14	8	**158**	1	49	26	15	272	**58.09**
C1	2	11	12	0	0	**183**	0	5	6	219	83.56
C2	2	0	28	4	12	0	**463**	9	17	535	86.54
C3	3	4	53	18	22	2	40	**213**	33	388	54.90
C4	30	2	41	25	12	1	24	12	**377**	524	71.95

A: Computer Science, B1: Computational Linguistics, B2: Bioinformatics, B3: Digital Construction, B4: Microelectronics, C1: Linguistics, C2: Biology, C3: Mechanical Engineering, C4: Electrical Engineering

Table 5: Confusion matrix with SVM for the 70/80s (SASCITEX)

	A	B1	B2	B3	B4	C1	C2	C3	C4	total	accuracy in %
A	**201**	1	0	9	7	1	0	2	9	230	87.39
B1	4	**97**	4	19	1	8	1	0	3	137	**70.80**
B2	5	0	**269**	14	6	0	18	6	1	319	**84.33**
B3	5	3	8	**168**	8	0	6	30	14	242	**69.42**
B4	2	2	10	17	**156**	0	8	9	1	205	**76.10**
C1	1	11	6	3	0	**90**	0	0	0	111	81.08
C2	0	0	7	2	2	1	**335**	3	1	351	95.44
C3	4	1	7	23	6	0	15	**229**	18	303	75.58
C4	18	2	3	42	7	0	4	34	**113**	223	50.67

A: Computer Science, B1: Computational Linguistics, B2: Bioinformatics, B3: Digital Construction, B4: Microelectronics, C1: Linguistics, C2: Biology, C3: Mechanical Engineering, C4: Electrical Engineering

Table 6: Confusion matrix with SVM for the early 2000s (DASCITEX)

pora (SASCITEX and DASCITEX), first, with decision trees, as they are based on Information Gain, and second, with support vector machines (SVMs), as they are used for text categorization tasks with many relevant features achieving very good results (cf. Joachims (1998)). Classification is performed on all features with 10 fold cross-validation. Table 4 shows the confusion matrix for all subcorpora for the 70/80s and classification accuracy for each subcorpus achieved by decision tree. The overall accuracy is 44.79% only, the correctly classified texts lying on the main diagonal of the matrix.

The confusion matrix produced by SVM is shown in Table 5, with an overall accuracy of **65.07%**. Apart from computational linguistics (B1), accuracy goes up by about 10% for digital contruction (B3) and linguistics (C1) and about 25-30% for the other subcorpora compared to decision tree. Accuracy with SVM for the contact disciplines (B1-B4) ranges from 20-60% and is much lower than the accuracy achieved for the seed disciplines (A and C1-C4) with around 54-86%. Thus, the contact disciplines are not clearly separated from the seed disciplines. Considering, for instance the triple A-B1-C1, we can see that more texts belonging to computational linguistics (B1) are classified into linguistics (C1) than into computational linguistics (27 texts in C1 vs. 26 in B1), i.e., texts in B1 seem to be quite similar to

B1 vs A		B2 vs A		B3 vs A		B4 vs A	
WL	0.629	WL	0.501	WL	0.399	LEX	0.883
STTR	0.509	LEX	0.355	LEX	0.331	WL	0.763
LEX	0.372	causal	0.334	n-grams_6	0.265	STTR	0.574
ADJ	0.261	n-grams_6	0.306	STTR	0.258	causal	0.560
VV	0.230	STTR	0.303	clauses/S	0.202	NN	0.458
n-grams_6	0.205	n-grams_4	0.284	adj-n-n	0.168	additive	0.440
causal	0.187	temporal	0.283	causal	0.160	temporal	0.433
types	0.174	n-grams_5	0.282	NN	0.13	mental	0.416
adj-c-adj-n	0.145	ADJ	0.273	n-grams_4	0.118	commun.	0.379
introduction	0.129	causative	0.197	ADJ	0.114	n-grams_4	0.364
B1 vs C1		**B2 vs C2**		**B3 vs C3**		**B4 vs C4**	
clauses/S	0.230	NN	0.269	LEX/S	0.260	LEX	0.469
ADV	0.204	MD	0.264	main	0.146	VV	0.311
LEX/C	0.196	WH	0.198	n-grams_main	0.132	WL	0.309
NN	0.179	permission	0.178	introduction	0.127	main	0.153
WH/S	0.122	volition	0.166	causative	0.114	NN	0.148
LEX	0.120	WL	0.147	exper-theme	0.113	introduction	0.142
occurrence	0.119	SL	0.145	obligation	0.087	LEX/S	0.115
commun.	0.112	WH/S	0.137	n-grams_intro	0.086	n-grams_main	0.096
MD	0.110	LEX	0.104	aspectual	0.081	causal	0.093
n-grams_abstr	0.108	LEX/C	0.098	LEX/C	0.077	n-grams_intro	0.088

A: Computer Science, B1: Computational Linguistics, B2: Bioinformatics, B3: Digital Construction, B4: Microelectronics, C1: Linguistics, C2: Biology, C3: Mechanical Engineering, C4: Electrical Engineering

Table 7: Feature ranking with IGain for the 70/80s (SASCITEX): Top 20 features contact vs seed disciplines

B1 vs A		B2 vs A		B3 vs A		B4 vs A	
WL	0.694	WL	0.701	WL	0.567	WL	0.791
STTR	0.631	main	0.680	causal	0.488	STTR	0.615
SL	0.441	STTR	0.678	STTR	0.385	VV	0.289
types	0.402	n-grams_main	0.634	temporal	0.347	main	0.233
causal	0.237	causal	0.621	n-grams_4	0.345	causal	0.230
n-grams_6	0.217	n-grams_4	0.577	n-grams	0.319	LEX	0.21
n-n	0.192	n-grams	0.552	n-grams_5	0.318	mental	0.196
adj-n	0.171	abstract	0.537	n-grams_main	0.282	temporal	0.190
adversative	0.128	bi-grams	0.521	LEX	0.280	n-of-n	0.189
adj-c-adj-n	0.125	introduction	0.487	bi-grams	0.262	aspectual	0.144
B1 vs C1		**B2 vs C2**		**B3 vs C3**		**B4 vs C4**	
occurrence	0.264	SL	0.566	WL	0.156	VV	0.436
adj-adj-n	0.193	abstract	0.518	VV	0.139	WL	0.410
ADV	0.189	n-grams_abstr	0.505	obligation	0.100	LEX/C	0.329
ADJ	0.137	main	0.412	LEX/C	0.100	ADV	0.243
NN	0.128	introduction	0.353	n-grams_5	0.097	n-grams_3	0.181
types	0.123	n-grams_main	0.344	MD	0.088	LEX/S	0.162
LEX/C	0.123	n-grams_intro	0.321	ADJ	0.075	activity	0.154
main	0.118	WH	0.204	aspectual	0.064	n-grams	0.147
commun.	0.107	MD	0.202	SL	0.061	STTR	0.135
abstract	0.107	WH/S	0.192	LEX/S	0.059	abstract	0.127

A: Computer Science, B1: Computational Linguistics, B2: Bioinformatics, B3: Digital Construction, B4: Microelectronics, C1: Linguistics, C2: Biology, C3: Mechanical Engineering, C4: Electrical Engineering

Table 8: Feature ranking with IGain for the early 2000s (DASCITEX): Top 20 features contact vs seed disciplines

texts in C1 in terms of the features investigated.

In order to check the separation of disciplines over time, we need to compare classification results across SASCITEX and DASCITEX. We again apply SVM, which returns an overall accuracy of **78.17%**.[2] Comparing the values for the individual subcorpora across SASCITEX and DASCITEX, we can observe that accuracies are now much higher for all subcorpora. Considering the contact disciplines, they have clearly gained distinctiveness in the 2000s in comparison to the 1970/80s, as texts in B1-B4 are classified correctly 69% to 84% of

[2]Decision tree performed poorly again in comparison achieving an accuracy of 57.24% only.

the time (instead of 20-60% in the 1970/80s).

In summary, the classification results match the results obtained by feature ranking, which have shown that the top 20 features increased discriminatory force over time. This is reflected by a higher classification accuracy overall and for the subcorpora.[3] The discriminatory force of features in the 1970s/80s instead, was not strong enough to clearly separate disciplines.

To see whether there are any particular features involved in the differentiation of the contact disciplines in particular vis à vis computer science on the one hand and the other seed disciplines on the other hand, we inspect the confusion matrix as well as the IGains of each B vs. A and each B vs. the respective C, both for SASCITEX and DASCITEX. In the comparison to computer science (A), we can see that the confusion matrixes produced with SVM (cf. Table 5 and 6) show few texts that are misclassified from the contact disciplines (Bs) into computer science (A) for both time slices. Thus, the features employed distinguish Bs from A quite well. Considering the IGain values (see Table 7 and 8 for the top 10 features), besides computational linguistics (B1; relatively low classification accuracy of 20% in the 70/80s), the contact disciplines have the following features in common: word length (WL), STTR, causal verbs in the top 10 as well as four-grams, lexical words (LEX) and temporal conjunctions in the top 20 features. Except lexical words (LEX), all features have a higher IGain in the 2000s. In the comparison to the other seed discipines (Cs), the confusion matrixes show more misclassifications of Bs into Cs. Considering the IGain values there are no tendencies uniformly applying to the contact disciplines (Bs). They rather show individual tendencies for each pair (B1 vs. C1, B2 vs. C2, B3 vs. C3, B4 vs. C4). Features that contribute to a better classification diachronically lie in the following parameters: (a) field (occurrence, term-patterns, ADV) for computational linguistics (B1), (b) document structure (abstract, main, intro), information density (SL) and conventionalization (n-grams_abstract) for bioinformatics (B2), (c) information density (WL) and technicality (VV) for digital construction (B3) and microelectronics (B4).

[3]There are only two exceptions: C1 (linguistics) goes slightly down (around 2.5%), C4 (electrical engineering) goes down by over 20% to 50.67% accuracy, i.e., it is not really distinguishable any more.

5 Summary and Conclusions

We have looked at disciplinary linguistic diversification in English scientific writing in terms of register, discourse styles and document structure. The results of our analysis provide evidence of major motifs of development in scientific writing over time, showing dynamicity over a time span of only thirty years. Diversification over time is clearly borne out for the contact disciplines but is also true for most of the other disciplines.

Considering the contact disciplines we have seen that (1) they can be distinguished quite well from computer science with the same features being involved in better classification results, (2) they show individual feature constellations in their distinction from their seed disciplines. Moreover, n-grams have gained discriminatory force over time and are ranked relatively high among our features in the 2000s subcorpus. As they are also relevant in terms of terminology, they give an insight in the relatedness of disciplines.

In terms of methods, we have combined state-of-the-art corpus processing with techniques of data analysis as developed in data mining. As such techniques become more accessible to linguistic, literary and cultural analysis, the repertoire of methods for such analysis will be greatly enhanced in that sounder empirical evidence can be sought in text-based socio-cultural and historical studies at large (cf. Jockers (2013)). The crucial factor in employing such methods is the motivation of the features to be used in analysis. Here, we have deliberately not relied on word-based features but instead mainly employed lexico-grammatical patterns. While bags-of-words are strong discriminators between texts/text classes, they can only tell us something about lexical variation (e.g., as an indicator of text topic). However, when register or style rather than topicality are in the focus (such as e.g. the linguistic construal of technical, dense or abstract discourse or the expression of field, tenor or mode relations), it will not be sufficient to study lexical word distributions (cf. Cohen et al. (2010); Teich and Fankhauser (2010) for some other studies). Instead, one needs to identify lexico-grammatical patterns that are potential indicators of the more abstract discoursive and contextual properties that are in focus.

The insight to be gained from our study for multilingually comparable corpora is that more elaborate definitions of 'comparability' might be required. Our approach offers such a definition of comparability by being firmly based on an established model of linguistic variation, which has also been widely applied in multilingual contexts, such as for example, automatic text generation (see e.g., Matthiessen and Bateman (1991); Bateman (1997); Kruijff et al. (2000)). The parameters of variation we employ (register: field, tenor, mode; discourse styles; time) provide a fine-grained grid of features involved in linguistic variation, which can be applied to other languages as well. For example, we can extract and analyze field features, such as term patterns (as produced for German by Weller et al. (2011)), tenor features, such as modal verbs, as well as the other features investigated using the same tools applied here (part-of-speech tagger, CQP, R-scripts and WEKA modules) with only little adaptations (e.g., tag sets, query formulation). Overall, we would expect that applying the concept of register to the problem of comparability will enable finer-tuned comparable corpora and thus contribute to their fuller potential for multilingual language technology.

Acknowledgments

We wish to thank the anonymous reviewers for their helpful comments. We are especially grateful to Peter Fankhauser for critically assessing our data and to Noam Ordan for valuable suggestions regarding the structure of the paper.

References

Shlomo Argamon, Jeff Dodick, and Paul Chase. Language use reflects scientific methodology: A corpus-based study of peer-reviewed journal articles. *Scientometrics*, 75(2):203–238, 2008.

Bogdan Babych, Anthony Hartley, and Serge Sharoff. Translating from under-resourced languages: Comparing direct transfer against pivot translation. In *Proceedings of the MT Summit XI*, pages 412–418, Copenhagen, Denmark, 2007.

Marco Baroni and Silvia Bernardini. A new approach to the study of translationese: Machine-learning the difference between original and translated text. *Literary and Linguistic Computing*, 21(3):259–274, 2006.

John A. Bateman. Enabling technology for multilingual natural language generation: The KPML development environment. *Journal of Natural Language Engineering*, 3(1):15–55, 1997.

Douglas Biber. *Variation Across Speech and Writing*. Cambridge University Press, Cambridge, 1988.

Douglas Biber. The multi-dimensional approach to linguistic analyses of genre variation: An overview of methodology and findings. *Computers and the Humanities*, 26(5-6):331–345, 1993.

Douglas Biber. *University Language: A Corpus-based Study of Spoken And Written Registers*, volume 23 of *Studies in Corpus Linguistics*. John Benjamins Publishing, Amsterdam/Philadelphia, 2006.

Douglas Biber. Register as a predictor of linguistic variation. *Corpus Linguistics and Linguistic Theory*, 8(1):9–37, 2012.

Douglas Biber, Stig Johansson, and Geoffrey Leech. *Longman Grammar of Spoken and Written English*. Longman, Harlow, 1999.

Yun-Chuang Chiao and Pierre Zweigenbaum. Looking for candidate translational equivalents in specialized, comparable corpora. In *Proceedings of the 19th international Conference on Computational Linguistics (COLING)*, Vol. 2, pages 1–5, Taipei, Taiwan, 2002.

Kevin Bretonnel Cohen, Helen Johnson, Karin Verspoor, Christophe Roeder, and Lawrence Hunter. The structural and content aspects of abstracts versus bodies of full text journal articles are different. *BMC bioinformatics*, 11(1): 492, 2010.

CWB. The IMS Open Corpus Workbench, 2010. http://www.cwb.sourceforge.net.

Stefania Degaetano-Ortlieb, Kermes Hannah, Ekaterina Lapshinova-Koltunski, and Teich Elke. SciTex a diachronic corpus for analyzing the development of scientific registers. In Paul Bennett, Martin Durrell, Silke Scheible, and Richard J. Whitt, editors, *New Methods in Historical Corpus Linguistics*, Corpus Linguistics and Interdisciplinary Perspectives on Language (CLIP), Vol. 3. Narr, Tübingen, forthcoming.

Stefan Evert. *The Statistics of Word Cooccurrences: Word Pairs and Collocations*. PhD thesis, IMS, University of Stuttgart, 2004.

M.A.K. Halliday. *An Introduction to Functional Grammar*. Arnold, London, 2004.

M.A.K. Halliday and J.R. Martin. *Writing science: Literacy and discursive power*. Falmer Press, London, 1993.

Thorsten Joachims. Text categorization with support vector machines: Learning with many relevant features. *Machine Learning: ECML-98*, pages 137–142, 1998.

Matthew L. Jockers. *Macroanalysis: Digital Methods and Literary History*. University of Illinois Press, 2013.

Hannah Kermes and Elke Teich. Formulaic expressions in scientific texts: Corpus design, extraction and exploration. *Lexicographica*, 28 (1):99–120, 2012.

Geert-Jan Kruijff, Elke Teich, John Bateman, Ivana Kruijff-Korbayová, Hana Skoumalová, Serge Sharoff, Lena Sokolova, Tony Hartley, Kamenka Staykova, and Jiří Hana. Multilinguality in a text generation system for three Slavic languages. In *Proceedings of the 18th international Conference on Computational Linguistics (COLING)*, Vol. 1, pages 474–480, Saarbrücken, Germany, 2000.

Christian M.I.M. Matthiessen and John A. Bateman. *Text generation and systemic-functional linguistics: Experiences from English and Japanese*. Communication in Artificial Intelligence Series. Pinter, 1991.

Randolph Quirk, Sidney Greenbaum, Geoffrey Leech, and Jan Svartvik. *A Comprehensive Grammar of the English Language*. Longman, London, 1985.

Elke Teich and Peter Fankhauser. Exploring a corpus of scientific texts using data mining. In S. Gries, S. Wulff, and M. Davies, editors, *Corpus-linguistic applications: Current studies, new directions*, pages 233–247. Rodopi, Amsterdam and New York, 2010.

Jean Ure. Lexical density and register differentiation. In G. E. Perren and J. L. M. Trim, editors, *Applications of Linguistics. Selected papers of the Second International Congress of Applied Linguistics, Cambridge 1969*, pages 443–452. Cambridge University Press, 1971.

Jean Ure. Introduction: Approaches to the study of register range. *International Journal of the Sociology of Language*, 35:5–23, 1982.

Vered Volansky, Noam Ordan, and Shuly Wintner. More human or more translated? Original texts vs. human and machine translations. In *Proceedings of the 11th Bar-Ilan Symposium on the Foundations of AI with Israeli Seminar on Computational Linguistics (ISCOL)*, Ramat Gan, Israel, 2011.

Marion Weller, Helena Blancafort, Anita Gojun, and Ulrich Heid. Terminology extraction and term variation patterns: a study of French and German data. In *Proceedings of the GSCL: German Society for Computational Linguistics and Language Technology*, Hamburg, Germany, 2011.

Casey Whitelaw and Jon Patrick. Selecting systemic features for text classification. In Ash Asudeh, Cécile Paris, and Stephen Wan, editors, *Proceedings of the Australasian Language Technology Workshop*, pages 93–100, Sydney, Australia, 2004.

Ian H. Witten and Frank Eibe. *Data Mining: Practical Machine Learning Tools and Techniques*. Elsevier, Morgan Kaufmann Publishers, Amsterdam, Boston, second edition, 2005.

Improving MT System Using Extracted Parallel Fragments of Text from Comparable Corpora

Rajdeep Gupta, Santanu Pal, Sivaji Bandyopadhyay
Department of Computer Science & Engineering
Jadavpur University
Kolkata – 700032, India
{rajdeepgupta20, santanu.pal.ju}@gmail.com,
sivaji_cse_ju@yahoo.com

Abstract

In this article, we present an automated approach of extracting English-Bengali parallel fragments of text from comparable corpora created using Wikipedia documents. Our approach exploits the multilingualism of Wikipedia. The most important fact is that this approach does not need any domain specific corpus. We have been able to improve the BLEU score of an existing domain specific English-Bengali machine translation system by 11.14%.

1 Introduction

Recently comparable corpora have got great attention in the field of NLP. Extracting parallel fragments of texts, paraphrases or sentences from comparable corpora are particularly useful for any statistical machine translation system (SMT) (Smith et al. 2010) as the size of the parallel corpus plays major role in any SMT performance. Extracted parallel phrases from comparable corpora are added with the training corpus as additional data that is expected to facilitate better performance of machine translation systems specifically for those language pairs which have limited parallel resources available. In this work, we try to extract English-Bengali parallel fragments of text from comparable corpora. We have developed an aligned corpus of English-Bengali document pairs using Wikipedia. Wikipedia is a huge collection of documents in many different languages. We first collect an English document from Wikipedia and then follow the inter-language link to find the same document in Bengali (obviously, if such a link exists). In this way, we create a small corpus. We assume that such English-Bengali document pairs from Wikipedia are already comparable since they talk about the same entity. Although each English-Bengali document pair talks about the same entity, most of the times they are not exact translation of each other. And as a result, parallel fragments of text are rarely found in these document pairs. The bigger the size of the fragment the less probable it is to find its parallel version in the target side. Nevertheless, there is always chance of getting parallel phrase, tokens or even sentences in comparable documents. The challenge is to find those parallel texts which can be useful in increasing machine translation performance.

In our present work, we have concentrated on finding small fragments of parallel text instead of rigidly looking for parallelism at entire sentential level. Munteanu and Marcu (2006) believed that comparable corpora tend to have parallel data at sub-sentential level. This approach is particularly useful for this type of corpus under consideration, because there is a very little chance of getting exact translation of bigger fragments of text in the target side. Instead, searching for parallel chunks would be more logical. If a sentence in the source side has a parallel sentence in the target side, then all of its chunks need to have their parallel translations in the target side as well.

It is to be noted that, although we have document level alignment in our corpus, it is somehow ad-hoc i.e. the documents in the corpus do not belong to any particular domain. Even with such a corpus we have been able to improve the performance of an existing machine translation system built on tourism domain. This also signifies our contribution towards domain adaptation of machine translation systems.

The rest of the paper is organized as follows. Section 2 describes the related work. Section 3 describes the preparation of the comparable corpus. The system architecture is described in section 4. Section 5 describes the experiments we conducted and presents the results. Finally the conclusion is drawn in section 6.

2 Related Work

There has been a growing interest in approaches focused on extracting word translations from comparable corpora (Fung and McKeown, 1997; Fung and Yee, 1998; Rapp, 1999; Chiao and Zweigenbaum, 2002; Dejean et al., 2002; Kaji, 2005; Gamallo, 2007; Saralegui et al., 2008). Most of the strategies follow a standard method based on context similarity. The idea behind this method is as follows: A target word t is the translation of a source word s if the words with which t co-occurs are translations of words with which s co-occurs. The basis of the method is to find the target words that have the most similar distributions with a given source word. The starting point of this method is a list of bilingual expressions that are used to build the context vectors of all words in both languages. This list is usually provided by an external bilingual dictionary. In Gamallo (2007), however, the starting list is provided by bilingual correlations which are previously extracted from a parallel corpus. In Dejean (2002), the method relies on a multilingual thesaurus instead of an external bilingual dictionary. In all cases, the starting list contains the "seed expressions" required to build context vectors of the words in both languages. The works based on this standard approach mainly differ in the coefficients used to measure the context vector similarity.

Otero et al. (2010) showed how Wikipedia could be used as a source of comparable corpora in different language pairs. They downloaded the entire Wikipedia for any two language pair and transformed it into a new collection: CorpusPedia. However, in our work we have showed that only a small ad-hoc corpus containing Wikipedia articles could be proved to be beneficial for existing MT systems.

3 Tools and Resources Used

A sentence-aligned English-Bengali parallel corpus containing 22,242 parallel sentences from a travel and tourism domain was used in the preparation of the baseline system. The corpus was obtained from the consortium-mode project "Development of English to Indian Languages Machine Translation (EILMT) System". The Stanford Parser and the CRF chunker were used for identifying individual chunks in the source side of the parallel corpus. The sentences on the target side (Bengali) were POS-tagged/chunked by using the tools obtained from the consortium mode project "Development of Indian Languages to Indian Languages Machine Translation (ILILMT) System".

For building the comparable corpora we have focused our attention on Wikipedia documents. To collect comparable English-Bengali document pairs we designed a crawler. The crawler first visits an English page, saves the raw text (in HTML format), and then finds the cross-lingual link (if exists) to find the corresponding Bengali document. Thus, we get one English-Bengali document pair. Moreover, the crawler visits the links found in each document and repeats the process. In this way, we develop a small aligned corpus of English-Bengali comparable document pairs. We retain only the textual information and all the other details are discarded. It is evident that the corpus is not confined to any particular domain. The challenge is to exploit this kind of corpus to help machine translation systems improve. The advantage of using such corpus is that it can be prepared easily unlike the one that is domain specific.

The effectiveness of the parallel fragments of text developed from the comparable corpora in the present work is demonstrated by using the standard log-linear PB-SMT model as our baseline system: GIZA++ implementation of IBM word alignment model 4, phrase extraction heuristics described in (Koehn et al., 2003), minimum-error-rate training (Och, 2003) on a held-out development set, target language model with Kneser-Ney smoothing (Kneser and Ney, 1995) trained with SRILM (Stolcke, 2002), and Moses decoder (Koehn et al., 2007).

4 System Architecture

4.1 PB-SMT(Baseline System)

Translation is modeled in SMT as a decision process, in which the translation $e_1^I = e_1..e_i..e_I$ of a source sentence $f_1^J = f_1..f_j..f_J$ is chosen to maximize (1)

$$\arg\max_{I,e_1^I} P(e_1^I \mid f_1^J) = \arg\max_{I,e_1^I} P(f_1^J \mid e_1^I).P(e_1^I) \quad (1)$$

where $P(f_1^J \mid e_1^I)$ and $P(e_1^I)$ denote respectively the translation model and the target language model (Brown et al., 1993). In log-linear phrase-based SMT, the posterior probability $P(e_1^I \mid f_1^J)$ is directly modeled as a log-linear combination of features (Och and Ney,

2002), that usually comprise of M translational features, and the language model, as in (2):

$$\log P(e_1^I \mid f_1^J) = \sum_{m=1}^{M} \lambda_m h_m(f_1^J, e_1^I, s_1^K)$$

$$+ \lambda_{LM} \log P(e_1^I) \quad (2)$$

where $s_1^k = s_1 ... s_k$ denotes a segmentation of the source and target sentences respectively into the sequences of phrases $(\hat{e}_1,...,\hat{e}_k)$ and $(\hat{f}_1,...,\hat{f}_k)$ such that (we set $i_0 = 0$) (3):

$$\forall 1 \le k \le K, \quad s_k = (i_k, b_k, j_k),$$

$$\hat{e}_k = e_{i_{k-1}+1} ... e_{i_k},$$

$$\hat{f}_k = f_{b_k} ... f_{j_k}. \quad (3)$$

and each feature $\hat{h}_m$ in (2) can be rewritten as in (4):

$$h_m(f_1^J, e_1^I, s_1^K) = \sum_{k=1}^{K} \hat{h}_m(\hat{f}_k, \hat{e}_k, s_k) \quad (4)$$

where $\hat{h}_m$ is a feature that applies to a single phrase-pair. It thus follows (5):

$$\sum_{m=1}^{M} \lambda_m \sum_{k=1}^{K} \hat{h}_m(\hat{f}_k, \hat{e}_k, s_k) = \sum_{k=1}^{K} \hat{h}(\hat{f}_k, \hat{e}_k, s_k) \quad (5)$$

where $\hat{h} = \sum_{m=1}^{M} \lambda_m \hat{h}_m$.

4.2 Chunking of English Sentences

We have used CRF-based chunking algorithm to chunk the English sentences in each document. The chunking breaks the sentences into linguistic phrases. These phrases may be of different sizes. For example, some phrases may be two words long and some phrases may be four words long. According to the linguistic theory, the intermediate constituents of the chunks do not usually take part in long distance reordering when it is translated, and only intra chunk reordering occurs. Some chunks combine together to make a longer phrase. And then some phrases again combine to make a sentence. The entire process maintains the linguistic definition of a sentence. Breaking the sentences into N-grams would have always generated phrases of length N but these phrases may not be linguistic phrases. For this reason, we avoided breaking the sentences into N-grams.

The chunking tool breaks each English sentence into chunks. The following is an example of how the chunking is done.

Sentence: India , officially the Republic of India , is a country in South Asia.

After Chunking: (India ,) (officially) (the Republic) (of) (India ,) (is) (a country) (in South Asia) (.)

We have further merged the chunks to form bigger chunks. The idea is that, we may sometimes find the translation of the merged chunk in the target side as well, in which case, we would get a bigger fragment of parallel text. The merging is done in two ways:

Strict Merging: We set a value 'V'. Starting from the beginning, chunks are merged such that the number of tokens in each merged chunk does not exceed V.

```
Procedure Strict_Merge()
begin
    Oline ← null
    Cur_wc ← 0
    repeat
        Iline←Next Chunk
        Length←Number of Tokens in Iline
        if(Cur_wc + Length > V)
            Output Oline as the next merged chunk
            Cur_wc←Length
        else
            Append Iline at the end of Oline
            Add Length to Cur_wc
        end if
    while (there are more chunks)
end
```

Figure 1. Strict-Merging Algorithm.

Figure 1 describes the pseudo-code for strict merging.

For example, in our example sentence the merged chunks will be as following, where V=4: (India , officially) (the Republic of) (India , is) (a country) (in South Asia .)

```
Procedure Window_Merging()
begin
    Set_Chunk←Set of all English Chunks
    L←Number of chunks in Set_Chunk
    for i = 0 to L-1
        Words←Set of tokens in i-th Chunk in Set_Chunk
        Cur_wc←number of tokens in Words
        Ol←i-th chunk in Set_Chunk
        for j = (i+1) to (L-1)
            C←j-th chunk in Set_Chunk
            w←set of tokens in C
            l←number of tokens in w
            if(Cur_wc + l ≤ V)
                Append C at the end of Ol
                Add l to Cur_wc
            end if
        end for
        Output Ol as the next merged chunk
    end for
end
```

Figure 2. Window-Based Merging Algorithm.

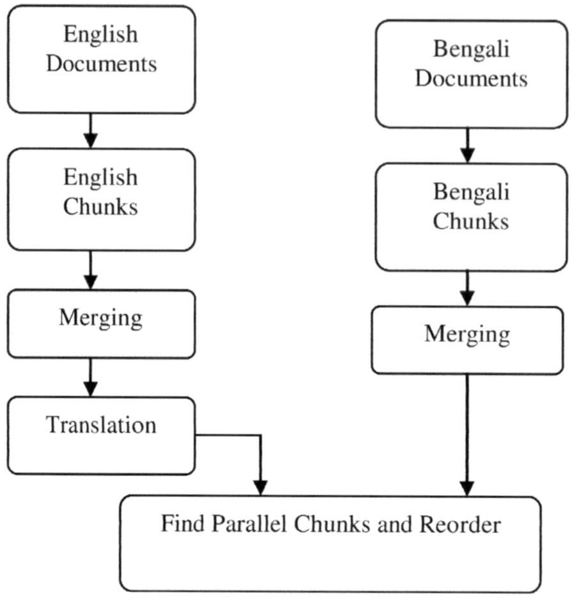

Figure 3. System Architecture for Finding Parallel Fragments

Window-Based Merging: In this type of chunking also, we set a value 'V', and for each chunk we try to merge as many chunks as possible so that the number of tokens in the merged chunk never exceeds V.

So, we slide an imaginary window over the chunks. For example, for our example sentence the merged chunks will be as following, where V = 4 :

(India , officially) (officially the Republic of) (the Republic of) (of India , is) (India , is) (is a country) (a country) (in South Asia .)

The pseudo-code of window-based merging is described in Figure 2.

4.3 Chunking of Bengali Sentences

Since to the best of our knowledge, there is no good quality chunking tool for Bengali we did not use chunking explicitly. Instead, strict merging is done with consecutive V number of tokens whereas window-based merging is done sliding a virtual window over each token and merging tokens so that the number of tokens does not exceed V.

4.4 Finding Parallel Chunks

After finding the merged English chunks they are translated into Bengali using a machine translation system that we have already developed. This is also the same machine translation system whose performance we want to improve. Chunks of each of the document pairs are then compared to find parallel chunks.

Each translated source chunk (translated from English to Bengali) is compared with all the target chunks in the corresponding Bengali-chunk document. When a translated source chunk is considered, we try to align each of its token to some token in the target chunk. Overlap between token two Bengali chunks B_1 and B_2, where B_1 is the translated chunk and B_2 is the chunk in the Bengali document, is defined as follows:

$Overlap(B_1,B_2)$ = Number of tokens in B_1 for which an alignment can be found in B_2.

It is to be noted that $Overlap(B_1,B_2) \neq Overlap(B_2 ,B_1)$. Overlap between chunks is found in both ways (from translated source chunk to target and from target to translated source chunk). If 70% alignment is found in both the overlap measures then we declare them as parallel. Two issues are important here: the comparison of two Bengali tokens and in case an alignment is found, which token to retrieve (source or target) and how to reorder them. We address these two issues in the next two sections.

4.5 Comparing Bengali Tokens

For our purpose, we first divide the two tokens into their *matra* (vowel modifiers) part and consonant part keeping the relative orders of characters in each part same. For example, Figure 4 shows the division of the word কলকাতা.

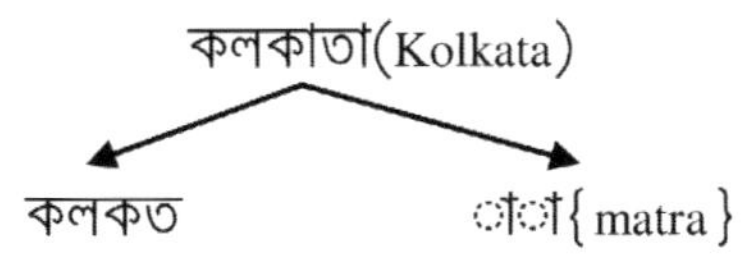

Figure 4. Division of a Bengali Word.

Respective parts of the two words are then compared. Orthographic similarities like minimum edit distance ratio, longest common subsequence ratio, and length of the strings are used for the comparison of both parts.

Minimum Edit Distance Ratio: It is defined as follows:

$$MEDR(B1, B2) = 1 - \frac{|ED(B1, B2)|}{max\ (|B1|, |B2|)}$$

where |B| is the length of the string B and ED is the minimum edit distance or *levenshtein distance* calculated as the minimum number of edit operations – insert, replace, delete – needed to transform B1 into B2.

Longest Common Subsequence Ratio: It is defined as follows:

$$LCSR(B1, B2) = \frac{|LCS(B1, B2)|}{max\ (|B1|, |B2|)}$$

where LCS is the longest common subsequence of two strings.

Threshold for matching is set empirically. We differentiate between shorter strings and larger strings. The idea is that, if the strings are short we cannot afford much difference between them to consider them as a match. In those cases, we check for exact match. Also, the threshold for consonant part is set stricter because our assumption is that consonants contribute more toward the word's pronunciation.

4.6 Reordering of Source Chunks

When a translated source chunk is compared with a target chunk it is often found that the ordering of the tokens in the source chunk and the target chunk is different. The tokens in the target chunk have a different permutation of positions with respect to the positions of tokens in the source chunk. In those cases, we reordered the positions of the tokens in the source chunk so as to reflect the positions of tokens in the target chunk because it is more likely that the tokens will usually follow the ordering as in the target chunk. For example, the machine translation output of the English chunk "*from the Atlantic Ocean*" is "*থেকে(theke) আটলান্টিক (atlantic) মহাসাগর (mahasagar)*". We found a target chunk "আটলান্টিক (*atlantic*) মহাসাগর (*mahasagar*) থেকে (*theke*) এবং (*ebong*)" with which we could align the tokens of the source chunk but in different relative order. Figure 5 shows the alignment of tokens.

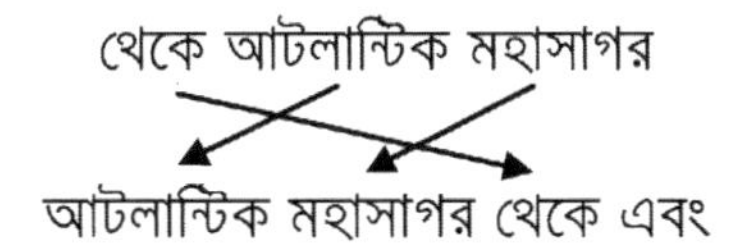

Figure 5. Alignment of Bengali Tokens.

We reordered the tokens of the source chunk and the resulting chunk was "আটলান্টিক মহাসাগর থেকে".Also, the token "এবং" in the target chunk could not find any alignment and was discarded. The system architecture of the present system is described in figure 3.

5 Experiments And Results

5.1 Baseline System

We randomly extracted 500 sentences each for the development set and test set from the initial parallel corpus, and treated the rest as the training corpus. After filtering on the maximum allowable sentence length of 100 and sentence length ratio of 1:2 (either way), the training corpus contained 22,492 sentences.

	V=4	V=7
Number of English Chunks(Strict-Merging)	579037	376421
Number of English Chunks(Window-Merging)	890080	949562
Number of Bengali Chunks(Strict-Merging)	69978	44113
Number of Bengali Chunks(Window-Merging)	230025	249330

Table 1. Statistics of the Comparable Corpus

	V=4	V=7
Number of Parallel Chunks(Strict-Merging)	1032	1225
Number of Parallel Chunks(Window-Merging)	1934	2361

Table 2. Number of Parallel Chunks found

		BLEU	NIST
Baseline System(PB-SMT)		10.68	4.12
Baseline + Parallel Chunks(Strict-Merging)	**V=4**	10.91	4.16
	V=7	11.01	4.16
Baseline + Parallel Chunks(Window-Merging)	**V=4**	11.55	4.21
	V=7	**11.87**	**4.29**

Table 3.Evaluation of the System

In addition to the target side of the parallel corpus, a monolingual Bengali corpus containing 406,422 words from the tourism domain was used for the target language model. We experimented with different n-gram settings for the language model and the maximum phrase length, and found that a 5-gram language model and a maximum phrase length of 7 produced the optimum baseline result. We therefore carried out the rest of the experiments using these settings.

5.2 Improving Baseline System

The comparable corpus consisted of 582 English-Bengali document pairs.

We experimented with the values V=4 and V=7 while doing the merging of chunks both in English and Bengali. All the single token chunks were discarded. Table 1 shows some statistics about the merged chunks for V=4 and V=7.It is evident that number of chunks in English documents is far more than the number of chunks in Bengali documents. This immediately suggests that Bengali documents are less informative than English documents. When the English merged chunks were passed to the translation module some of the chunks could not be translated into Bengali. Also, some chunks could be translated only partially, i.e. some tokens could be translated while some could not be. Those chunks were discarded. Finally, the number of (Strict-based) English merged-chunks and number of (Window-based) English merged-chunks were 285756 and 594631 respectively.

Two experiments were carried out separately. Strict-based merged English chunks were compared with Strict-Based merged Bengali chunks. Similarly, window-based merged English chunks were compared with window-based merged Bengali chunks. While searching for parallel chunks each translated source chunk was compared with all the target chunks in the corresponding document. Table 2 displays the number of parallel chunks found. Compared to the number of chunks in the original documents the number of parallel chunks found was much less. Nevertheless, a quick review of the parallel list revealed that most of the chunks were of good quality.

5.3 Evaluation

We carried out evaluation of the MT quality using two automatic MT evaluation metrics: BLEU (Papineni et al., 2002) and NIST (Doddington, 2002). Table 3 presents the experimental results. For the PB-SMT experiments, inclusion of the extracted strict merged parallel fragments from comparable corpora as additional training data presented some improvements over the PB-SMT baseline. Window based extracted fragments are added separately with parallel corpus and that also provides some improvements over the PB baseline; however inclusion of window based extracted phrases in baseline system with phrase length 7 improves over both strict and baseline in term of BLEU score and NIST score.

Table 3 shows the performance of the PB-SMT system that shows an improvement over baseline with both strict and window based merging even if, we change their phrase length from 4 to 7. Table 3 shows that the best improvement is achieved when we add parallel chunks as window merging with phrase length 7. It gives 1.19 BLEU point, i.e., 11.14% relative improvement over baseline system. The NIST score could be improved up to 4.12%. Bengali is a morphologically rich language and has relatively free phrase order. The strict based extraction does not reflect much improvement compared to the window based extraction because strict-merging (Procedure Strict_Merge) cannot cover up all the segments on either side, so very few parallel extractions have been found compared to window based extraction.

6 Conclusion

In this work, we tried to find English-Bengali parallel fragments of text from a comparable corpus built from Wikipedia documents. We have successfully improved the performance of an existing machine translation system. We have also shown that out-of-domain corpus happened to be useful for training of a domain specific MT system. The future work consists of working on larger amount of data. Another focus could be on building ad-hoc comparable corpus from WEB and using it to improve the performance of an existing out-of-domain MT system. This aspect of work is particularly important because the main challenge would be of domain adaptation.

Acknowledgements

This work has been partially supported by a grant from the English to Indian language Machine Translation (EILMT) project funded by the Department of Information and Technology (DIT), Government of India.

Reference

Chiao, Y. C., & Zweigenbaum, P. (2002, August). Looking for candidate translational equivalents in specialized, comparable corpora. In *Proceedings of the 19th international conference on Computational linguistics-Volume 2* (pp. 1-5). Association for Computational Linguistics.

Déjean, H., Gaussier, É., & Sadat, F. (2002). Bilingual terminology extraction: an approach based on a multilingual thesaurus applicable to comparable corpora. In *Proceedings of the 19th International Conference on Computational Linguistics COLING* (pp. 218-224).

Doddington, G. (2002, March). Automatic evaluation of machine translation quality using n-gram co-occurrence statistics. In Proceedings of the second international conference on Human Language Technology Research (pp. 138-145). Morgan Kaufmann Publishers Inc..

Fung, P., & McKeown, K. (1997, August). Finding terminology translations from non-parallel corpora. In *Proceedings of the 5th Annual Workshop on Very Large Corpora* (pp. 192-202).

Fung, P., & Yee, L. Y. (1998, August). An IR approach for translating new words from nonparallel, comparable texts. In *Proceedings of the 17th international conference on Computational linguistics-Volume 1* (pp. 414-420). Association for Computational Linguistics.

Hiroyuki, K. A. J. I. (2005). Extracting translation equivalents from bilingual comparable corpora. *IEICE Transactions on information and systems, 88*(2), 313-323.

Kneser, R., & Ney, H. (1995, May). Improved backing-off for m-gram language modeling. In *Acoustics, Speech, and Signal Processing, 1995. ICASSP-95., 1995 International Conference on* (Vol. 1, pp. 181-184). IEEE.

Koehn, P., Hoang, H., Birch, A., Callison-Burch, C., Federico, M., Bertoldi, N., ... & Herbst, E. (2007, June). Moses: Open source toolkit for statistical machine translation. In *Proceedings of the 45th Annual Meeting of the ACL on Interactive Poster and Demonstration Sessions* (pp. 177-180). Association for Computational Linguistics.

Koehn, P., Och, F. J., & Marcu, D. (2003, May). Statistical phrase-based translation. In *Proceedings of the 2003 Conference of the North American Chapter of the Association for Computational Linguistics on Human Language Technology-Volume 1* (pp. 48-54). Association for Computational Linguistics.

Munteanu, D. S., & Marcu, D. (2006, July). Extracting parallel sub-sentential fragments from non-parallel corpora. In *Proceedings of the 21st International Conference on Computational Linguistics and the 44th annual meeting of the Association for Computational Linguistics* (pp. 81-88). Association for Computational Linguistics..

Och, F. J. (2003, July). Minimum error rate training in statistical machine translation. In *Proceedings of the 41st Annual Meeting on Association for Computational Linguistics-Volume 1* (pp. 160-167). Association for Computational Linguistics.

Och, F. J., & Ney, H. (2000). Giza++: Training of statistical translation models.

Otero, P. G. (2007). Learning bilingual lexicons from comparable english and spanish corpora. *Proceedings of MT Summit xI*, 191-198.

Otero, P. G., & López, I. G. (2010). Wikipedia as multilingual source of comparable corpora. In *Proceedings of the 3rd Workshop on Building and Using Comparable Corpora, LREC* (pp. 21-25).

Papineni, K., Roukos, S., Ward, T., & Zhu, W. J. (2002, July). BLEU: a method for automatic evaluation of machine translation. In *Proceedings of the 40th annual meeting on association for computa-*

tional linguistics (pp. 311-318). Association for Computational Linguistics.

Rapp, R. (1999, June). Automatic identification of word translations from unrelated English and German corpora. In *Proceedings of the 37th annual meeting of the Association for Computational Linguistics on Computational Linguistics* (pp. 519-526). Association for Computational Linguistics.

Saralegui, X., San Vicente, I., & Gurrutxaga, A. (2008). Automatic generation of bilingual lexicons from comparable corpora in a popular science domain. In *LREC 2008 workshop on building and using comparable corpora*.

Smith, J. R., Quirk, C., & Toutanova, K. (2010, June).Extracting parallel sentences from comparable corpora using document level alignment. In Human Language Technologies: The 2010 Annual Conference of the North American Chapter of the Association for Computational Linguistics (pp. 403-411). Association for Computational Linguistics.

Stolcke, A. (2002, September). SRILM-an extensible language modeling toolkit. In *Proceedings of the international conference on spoken language processing* (Vol. 2, pp. 901-904).

VARTRA: A Comparable Corpus for Analysis of Translation Variation

Ekaterina Lapshinova-Koltunski
Universität des Saarlandes
A 2.2 Universität Campus
66123 Saarbrücken
Germany
e.lapshinova@mx.uni-saarland.de

Abstract

This paper presents a comparable translation corpus created to investigate translation variation phenomena in terms of contrasts between languages, text types and translation methods (machine vs. computer-aided vs. human). These phenomena are reflected in linguistic features of translated texts belonging to different registers and produced with different translation methods. For their analysis, we combine methods derived from translation studies, language variation and machine translation, concentrating especially on textual and lexico-grammatical variation. To our knowledge, none of the existing corpora can provide comparable resources for a comprehensive analysis of variation across text types and translation methods. Therefore, the corpus resources created, as well as our analysis results will find application in different research areas, such as translation studies, machine translation, and others.

1 Introduction: Aims and Motivation

Comparable corpora serve as essential resources for numerous studies and applications in both linguistics (contrastive language, text analysis), translation studies and natural language processing (machine translation, computational lexicography, information extraction). Many comparable corpora are available and have been being created for different language pairs like (a) English, German and Italian (Baroni et al., 2009); (b) English, Norwegian, German and French (Johansson, 2002); (c) written or spoken English and German (Hansen et al., 2012) or (Lapshinova et al., 2012).

However, comparable corpora may be of the same language, as the feature of 'comparability' may relate not only to corpora of different languages but also to those of the same language. The main feature that makes them comparable is that they cover the same text type(s) in the same proportions, cf. for instance, (Laviosa, 1997) or (McEnery, 2003), and thus, can be used for a certain comparison task.

As our research goal is the analysis of translation variation, we need a corpus which allows us to compare translations, which differ in the source/target language, the type of the text translated (genre or register) and the method of translation (human with/without CAT[1] tools, machine translation). There are a number of corpus-based studies dedicated to the analysis of variation phenomena, cf. (Teich, 2003; Steiner, 2004; Neumann, 2011) among others. However, all of them concentrate on the analysis of human translations only, comparing translated texts with non-translated ones. In some works on machine translation, the focus does lie on comparing different translation variants (human vs. machine), e.g. (White, 1994; Papineni et al., 2002; Babych and Hartley, 2004; Popović, 2011). However, they all serve the task of automatic machine translation (MT) systems evaluation and use the human-produced translations as references or training material only. None of them provide analysis of specifc (linguistic) features of different text types translated with different translation methods.

The same tendencies are observed in the corpus resources available, as they are mostly built for certain research goals. Although there exists a number of translation corpora, none of them fits our research task: most of them include one translation method only: EUROPARL (Koehn, 2005) and JRC-Acquis (Steinberger et al., 2006) – translations produced by humans, or DARPA-94 (White, 1994) – machine-translated texts only.

[1] CAT = computer-aided translation

Moreover, they all contain one register only and, therefore, cannot be applied to a comprehensive analysis of variation phenomena.

Therefore, we decided to compile our own comparable corpus which contains translations from different languages, of different text types, produced with different translation methods (human vs. machine). Furthermore, both human and machine translations contain further varieties: they are produced by different translators (both professional and student), with or without CAT tools or by different MT systems.

This resource will be valuable not only for our research goals, or for research purposes of further translation researchers. It can also find further applications, e.g. in machine translation or CAT tool development, as well as translation quality assesment.

The remainder of the paper is structured as follows. Section 2 presents studies we adopt as theoretical background for the selection of features and requirements for corpus resources. In section 4, we describe the compilation and design of the comparable translation corpus at hand. In section 5, we demonstrate some examples of corpus application, and in section 6, we draw some conclusions and provide more ideas for corpus extension and its further application.

2 Theoretical Background and Resource Requirements

To design and annotate a corpus reflecting variation phenomena, we need to define (linguistic) features of translations under analysis. As sources for these features, we use studies on translation and *translationese*, those on language variation, as well as works on machine translation, for instance MT evaluation and MT quality assessment.

2.1 Translation analysis and translationese

As already mentioned in section 1 above, translation studies either analyse differences between original texts and translations, e.g. (House, 1997; Matthiessen, 2001; Teich, 2003; Hansen, 2003; Steiner, 2004), or concentrate on the properties of translated texts only, e.g. (Baker, 1995). However, it is important that most of them consider translations to have their own specific properties which distinguish them from the originals (both of the source and target language), and thus, establish specific language of translations – the *translationese*.

Baker (1995) excludes the influence of the source language on a translation altogether, analysing characteristic patterns of translations independent of the source language. Within this context, she proposed translation universals – hypotheses on the universal features of translations: *explicitation* (tendency to spell things out rather than leave them implicit), *simplification* (tendency to simplify the language used in translation), *normalisation* (a tendency to exaggerate features of the target language and to conform to its typical patterns) and *levelling out* (individual translated texts are alike), cf. (Baker, 1996). Additionally, translations can also have features of "*shining through*" defined by Teich (2003) – in this case we observe some typical features of the source language in the translation. The author analyses this phenomena comparing different linguistic features (e.g. passive and passive-like constructions) of originals and translations in English and German.

In some recent applications of *translationese* phenomena, e.g. those for cleaning parallel corpora obtained from the Web, or for the improvement of translation and language models in MT (Baroni and Bernardini, 2005; Kurokawa et al., 2009; Koppel and Ordan, 2011; Lembersky et al., 2012), authors succeeded to automatically identify these features with machine learning techniques.

We aim at employing the knowledge (features described) from these studies, as well as techniques applied to explore these features in the corpus.

2.2 Language variation

Features of translated texts, as well as those of their sources are influenced by the text types they belong to, see (Neumann, 2011). Therefore, we also refer to studies on language variation which focus on the analysis of variation across registers and genres, e.g. (Biber, 1995; Conrad and Biber, 2001; Halliday and Hasan, 1989; Matthiessen, 2006; Neumann, 2011) among others. Register is described as functional variation, see Quirk et al. (1985) and Biber et al. (1999). For example, language may vary according to the activitiy of the involved participants, production varieties (written vs. spoken) of a language or the relationship between speaker and addressee(s). These parameters correspond to the variables of *field*, *tenor* and *mode* defined in the framework of Systemic Functional Linguistics (SFL), which describes language variation according to situational contexts, cf. e.g. Halliday and Hasan (1989), and Halliday (2004).

In SFL, these variables are associated with the corresponding lexico-grammatical features, e.g. field of discourse is realised in functional verb classes (e.g., activity, communication, etc) or term patterns, tenor is realised in modality (expressed e.g. by modal verbs) or stance expressions, mode is realised in information structure and textual cohesion (e.g. personal and demonstrative reference). Thus, differences between registers or text types can be identified through the analysis of occurrence of lexico-grammatical features in these registers, see Biber's studies on linguistic variation, e.g. (Biber, 1988; Biber, 1995) or (Biber et al., 1999).

Steiner (2001) and Teich (2003) refer to registers as one of the influencing sources of the properties of translated text. Thus, we attempt to study variation in translation variants by analysing distributions of lexico-grammatical features in our corpus.

2.3 Machine translation

We also refer to studies on machine translation in our analysis, as we believe that translation variation phenomena should not be limited to those produced by humans. Although most studies comparing human and machine translation serve the task of automatic MT evaluation only, cf. (White, 1994; Papineni et al., 2002; Babych and Hartley, 2004), some of them do use linguistic features for their analysis.

For instance, Popović and Burchardt (2011) define linguistically influenced categories (inflections, word order, lexical choices) to automatically classify errors in the output of MT systems. Specia (2011) and Specia et al. (2011) also utilise linguistic features as indicators for quality estimation in MT. The authors emphasize that most MT studies ignored the MT system-independent features, i.e. those reflecting the properties of the translation and the original. The authors classify them into *source complexity* features (sentence and word length, type-token-ratio, etc.), *target fluency* features (e.g. translation sentence length or coherence of the target sentence) and *adequacy* features (e.g. absolute difference between the number of different phrase types in the source and target or difference between the depth of their syntactic trees, etc.).

3 Methodology

Consideration of the features described in the above mentioned frameworks will give us new insights on variation phenomena in translation. Thus, we collect these features and extract information on their distribution across translation variants of our corpus to evaluate them later with statistical methods.

Some of the features described by different frameworks overlap, e.g. type-token-ratio (TTR) or sentence length as indicator for simplification in translationese analysis and as a target fluency feature in MT quality estimation; modal meanings and theme-rheme distribution in register analysis and SFL, or alternation of passive verb constructions in register analysis and translation studies.

Investigating language variation in translation, we need to compare translations produced by different systems with those produced by humans (with/without the help of CATs). Furthermore, we need to compare translated texts either with their originals in the source or comparable originals in the target language. Moreover, as we know that text type has influence on both source and target text (Neumann, 2011), we need to compare different text registers of all translation types.

This requires a certain corpus design: we need a linguistically-annotated corpus for extraction of particular features (e.g. morpho-syntactic constructions); we need to include meta-information on (a) translation type (human vs. computer-aided vs. machine, both rule-based and statistical), (b) text production type (original vs. translation) and (c) text type (various registers and domains of discourse). This will enable the following analysis procedures: (1) automatic extraction, (2) statistical evaluation and (3) classification (clustering) of lexico-grammatical features.

4 Corpus Resources

4.1 Corpus data collection

Due to the lack of resources required for the analysis of translation variation, we have compiled our own translation corpus VARTRA (VARiation in TRAnslation). In this paper, we present the first version of the corpus – VARTRA-SMALL, which is the small and normalised version used for our first analyses and experiments. The compilation of the full version of VARTRA is a part of our future work, cf. section 6.

VARTRA-SMALL contains English original texts and variants of their translations (to each text) into German which were produced by: (1) human professionals (PT), (2) human student translators with the help of computer-aided translation tools (CAT), (3) rule-based MT systems (RBMT) and (4) statistical MT systems (SMT).

The English originals (EO), as well as the translations by profesionals (PT) were exported from the already existing corpus CroCo mentioned in section 1 above. The CAT variant was produced by student assistents who used the CAT tool ACROSS in the translation process[2]. The current RBMT variant was translated with SYSTRAN (RBMT1)[3], although we plan to expand it with a LINGUATEC-generated version[4]. For SMT, we have compiled two versions – the one produced with Google Translate[5] (SMT1), and the other one with a Moses system (SMT2).

Each translation variant is saved as a subcorpus and covers seven registers of written language: political essays (ESSAY), fictional texts (FICTION), manuals (INSTR), popular-scientific articles (POPSCI), letters of share-holders (SHARE), prepared political speeches (SPEECH), and touristic leaflets (TOU), presented in Table 1. The total number of tokens in VARTRA-SMALL comprises 795,460 tokens (the full version of VARTRA will comprise at least ca. 1,7 Mio words).

4.2 Corpus annotation

For the extraction of certain feature types, e.g. modal verbs, passive and active verb constructions, Theme types, textual cohesion, etc. our corpus should be linguistically annotated. All subcorpora of VARTRA-SMALL are tokenised, lemmatised, tagged with part-of-speech information, segmented into syntactic chunks and sentences. The annotations were obtained with Tree Tagger (Schmid, 1994).

In Table 2, we outline the absolute numbers for different annotation levels per subcorpus (translation variant) in VARTRA-SMALL.

VARTRA-SMALL is encoded in CWB and can be queried with the help of Corpus Query Processor (CQP) (Evert, 2005). We also encode a part of the meta-data, such as information on register, as well as translation method, tools used and the source language. A sample output encoded in CQP format that is subsequently used for corpus query is shown in Figure 1.

subc	token	lemma	chunk	sent
PT	132609	9137	55319	6525
CAT	139825	10448	58669	6852
RBMT	131330	8376	55714	6195
SMT1	130568	9771	53935	6198
SMT2	127892	7943	51599	6131

Table 2: Annotations in VARTRA-SMALL

In this way, we have compiled a corpus of different translation variants, which are comparable, as they contain translations of the same texts produced with different methods and tools. Thus, this comparable corpus allows for analysis of contrasts in terms of (a) text typology (e.g. fiction vs. popular-scientific articles); (b) text production types (originals vs. translations) and (c) translation types (human vs. machine and their subtypes).

Furthermore, examination of some translation phenomena requires parallel components – alignment between originals and translations. At the moment, alignment on the sentence level (exported from CroCo) is available for the EO and PT subcorpora. We do not provide any alignment for further translation variants at the moment, although we plan to align all of them with the originals on word and sentence level.

4.3 Corpus querying

As already mentioned in 4.2, VARTRA-SMALL can be queried with CQP, which allows definition of language patterns in form of regular expressions based on string, part-of-speech and chunk tags, as well as further constraints. In Table 3, we illustrate an example of a query which is built to extract cases of processual finite passive verb constructions in German: lines 1 - 5 are used for passive from a *Verbzweit* sentence (construction in German where the finite verb occupies the position after the subject), and lines 6 - 10 are used for *Verbletzt* constructions (where the finite verb occupies the final position in the sentence). In this example, we make use of part-of-speech (lines 3a, 5, 8 and 9a), lemma (lines 3b and 9b) and

[2] `www.my-across.net`
[3] SYSTRAN 6
[4] `www.linguatec.net`
[5] `http://translate.google.com/`

	EO	PT	CAT	RBMT	SMT1	SMT2
ESSAY	15537	15574	15795	15032	15120	14746
FICTION	11249	11257	12566	11048	11028	10528
INSTR	20739	21009	19903	20793	20630	20304
POPSCI	19745	19799	22755	20894	20353	19890
SHARE	24467	24613	24764	22768	22792	22392
SPEECH	23308	23346	24321	23034	22877	22361
TOU	17564	17638	19721	17761	17768	17671
TOTAL	132609	133236	139825	131330	130568	127892

Table 1: Tokens per register in VARTRA-SMALL

chunk type (lines 2b and 6b) information, as well as chunk (lines 2a, 2c, 6a and 6c) and sentence (lines 1 and 10) borders.

	query block	example
1.	<s>	
2a.	<chunk>	
2b.	[_.chunk_type=“NC”]+	*Ein Chatfenster*
2c.	</chunk>	
3a.	[pos=“VAFIN”&	
3b.	lemma=“werden”]	*wird*
4.	[word!=“.”]*	*daraufhin*
5.	[pos=“V.*PP”];	*angezeigt*
6a.	<chunk>	
6b.	[_.chunk_type=“NC”]+	*das Transportgut*
6c.	</chunk>	
7.	[word!=“.”]*	*nicht*
8.	[pos=“V.*PP”]	*akzeptiert*
9a.	[pos=“VAFIN”&	
9b.	lemma=“werden”]	*wird*
10.	</s>	

Table 3: Example queries to extract processual finite passive constructions

CQP also allows us to sort the extracted information according to the metadata: text registers and IDs or translation methods and tools. Table 4 shows an example of frequency distribution according to the metadata information. In this way, we can obtain data for our analyses of translation variation.

5 Preliminary Analyses

5.1 Profile of VARTRA-SMALL in terms of shallow features

We start our analyses with the comparison of translation variants only saved in our subcorpora: PT, CAT, RBMT, SMT1 and SMT2. The structure of the corpus, as well as the annotations available already allow us to compare subcorpora (translation variants) in terms of shallow features, such as type-token-ration (TTR), lexical density (LD) and part-of-speech (POS) distributions. These features are among the most frequently used variables which characterise linguistic variation in corpora, cf. (Biber et al., 1999) among others. They also deliver the best scores in the identification of translationese features. We calculate TTR as the percentage of different lexical word forms (types) per subcorpus. LD is calculated as percentage of content words and the percentages given in the POS distribution are the percentages of given word classes per subcorpus, all normalised per cent. The numerical results for TTR and LD are given in Table 5.

method	tool	register	freq
CAT	Across	POPSCI	101
CAT	Across	SHARE	90
CAT	Across	SPEECH	89
CAT	Across	INSTR	73
RBMT	SYSTRAN	SHARE	63
RBMT	SYSTRAN	POPSCI	62
CAT	Across	TOU	58

Table 4: Example output of V2 processual passive across translation method, tool and text register (absolute frequencies)

subc	TTR	LD
PT	15.82	48.33
CAT	14.10	44.60
RBMT	15.04	45.08
SMT1	14.32	46.03
SMT2	14.68	47.86

Table 5: TTR and LD in VARTRA-SMALL

```
<translation method="CAT" tool="Across" sourceLanguage="English">
<text "CAT_ESSAY_001.txt" register="ESSAY">
<s>
<chunk type="NC">
Die                 ART        d
weltweiten          ADJA       weltweit
Herausforderungen   NN         Herausforderung
</chunk>
<chunk type="PC">
im                  APPRART    im
Bereich             NN         Bereich
</chunk>
<chunk type="NC">
der                 ART        d
Energiesicherheit   NN         Energiesicherheit
</chunk>
<chunk type="VC">
erfordern           VVFIN      erfordern
</chunk>
<chunk type="PC">
über                APPR       über
einen               ART        ein
Zeitraum            NN         Zeitraum
</chunk>
<chunk type="PC">
von                 APPR       von
vielen              PIAT       viel
Jahrzehnten         ADJA       jahrzehnte
nachhaltige         ADJA       nachhaltig
Anstrengungen       NN         Anstrengung
</chunk>
<chunk type="PC">
auf                 APPR       auf
```

Figure 1: Example of an annotated sample from VARTRA-SMALL

For the analysis of POS distribution, we decide to restrict them to nominal and verbal word classes. Tables 6 and 7 illustrate distribution of nominal – nouns, pronouns (pron), adjectives (adj) and adpositions (adp), and verbal word classes – verbs, adverbs (adv) and conjunctions (conj) – across different translation variants.

subc	noun	pron	adj	adp	total
PT	27.18	8.23	9.38	8.31	53.10
CAT	24.80	8.53	8.08	9.52	50.93
RBMT	24.80	8.61	8.91	9.01	51.32
SMT1	27.18	8.04	8.67	9.02	52.89
SMT2	29.78	7.28	10.42	8.64	56.11

Table 6: Nominal word classes in % in VARTRA-SMALL

subc	verb	adv	conj	total
PT	11.80	3.95	5.32	21.06
CAT	13.58	3.69	5.83	23.10
RBMT	12.90	2.74	6.34	21.99
SMT1	11.88	2.81	6.32	21.02
SMT2	9.09	2.52	6.06	17.67

Table 7: Verbal word classes in % in VARTRA-SMALL

5.2 Interpretation of results

According to Biber (1999), high proportion of variable lexical words in a text is an indicator of richness and density of experiential meanings. This characterises the field of discourse (see section 2.2 above), and TTR, thus, indicates informational density. In terms of translationese (see section 2.1), TTR reveals simplification features of translations. Translations always reveal lower TTR and LD than their originals, cf. (Hansen, 2003).

The highest TTR, thus, the most lexically rich translation variant in VARTRA is the one produced by human translators: PT > RBMT > SMT2 > SMT1 > CAT. It is interesting that the other human-produced variant demonstrates the lowest lexical richness which might be explained by the level of experience of translators (student translators). Another reason could be the strength of pronominal cohesion and less explicit specification of domains. However, the comparison of the distribution of pronouns (devices for pronominal cohesion) does not reveal big differences between PT and CAT, cf. Table 6.

Another simplification feature is LD, which is also the lowest in CAT-subcorpus of VARTRA: PT > SMT2 > SMT1 > RBMT > CAT. Steiner (2012) claims that lower lexical density can indicate increased logical explicitness (increased use of conjunctions and adpositions) in translations. CAT does demonstrate the highest number of adpositions in the corpus, although the difference across subcorpora is not high, see Table 6.

The overall variation between the subcorpora in terms of TTR and LD is not high, which can be interpreted as indicator of levelling out (see section 2.1 above): translations are often more alike in terms of these features than the individual texts in a comparable corpus of source or target language.

In terms of nominal vs. verbal word classes, there seems to be a degree of dominance of nominal classes (56.11% vs. 17.67%) in SMT2 resulting in a ratio of 3.18 compared to other subcorpora, cf. Table 8.

subc	**nominal vs. verbal**	**ratio**
PT	53.10 : 21.06	2.52
CAT	50.93 : 23.10	2.20
RBMT	51.32 : 21.99	2.33
SMT1	52.89 : 21.02	2.52
SMT2	56.11 : 17.67	3.18

Table 8: Proportionality of nominal vs. verbal opposition in VARTRA-SMALL

The greatest contributors to this dominance are nouns and adjectives (Table 6 above). For CAT, we again observe the lowest numbers (the lowest noun vs. verb ratio) which means that this translation variant seems to be the most "verbal" one. According to Steiner (2012), German translations are usually more verbal than German originals. Comparing German and English in general, the author claims that German is less "verbal" than English. Thus, a higher "verbality" serves as an indicator of "shining though" (see 2.1 above), which we observe in case of CAT. However, to find this out, we would need to compare our subcorpora with their originals, as well as the comparable German originals.

5.3 First statistical experiments

We use the extracted shallow features for the first steps in feature evaluation. As our aim is to investigate the relations between the observed feature frequencies and the respective translation variants, we decide for *correspondence analysis*, a multivariate technique, which works on observed frequencies and provides a map of the data usually plotted in a two dimensional graph, cf. (Baayen, 2008).

As input we use the features described in 5.1 above: TTR, LD, nouns, adjectives (adj), adpositions (adp), verbs, adverbs (adv), conjunctions (conj). Additionally, we divide the class of pronouns into two groups: personal (pers.P) and demonstrative (dem.P) – devices to express pronominal cohesion. We also extract frequency information on modal verbs which express modality.

The output of the correspondence analysis is plotted into a two dimensional graph with arrows representing the observed feature frequencies and points representing the translation variants. The length of the arrows indicates how pronounced a particular feature is. The position of the points in relation to the arrows indicates the relative importance of a feature for a translation variant. The arrows pointing in the direction of an axis indicate a high contribution to the respective dimension. Figure 2 shows the graph for our data.

In Table 9, we present the Eigenvalues calculated for each dimension to assess how well our data is represented in the graph[6]. We are able to obtain a relatively high cumulative value by the first two dimensions (representing *x* and *y*-axis in Figure 2), as they are the ones used to plot the two-dimensional graph. The cumulative value for the first two dimensions is 94,3%, which indicates that our data is well represented in the graph.

If we consider the *y*-axis in Figure 2, we see that there is a separation between human and machine translation, although SMT2 is on the borderline. CAT is also closer to MT, as it is plotted much closer to 0 than PT. Conjunctions, personal pronouns and adverbs seem to be most prominent contributors to this separation, as their arrows are

[6] 'dim' lists dimensions, 'value' – Eigenvalues converted to percentages of explained variation in '%' and calculated as cumulative explained variation with the addition of each dimension in 'cum'.

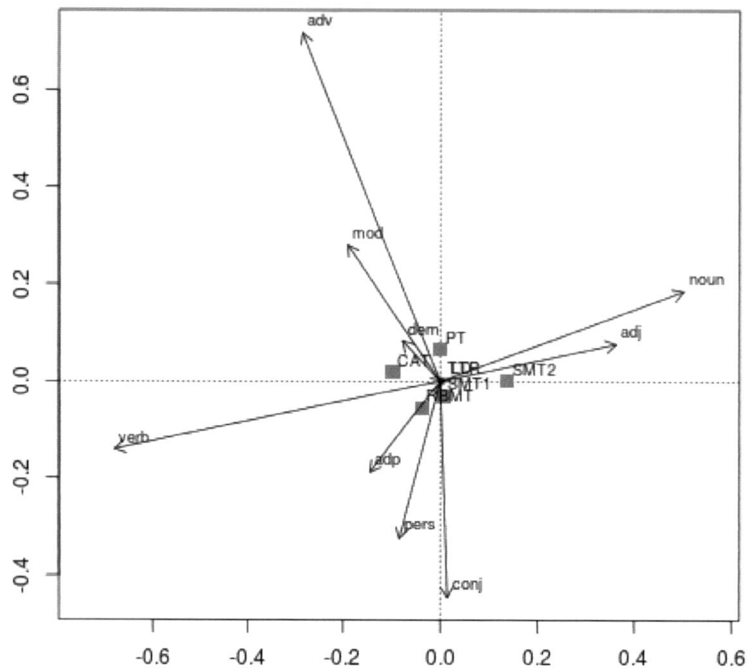

Figure 2: Graph for correspondence analysis on translation variants

dim	value	%	cum%	scree plot
1	0.005939	73.0	73.0	************************
2	0.001726	21.2	94.3	*******
3	0.000352	4.3	98.6	*
4	0.000114	1.4	100.0	
	———	——		
Total:	0.008131	100.0		

Table 9: Contribution of dimensions

the longest ones, and they point in the direction of the *y*-axis.

Verbs, adjectives and nouns seem to be most prominent contributors to the other division (considering the *x*-axis). Here, we can observe three groups of subcorpora: CAT and RBMT share certain properties which differ them from SMT2. PT remains on the borderline, whereas SMT1 tend slightly to SMT2.

6 Conclusion and Future Work

In this paper, we presented a comparable corpus of translations from English into German, which contains multiple variants of translation of the same texts. This corpus is an important resource for the investigation of variation phenomena reflected in linguistic features of translations. The corpus architecture allows us to extract these features automatically. Our preliminary results show that there are both similarities and differences between translation variants produced by humans and machine systems. We expect even more variation, if we compare the distribution of these features across text registers available in all subcorpora.

However, there is a need to inspect the reasons for this variation, as they can be effected by translator experience, restrictions of the CAT system applied or the training material used in MT.

We believe that our resources, as well as our research results will find application not only in contrastive linguistics or translation studies. On the one hand, our corpus provides a useful dataset to investigate translation phenomena and processes, but on the other, it can be used for the development, optimisation and evaluation of MT systems, as well as CAT tools (e.g. translation memories).

In the future, we aim at expanding it with more data: (1) more texts for the existing registers (each register should contain around 30,000 words), (2) further text registers (e.g. academic, web and news texts). We also plan to produce further human and machine-generated translations, i.e. (3) machine translations post-edited by humans, as well as translation outputs of (4) further MT systems. Moreover, we aim at adding translations from German into English to trace variation influenced by language typology.

As the automatic tagging of part-of-speech and chunk information might be erroneous, we plan to evaluate the output of the TreeTagger and compare it with the output of further tools available, e.g. MATE dependency parser, cf. (Bohnet, 2010). Furthermore, the originals will be aligned with their translations on word and sentence level. This annotation type is particularly important for the analysis of variation in translation of certain lexico-grammatical structures.

A part of the corpus (CAT, RBMT and SMT subcorpora) will be available to a wider academic public, e.g. via the CLARIN-D repository.

Acknowledgments

The project "VARTRA: Translation Variation" was supported by a grant from Forschungsausschuß of the Saarland University. We are especially grateful to Anne-Katrin Schumann, Elke Teich and Noam Ordan for their comments. Also, we wish to thank the anonymous reviewers for their suggestions for improving our paper. All remaining errors remain ours.

References

Across Personal Edition: Free CAT Tool for Freelance Translators. `http://www.my-across.net/en/translation-workbench.aspx`.

Harald Baayen. 2008. *Analyzing Linguistic Data. A Practical Introduction to Statistics Using R*. Cambridge University Press.

Bogdan Babych and Anthony Hartley. 2004. Modelling legitimate translation variation for automatic evaluation of MT quality. *Proceedings of LREC-2004*, Vol. 3.

Mona Baker. 1995. Corpora in Translation Studies: An Overview and Some Suggestions for Future Research. *Target*, 7(2):223–43.

Mona Baker. 1996. Corpus-based translation studies: The challenges that lie ahead. Harold Somers (ed.). Terminology, LSP and Translation. Studies in language engineering in honour of Juan C. Sager. Amsterdam and Philadelphia: Benjamins: 175–186.

Marco Baroni and Silvia Bernardini. 2005. A New Approach to the Study of Translationese: Machine-learning the Difference between Original and Translated Text. *Literary and Linguistic Computing*, 21 (3): 259–274.

Marco Baroni, Silvia Bernardini, Adriano Ferraresi and Eros Zanchetta. 2009. The WaCky Wide Web: A Collection of Very Large Linguistically Processed Web-Crawled Corpora. *Language Resources and Evaluation*, 43(3): 209–226.

Douglas Biber. 1988. *Variation across speech and writing*. Cambridge: Cambridge University Press.

Douglas Biber. 1995. *Dimensions of Register Variation. A Cross-linguistic Comparison*. Cambridge: Cambridge University Press.

Douglas Biber, Stig Johansson, Geoffrey Leech, Susan Conrad and Edward Finegan. 1999. *Longman Grammar of Spoken and Written English*. Longman, London.

Bernd Bohnet. 2010. Top Accuracy and Fast Dependency Parsing is not a Contradiction. *The 23rd International Conference on Computational Linguistics (COLING 2010)*. Beijing, China.

Susan Conrad and Douglas Biber (eds.). 2001. *Variation in English: Multi-Dimensional studies*. Longman, London.

The IMS Open Corpus Workbench. 2010. http://www.cwb.sourceforge.net

Stefan Evert. 2005. *The CQP Query Language Tutorial*. IMS Stuttgart, CWB version 2.2.b90.

Google Translate. Accessed July 2012. http://translate.google.com

Michael A.K. Halliday. 1985. *Spoken and written language*. Deakin University Press, Victoria.

Michael A.K. Halliday, and Riquaya Hasan. 1989. *Language, context and text: Aspects of language in a social semiotic perspective*. Oxford University Press.

Michael A.K. Halliday. 2004. *An Introduction to Functional Grammar*, 3. edition. Hodder Education.

Silvia Hansen-Schirra, Stella Neumann, and Erich Steiner. 2013. *Cross-linguistic Corpora for the Study of Translations. Insights from the Language Pair English-German*. Berlin, New York: de Gruyter.

Silvia Hansen. 2003. *The Nature of Translated Text – An Interdisciplinary Methodology for the Investigation of the Specific Properties of Translations*. Ph.D. Theses.

Juliane House. 1997. *Translation Quality Assessment: A Model Revisited*. Ph.D. Thesis.

Stig Johansson. Towards a multilingual corpus for contrastive analysis and translation studies. *Language and Computers*, 43 (1): 47–59.

Adam Kilgariff. 2010. Comparable Corpora Within and Across Languages, Word Frequency Lists and the KELLY Project. *BUCC, 6th Workshop on Building and Using Comparable Corpora*, Valletta, Malta.

Phillip Koehn. 2005 Europarl: A Parallel Corpus for Statistical Machine Translation. *MT Summit*.

Moshe Koppel and Noam Ordan. 2011. Translationese and its dialects. *Proceedings of the 49th Annual Meeting of the Association for Computational Linguistics (ACL11)*.

David Kurokawa, Cyril Goutte and Pierre Isabelle. 2009. Automatic Detection of Translated Text and its Impact on Machine Translation. *Proceedings of MT-Summit-XII*.

Ekaterina Lapshinova-Koltunski, Kerstin Kunz and Marilisa Amoia. 2012. Compiling a Multilingual Spoken Corpus. *Proceedings of the VIIth GSCP International Conference : Speech and Corpora*. Firenze : Firenze University Press.

Sara Laviosa. 1997. How Comparable Can 'Comparable Corpora' Be? *Target*, 9(2): 289–319.

Gennady Lembersky, Noam Ordan and Shuly Wintner. 2012. Language models for machine translation: Original vs. translated texts. *Computational Linguistics*.

Linguatec Personal Translator 14. http://www.linguatec.net/products/tr/pt

Christian M.I.M. Matthiessen. 2001. The environment of translation. Erich Steiner and Colin Yallop (eds). *Exploring Translation and Multilingual Text Production: Beyond Content*. Berlin and New York: Mouten de Gruyter.

Christian M.I.M. Matthiessen. 2006. Frequency profiles of some basic grammatical systems: an interim report. Geoffrey Thompson and Susan Hunston (eds). *System and Corpus: Exploring connections*. Equinox, London.

Tony McEnery. 2003. *Oxford Handbook of Computational Linguistics*, chapter Corpus Linguistics: 448–463. Oxford: Oxford University Press.

Stella Neumann. 2011. *Contrastive Register Variation. A Quantitative Approach to the Comparison of English and German*. Berlin and New York: de Gruyter.

Kishore Papineni, Salim Roukus, Todd Ward and Wei-Jing Zhu. 2002. BLEU: a method for automatic evaluation of machine translation *Proceedings of the 40th annual meeting on association for computational linguistics*, 311–318.

Maja Popović and Aljoscha Burchardt. 2011. From Human to Automatic Error Classification for Machine Translation Output. *15th International Conference of the European Association for Machine Translation (EAMT 11)*.

Randolph Quirk, Sidney Greenbaum, Geoffrey Leech and Jan Svartvik. 1985. *A Comprehensive Grammar of the English Language*. Longman, London.

Helmut Schmid. 1994. Probabilistic Part-of-Speech Tagging Using Decision Trees. *International Conference on New Methods in Language Processing*, Manchester (UK): 44–49.

Lucia Specia. 2011. Exploiting objective annotations for measuring translation post-editing effort. *Proceedings of the 15th Conference of the European Association for Machine Translation*: 73–80.

Lucia Specia, Najeh Hajlaoui, Catalina Hallett and Wilker Aziz. 2011. Predicting machine translation adequacy. *Machine Translation Summit XIII (2011)*: 19–23.

Ralf Steinberger, Bruno Pouliquen, Anna Widiger, Camelia Ignat, Tomaz Erjavec, Dan Tufis and Daniel Varga. 2006. The JRC-Acquis: A multilingual aligned parallel corpus with 20+ languages. *Proceedings of the 5th International Conference on Language Resources and Evaluation (LREC'2006)*. Genoa, Italy, 24-26 May 2006.

Erich Steiner. 2001. Translations English-German: Investigating the Relative Importance of Systemic Contrasts and of the Text Type translation. *SPRIKreports* 7:1–49.

Erich Steiner. 2004. *Translated texts: Properties, Variants, Evaluations*. Frankfurt a.Main: Peter Lang.

Erich Steiner. 2012. A characterization of the resource based on shallow statistics. Hansen-Schirra, Silvia, Stella Neumann and Erich Steiner (eds). *Cross-linguistic Corpora for the Study of Translations. Insights from the Language Pair English-German*. Berlin, New York: de Gruyter.

SYSTRAN Enterprise Server 6. Online Tools User Guide.

Elke Teich. 2003. *Cross-linguistic Variation in System and Text. A Methodology for the Investigation of Translations and Comparable Texts*. Berlin and New York: Mouton de Gruyter.

John S. White. 1994. The ARPA MT Evaluation Methodologies: Evolution, Lessons, and Further Approaches. *Proceedings of the 1994 Conference of the Association for Machine Translation in the Americas*, 193–205.

Building Ontologies from Collaborative Knowledge Bases to Search and Interpret Multilingual Corpora

Yegin Genc **Elizabeth A. Lennon** **Winter Mason** **Jeffrey V. Nickerson**
Stevens Institute of Technology
Center for Decision Technologies
Castle Point on Hudson, Hoboken, NJ USA
{ygenc, elennon, wmason, jnickerson}@stevens.edu

Abstract

Tools and techniques that automate the interpretation of multilingual corpora are useful on many fronts; scholars, as an example, could use such tools to more readily pinpoint relevant articles from journals in a wide variety of languages. This work describes techniques to build and characterize ontologies using collaborative knowledge bases, e.g., Wikipedia. These ontologies can then be used to search and classify texts. Originally developed for monolingual corpora, we extend the approach to multilingual texts and test the methods with Mandarin scientific abstracts. The presented techniques provide a novel and efficient mechanism to obtain contextually rich ontologies and measure document relevancy within multilingual corpora.

1 Introduction

The wealth of data available online in the form of unstructured text drives the development of tools that automatically extract meaning from cross-lingual corpora. Techniques that quantify the degree to which texts exhibit similar meaning improve a variety of search processes – for example, academic research. However, automating the interpretation of multilingual corpora requires detecting similarities in meaning, while ignoring irrelevant linguistic differences. For example, the understanding that emerges from the connections and associations among words, i.e. context, can manifest very differently in different languages (Goddard, 2011). Furthermore, the meanings of words used in natural language are often context dependent, and context itself both shapes and reveals meaning (Gennaro et al., 2007).

For the purposes of this work, an ontology is defined as a model that represents word entities as concepts and their interrelationships (Lanzenberger et al., 2010). In this sense, ontologies represent the relevant aspects of context. To effectively comprehend cross-lingual corpora, tools that can explore the dependencies between language and context are needed.

One way to do this is to make use of well-understood existing texts that have explicitly linked concept graphs. Examples of such texts are collaborative knowledge stores, databases built up through the contributions of many individuals.

The techniques described here use Wikipedia to build ontologies from journal article abstracts in different languages, which we test on text written in Mandarin. In order to compare alternative ways of deriving ontologies, a set of articles that have both Mandarin and English abstracts are used as the test corpus.

The rest of the paper is organized into four sections. The background section briefly summarizes prior research relevant to this work. Next, the methods section details the processing steps used to create and visualize the ontologies for three experimental conditions. Sample ontology visualizations for each of the experimental conditions are shown. A discussion comparing some of the emergent features in each of the three generated ontologies follows. Finally, we outline next steps for the extension of these techniques.

2 Background

Translation is used to convey the meaning represented in one language in another language. Automated text translation was a goal of early computing (Locke and Booth, 1955), and is still challenging today. Approaches taken include dictionary look-ups, cognate matching, and parallel corpora based methods (Kishida, 2005). Cognate matching uses untranslatable terms such as proper nouns or technical terminology as the bases of cross-lingual connections. For example, Freitas-Juniar et al. (2006) leveraged medical terms, commonly used across languages, to classify medical documents from multiple languages.

Landauer and Littman (1991) used parallel corpora based methods when they created a language independent indexing space via Singular Value Decomposition to generate a comparable corpus. This permitted texts to be represented in a language-independent space, solely using the terms of the presentation language.

One early machine translation system, DIONYSUS, used three static knowledge sources: a lexicon, an ontological domain model, and a text-meaning-representation language in an effort to automate translation. The DIONYSUS researchers noted the challenge of developing an ontology based on a detailed version of a "constructed reality" (Onyshkevych and Nirenburg 1992). In other words, an ontological model of concepts representing a worldview is only as good as its ability to capture the breadth and depth of the world it attempts to model. Creating ontologies for machine translation applications arguably require knowledge stores as rich, expansive, and comprehensive as human language itself (Hovy, 2005).

One challenge related to reliable ontology creation is the relevance of the produced ontology in the future (Hovy, 2005). That is, word meanings morph over time, and so the ontology needs to shift also. Moreover, shifts in word meanings happen differently in different languages. Nichols et al. (2006) explored multilingual ontology acquisition using robust minimal recursion semantics and machine-readable dictionaries. Though they demonstrated a language-agnostic tool for automated ontology generation, it was still limited to the static database of words contained in the dictionaries.

Attempting to overcome the limitations of dictionaries, Gabrilovich and Markovitch (2009) turned to Wikipedia to perform what they called *explicit semantic analysis* (ESA). They drew upon both the reference and contextual knowledge embedded throughout Wikipedia with the goal of outperforming statistical methods, like latent semantic analysis (LSA), in computing semantic relatedness of texts (Gabrilovich and Markovitch, 2009). However, in explicit semantic analysis, the semantic interpreter, which consists of weighted lists of concepts, i.e. Wikipedia articles, is built directly from Wikipedia's text, a time-consuming process. Sorg and Cimiano (20 - 12) developed an approach leveraging explicit semantic analysis for cross-lingual information retrieval using Wikipedia.

Building on the premise that collaborative knowledge stores, like Wikipedia, are superior for semantic-analysis related tasks, other researchers have mapped extracted word entities from Twitter tweets directly to the titles of Wikipedia pages. The reported technique outperformed statistically-based, semantic categorization methods, specifically LSA and string-edit-distance (Genc et al. 2011). In addition, the approach could categorize concepts in short text strings, a widely known challenge in semantics (Michelson and Macskassy, 2010). In addition, using the Wikipedia title pages instead of the actual article content enabled a faster semantic transform (Genc et al. 2012). Mapping extracted entities to online collaborative knowledge bases, like Wikipedia, also presents a path to accessing an ever-relevant contextual framework based upon the most current human knowledge base (Michelson and Macskassy 2010).

3 Methods

This study compares simplified Chinese Wikipedia and English Wikipedia in their resourcefulness to build ontologies. For the comparison, we used a sample abstract that is available in both Mandarin and English (Figure 1). We constructed ontologies from our sample using both Chinese and English Wikipedia according to the experimental conditions detailed in section 3.2.

3.1 Text Segmentation and Entity Extraction

To extract entities, atomic, meaningful elements of text, we first segmented the texts into phrases – single words, bi-grams, and tri-grams – that overlap in a sliding window fashion. To give an example: the first few words of the English abstract, 'In recent years, there have', yielded: {'in', 'in recent', 'in recent years', 'recent', 'recent years', 'recent years there', 'years'}. In Mandarin, word boundaries are not explicit. Thus, we segmented the Chinese version of the abstract into words first with the tools from (Youli, 2011), and then proceeded to phrase segmentation.

Journal Abstract in Mandarin

文本自动分类是信息检索与数据挖掘领域的研究热点与核心技术,近年来得到了泛的关注和快速的发展.提出了基于机器学习的文本分类技术所面临的互联网内容信息处理等复杂应用的挑战,从模型、算法和评测等方面对其研究进展进行综述评论.认为非线性、数据集偏斜、标注瓶颈、多层分类、算法的扩展性及 Web 页分类等问题是目前文本分类研究的关键问题,并讨论了这些问题可能采取的方法.最后对研究的方向进行了展望.

Journal Abstract in English

In recent years, there have been extensive studies and rapid progresses in automatic text categorization, which is one of the hotspots and key techniques in the information retrieval and data mining field. Highlighting the state-of-art challenging issues and research trends for content information processing of Internet and other complex applications, this paper presents a survey on the up-to-date development in text categorization based on machine learning, including model, algorithm and evaluation. It is pointed out that problems such as nonlinearity, skewed data distribution, labeling bottleneck, hierarchical categorization, scalability of algorithms and categorization of Web pages are the key problems to the study of text categorization. Possible solutions to these problems are also discussed respectively. Finally, some future directions of research are given.

Figure 1: Sample journal abstract in Mandarin and English (from Su et al. 2006)

The words and word phrases resulting from text segmentation are potential entities. We then check which of these phrases match a title in Wikipedia. These titles are either a page name in Wikipedia domain or a redirection page to an entity with an alternate title. Redirections happen for alternative names, plurals, closely related words, adjectives/adverbs pointing to the corresponding noun, less or more specific forms of names, abbreviations, alternative spellings, or punctuation and likely misspellings. The potential entities that have matches to Wikipedia titles are then considered existing entities, and are used in the ontology generation.

3.2 Ontology Generation

Wikipedia offers a network of networks: each language domain provides concepts and their relationships. These language-specific networks connect through the language links given on a Wikipedia page for a particular concept, and point users to pages with the same conceptual meaning in the alternate, target language. It is important to note that language links in Wikipedia do not direct the reader to the translation of the original content but to another Wikipedia page created for the same concept in the designated language. To give an example, machine learning page in English is linked to 机器学习 (Machine learning) in the Chinese Wikipedia, but the contents of these two pages are different; the two pages are created and updated by different users at different times.

We build the ontology of a document using the entities extracted from the text (see 3.1) and the Wikipedia categories of those entities. More specifically, we captured the immediate first level categories of the entities with existing Wikipedia title pages via Wikipedia's API. During the process, hidden categories were excluded since they are used for administrative purposes. Ontologies were constructed according to the following experimental conditions. For experiment A, Mandarin entities were extracted from the Mandarin version of the abstract, and the Chinese Wikipedia (http://zh.wikipedia.org/wiki/Wikipedia:首页) was used to build an ontology. For experiment B, Mandarin entities were extracted from the Mandarin version of the abstract. Next, we identified the corresponding English Wikipedia pages for the Mandarin entities and used the English entities to build the ontology from English Wikipedia. Entities without a corresponding English page were ignored. For experiment C, English entities were extracted from the English version of the abstract, and English Wikipedia (http://en.wikipedia.org/wiki/Main_Page) was used to build the ontology. These experimental conditions are summarized in Table 1.

Experiment	Language of Entities	Wikipedia Language
A	Mandarin	Mandarin
B	Mandarin	English
C	English	English

Table 1: Summary of Experimental Conditions

3.3 Ontology Visualization

For the visualizations, the python library, pyprocessing, was used to apply Processing (www.processing.org), a platform that allows for the creation of interactive visualizations. Orange circles show extracted entities that landed on Wikipedia titles with existing pages in the respective language. The first-level categories associated with those pages were visualized as blue circles. A line shows the link back to the corresponding entity represented as a Wikipedia title. At this time a spring weighting function is used to automate the positioning of the items in the bipartite graphs constituting the ontology visualizations.

4 Results and Discussion

Figures 2 (below), 3, and 4 (following pages) display the ontologies resulting from experimental conditions A, B, and C respectively. Figure 2 shows several key concepts from the journal abstract about machine learning in NLP have been effectively captured as entities using the collective knowledge base of Chinese Wikipedia. In Figure 2 the English entity names are given in

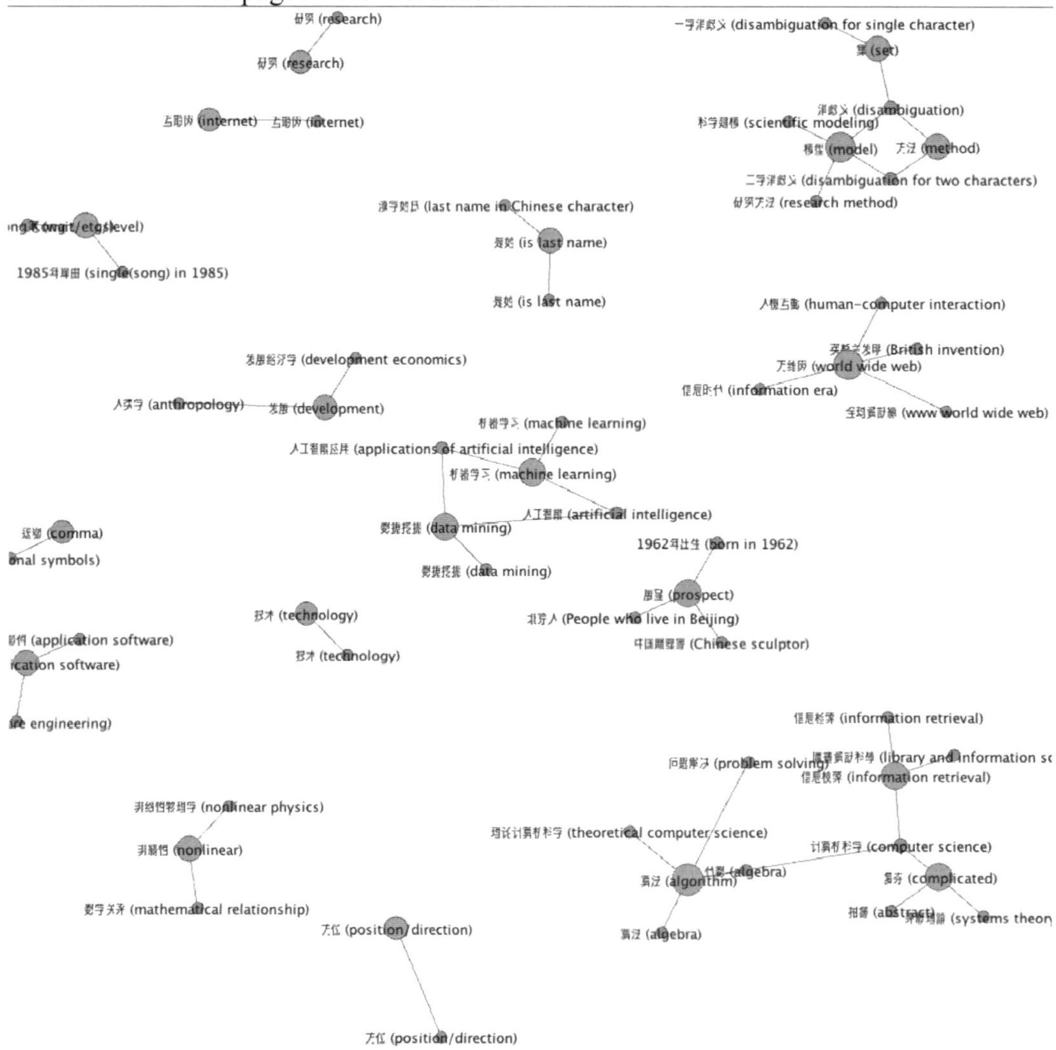

Figure 2: Ontology generated using experimental condition A, in which Chinese Wikipedia is used to build an ontology from Mandarin entities. The English translation of the entities are given for reference. Note that all nodes display, but the current algorithm uses the edge of the canvas as x=0, so some of the entities may not display as complete circles.

parentheses for reference. A native Mandarin speaker translated the Mandarin characters, which had been presented as a list of terms. Figure 3 contains many of the same concepts seen in Figure 2. Figure 4, created from the English abstract and English Wikipedia, displays approximately fifty percent more entities (excluding disambiguation). The entities associated with the disambiguation category currently in figure 4 can be filtered out as needed.

Table 2 summarizes the number of entities and maximum number of categories for each of the experiments. A total of eight entities were shared among all three experimental conditions.

Experiment	# of Entities	Max # of 1st level Categories
A	20	4
B	16	10
C	33 *	11

Table 2: Summary of Ontology Metrics, (* Excludes entities connected to disambiguation categories)

Figure 3: Ontology generated using experimental condition B, in which Chinese Wikipedia's links to the English Wikipedia in order to build an ontology from Mandarin entities.

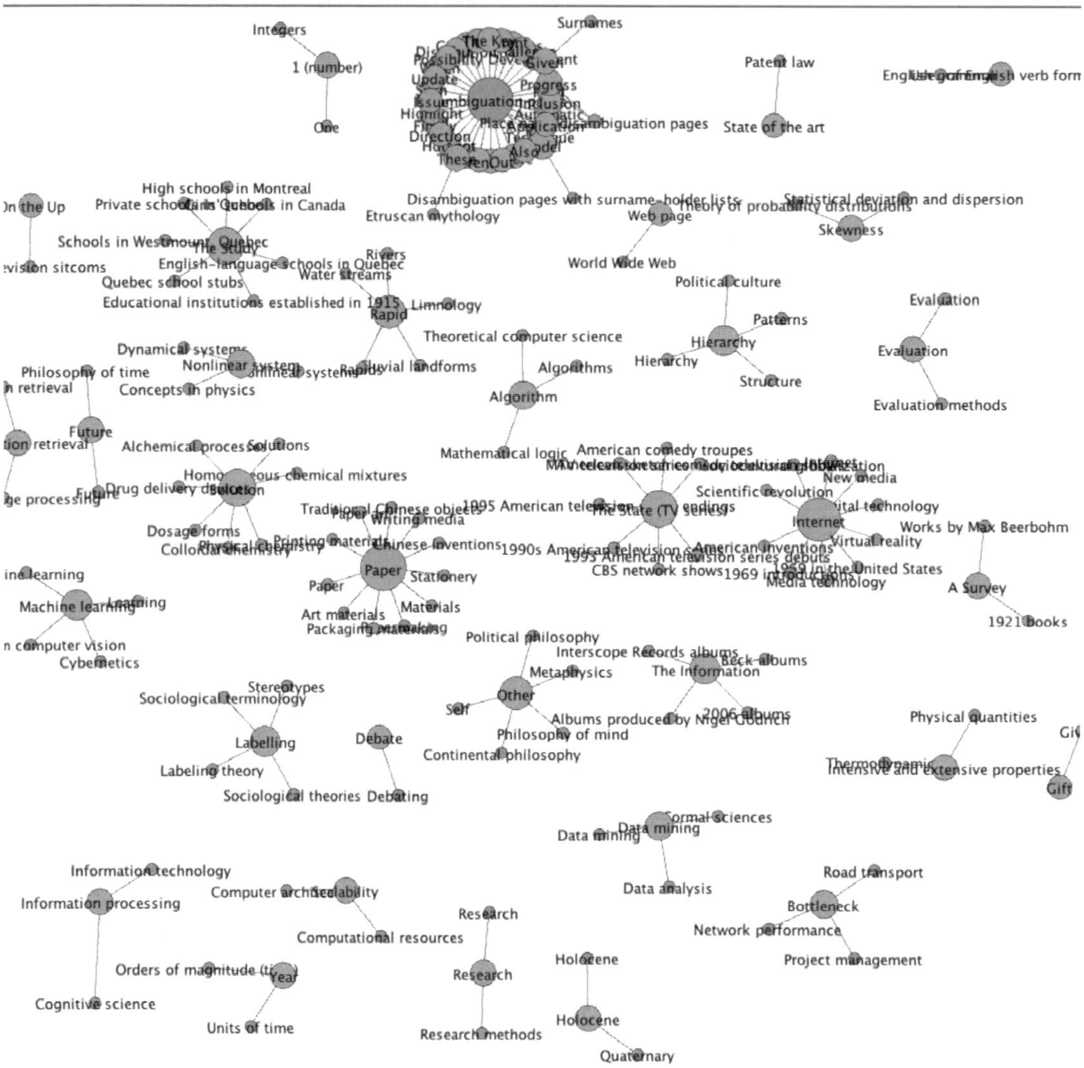

Figure 4: Ontology generated using experimental condition C, in which English Wikipedia is used to build an ontology from English entities.

These visualizations yield preliminary insights into the manner in which varying languages represent concepts in Wikipedia. Comparing the ontologies in Figures 2-4 reveals different languages in Wikipedia exhibit different breadth. English Wikipedia provided more concepts than the Chinese counterpart for this text sample. This is not surprising given the English Wikipedia is larger. However, the Mandarin entities shown in Figure 2 offer a satisfactory representation of the text. In addition, the extra concepts from English Wikipedia add little to the general understanding of the text, and may even distract from the abstract's key concepts.

Wikipedia pages from different languages generate different ontologies for seemingly similar concepts. For example, in Experiment A (Figure 2), *algorithm*, *information retrieval*, and *complexity* (which has the English label 'complicated') are connected through the *computer science* category. However, the corresponding English pages of these entities used in experiment B (Figure 3) are not connected through any shared first-level categories. This suggests English Wikipedia pages are categorized in greater detail, making it difficult to capture relationships among concepts through the immediate, first-level categories. In other words, the detailed ontology of English Wikipedia may not be as effective a reference as the simple ontology in Chinese Wikipedia. It could also be that the translation process introduces noise. Identifying and visualizing the second-level category connections might provide further insight into the differences between the two methods.

5 Summary and Next Steps

As a context-rich, collaborative knowledge base, Wikipedia is ideal for building ontologies. This study presented varying approaches to constructing ontologies from simplified Chinese and English Wikipedias, as a first step in evaluating cross-lingual corpora. The methods employed in this study can be further adopted to extract ontologies across multiple languages provided the analogous collaborative knowledge stores exist in the target languages. The sample ontology visualizations generated in this work demonstrated there are multiple ways to pursue concept representation using the Chinese and English versions of Wikipedia.

Wikipedia offers networks of concepts in different languages. Networks of different languages in Wikipedia are mapped through language links within pages, but this is rarely a one-to-one mapping. Thus, we also need ways to align ontologies with different levels of explicitness and formalization.

Future research might build on the visualization techniques discussed here in order to explore mechanisms for ontology alignment. For example, the percentage of entity coexistence within a set of ontologies could be used as a metric for the alignment of ontologies. In addition, the techniques described here could be used to assess semantic similarity using ontologies coming from different collaborative data stores in different languages.

Finally, there are two approaches to extracting ontologies from cross-lingual corpora: work can be translated first and then ontologies extracted, or ontologies can be extracted, and then the ontologies translated. With more experiments, it may be possible to determine which is the best order to use, taking into account the corpus, the languages involved, and the collaborative data stores available.

Acknowledgments

The authors acknowledge and thank Dorian Zaccaria for helping with the ontology visualizations and Yue Han for help with verification of Chinese character translations.

References

Freitas-Junior, H. R., Ribeiro-Neto, B., Vale, R. F., Laender, A. H. F., & Lima, L. R. S. (2006). Categorization-driven cross-language retrieval of medical information. *Journal of the American Society for Information Science and Technology*, 57(4), 501–510. doi:10.1002/asi.20320

Gabrilovich, E., & Markovitch, S. (2009). Wikipedia-based semantic interpretation for natural language processing. *Journal of Artificial Intelligence Research, 34*(2), 443-498.

Genc, Y., Mason, W., & Nickerson, J. (2012). Semantic transforms using collaborative knowledge bases. Paper presented at *Workshop on Information in Networks*, New York University, September 28-29, 2012. Available at SSRN 2154367.

Genc, Y., Sakamoto, Y., & Nickerson, J. V. (2011). Discovering context: Classifying tweets through a semantic transform based on Wikipedia, In *Proceedings on Foundations of Augmented Cognition. Directing the Future of Adaptive Systems*. Orlando, FL. pp. 484-492.

Gennari, S. P., MacDonald, M. C., Postle, B. R., & Seidenberg, M. S. (2007). Context-dependent interpretation of words: Evidence for interactive neural processes. *Neuroimage, 35*(3), 1278-1286. doi:10.1016/j.neuroimage.2007.01.015

Goddard, C. (2011). *Semantic Analysis: A Practical Introduction* (2nd Ed.). Oxford University Press, New York, NY.

Hovy, E. (2005). Methodologies for the reliable construction of ontological knowledge. In *Proceedings of the 13th international conference on Conceptual Structures: Common Semantics for Sharing Knowledge (ICCS '05)*. pp. 91–106. doi:10.1007/11524564_6

Kishida, K. (2005). Technical issues of cross-language information retrieval: a review. *Information Processing & Management*, 41(3), 433–455.

Landauer, T. K., & Littman, M. L. (1991). A statistical method for language-independent representation of the topical content of text segments. In *Proceedings of the Eleventh International Conference: Expert Systems and Their Applications*, 8, pp. 77-85.

Lanzenberger, M., Sampson, J., & Rester, M. (2010). Ontology visualization: Tools and techniques for visual representation of semi-structured meta-data. *Journal of Universal Computer Science,* 16(7), 1036-1054.

Locke, W. N., & Booth, A. D. (Eds.). (1955). *Machine translation of languages: fourteen essays*. Published jointly by Technology Press of the Massachusetts Institute of Technology and Wiley, New York, NY.

Michelson, M. & Macskassy, S. A. (2010). Discovering users' topics of interest on Twitter: A first look. In *Proceedings of the fourth workshop on Analytics for noisy unstructured text data (AND '10)* Toronto, Canada. doi:10.1145/1871840.1871852

Nichols, E., Bond, F., Tanaka, T., & Fujita, S. (2006). Multilingual ontology acquisition from multiple MRDS. In *Proceedings of the 2nd Workshop on Ontology Learning and Population,* Sydney, Australia pp. 10–17.

Onyshkevych, B. A., & Nirenburg, S. (1992). Lexicon, ontology, and text meaning, 289–303. doi:10.1007/3-540-55801-2_42

Sorg, P., & Cimiano, P. (2012). Exploiting Wikipedia for cross-lingual and multilingual information retrieval. *Data & Knowledge Engineering, 74 (2012) 26–45*. doi:10.1016/j.datak.2012.02.003

Su J.S., Zhang B.F., & Xu X. (2006). Advances in machine learning based text categorization. *Journal of Software*, 2006,17(9), 1848-1859. doi: 10.1360/jos171848

Youli, D. (2011). Chinese Segmentation Analysis [Software]. Available from http://trac.xapian.org/wiki/GSoC2011/ChineseSegmentationAnalysis

Using a Random Forest Classifier to recognise translations of biomedical terms across languages

Georgios Kontonatsios[1,2] **Ioannis Korkontzelos**[1,2] **Jun'ichi Tsujii**[3] **Sophia Ananiadou**[1,2]
National Centre for Text Mining, University of Manchester, Manchester, UK[1]
School of Computer Science, University of Manchester, Manchester, UK[2]
Microsoft Research Asia, Beijing, China[3]
{gkontonatsios,ikorkontzelos,sananiadou}@cs.man.ac.uk
jtsujii@microsoft.com

Abstract

We present a novel method to recognise semantic equivalents of biomedical terms in language pairs. We hypothesise that biomedical term are formed by semantically similar textual units across languages. Based on this hypothesis, we employ a Random Forest (RF) classifier that is able to automatically mine *higher order associations* between textual units of the source and target language when trained on a corpus of both positive and negative examples. We apply our method on two language pairs: one that uses the same character set and another with a different script, English-French and English-Chinese, respectively. We show that English-French pairs of terms are highly transliterated in contrast to the English-Chinese pairs. Nonetheless, our method performs robustly on both cases. We evaluate RF against a state-of-the-art alignment method, GIZA++, and we report a statistically significant improvement. Finally, we compare RF against Support Vector Machines and analyse our results.

1 Introduction

Given a term in a source language and term in a target language the task of this paper is to classify this pair as a translation or not. We investigate the performance of the proposed classifier by applying it on a balanced classification problem, i.e. our experimental datasets contain an equal number of positive and negative examples. The proposed classification model can be used as a component of a larger system that automatically compiles bilingual dictionaries of technical terms across languages. Bilingual dictionaries of terms are important resources for many *Natural Language Processing* (NLP) applications including *Statistical Machine Translation* (SMT) (Feng et al., 2004; Huang and Vogel, 2002; Wu et al., 2008), *Cross-Language Information Retrieval* (Ballesteros and Croft, 1997) and *Question Answering* systems (Al-Onaizan and Knight, 2002). Especially in the biomedical domain, manually creating and more importantly updating such resources is an expensive process, due to the vast amount of *neologisms*, i.e. newly introduced terms (Pustejovsky et al., 2001). The UMLS metathesaurus which is one the most popular *hub* of multilingual resources in the biomedical domain, contains technical terms in 21 languages that are linked together using a *concept* identifier. In Spanish, the second most popular language in UMLS, only 16.44% of the 7.6M English terms are covered while other languages fluctuate between 0.0052% (for Hebrew terms) to 3.26% (for Japanese terms). Hence, these lexica are far for complete and methods that *semi-automatically* (i.e., in a post-processing step, curators can manually remove erroneous dictionary entries) discover pairs of terms across languages are needed to enrich such multilingual resources. Our method can be applied to parallel, aligned corpora, where we expect approximately the same, balanced classification problem. However, in comparable corpora the search space of candidate alignments is of vast size, i.e., quadratic the the size of the input data. To cope with this heavily unbalanced classification problem, we would need to narrow down the number of negative instances before classification.

We hypothesise that there are *language independent* rules that apply to biomedical terms across many languages. Often the same or similar textual units (e.g., morphemes and suffixes) are concatenated to realise the same terms in different languages. For example, Table 1 illustrates how a morpheme expressing *pain* (*ache* in English) is used to realise the same terms in English, Chinese and French. The realisations of the term "head-

English Morpheme: **-ache**	Chinese Morpheme: 痛	French Morpheme: **-mal**
head-**ache**	头-痛	**mal** de tête
back-**ache**	腰-痛	**mal** au dos
ear-**ache**	耳朵-痛	**mal** d'oreille

Table 1: An example of English, Chinese and French terms consisting of the same morphemes

ache" is expected to consist of the units for "head" and "ache" regardless of the language of realisation. Hence, knowing the translations of "head" and "ache" allows the reconstruction "headache" in a target language.

In our method, we use a *Random Forest (RF)* classifier (Breiman, 2001) to learn the underlying rules according to which terms are being constructed across languages. An RF is an ensemble of Decision Trees voting for the most *popular* class. RF classifiers are popular in the biomedical domain for various tasks: classification of microarray data (Díaz-Uriarte and De Andres, 2006), compound classification in cheminformatics (Svetnik et al., 2003), classification of microRNA data (Jiang et al., 2007) and protein-protein interactions in Systems Biology (Chen and Liu, 2005). In NLP, RF classifiers have been used for: Language Modelling (Xu and Jelinek, 2004) and semantic parsing (Nielsen and Pradhan, 2004). To the best of the authors' knowledge, this is the first attempt to employ RF for identifying translation equivalents of biomedical terms.

We prefer RF over other traditional machine learning approaches such as *Support Vector Machines (SVMs)* for a number of reasons. Firstly, RF is able to automatically construct *correlation paths* from the feature space, i.e. decision rules that correspond to the translation rules that we intend to capture. Secondly, RF is considered one of the most accurate classifier available (Díaz-Uriarte and De Andres, 2006; Jiang et al., 2007). Finally, RF is reported to cope well with datasets where the number of features is larger than the number of observations (Díaz-Uriarte and De Andres, 2006). In our dataset, the number of features is almost four times more than that of the observations.

We represent pairs of terms using character gram features (i.e., *first order* features). Such shallow features have been proven effective in a number of NLP applications including: Named Entity Recognition (Klein et al., 2003), *Multilingual Named Entity Transliteration* (Klementiev and Roth, 2006; Freitag and Khadivi, 2007) and predicting authorship (Stamatatos, 2006). In addition, by selecting character n-grams instead of word n-grams, one avoids to segment words in Chinese which has been proven to be a challenging topic (Sproat and Emerson, 2003). We evaluate our proposed method on two datasets of biomedical terms (English-French and English-Chinese) that contain equal numbers of positive and negative instances. RF achieves higher classification performance than baseline methods. To boost SVM's performance further, we used a *second order* feature space to represent the data. It consists of pairs of character grams that co-occur in translation pairs. In the second order feature space, the performance of SVMs improved significantly.

The rest of the paper is structured as follows. In Section 2, we present previous approaches in identifying translation equivalents of terms or named entities. In Section 3, we define the classification problem, we formulate the RF classifier and we discuss the first and second order feature space that we use to represent pairs of terms. In Section 4, we show that RF achieves superior classification performance. In Section 5, we overview our method and we discuss how it can be used to compile large-scale bilingual dictionaries of terms from comparable corpora.

2 Related Work

In this section, we review previous approaches that exploit the internal structure of sequences to align terms or named entities across languages. (Klementiev and Roth, 2006; Freitag and Khadivi, 2007) use character gram features, similar to the feature space that we propose in this paper, to train discriminative, supervised models. Klementiev and Roth (2006) introduce a supervised *Perceptron* model for English and Russian named entities. They construct a character gram feature space as follows: firstly, they extract all distinct character grams from both source and target named entity. Then, they pair character grams of the source named entity with character grams of the corresponding target named entity into features. In order to reduce the number of features, they link only those character grams whose position offsets in the source and target sequence differs by -1, 0 or 1. Freitag and Khadivi (2007) employ the same character gram feature space but they do not constraint the included character-grams to their relative position offsets in the source and target sequence. The *boolean* features are defined for every distinct character-grams observed in the data of length k or shorter. Using this feature space they train an *Averaged Perceptron* model, able to incorporate an arbitrary number of features in the input vectors, for English and Arabic named entities. The above character gram based methods mainly focused on *aligning* named entities of the general domain, i.e. person names, locations, organizations, etc., that are transliterated, i.e. present phonetic similarities, across languages.

SMT-based approaches built on top of existing SMT frameworks to identify translation pairs of terms (Tsunakawa et al., 2008; Wu et al., 2008). Tsunakawa et al. (2008), align terms between a source language L_s and a target language L_t using a pivot language L_p. They assume that two bilingual dictionaries exist: from L_s to L_p and from L_p to L_t. Then, they train *GIZA++* (Och and Ney, 2003) on both directions and they merge the resulting phrase tables into one table between L_s and L_t, using grow-diag-final heuristics (Koehn et al., 2007). Wu et al. (2008), use morphemes instead of words as translation units to train a phrase based SMT system for technical terms in English and Chinese. The use of shorter lexical fragments, e.g. lemmas, stems and suffixes, as translation units has reportedly reduced the *Out-Of-Vocabulary* problem (Virpioja et al., 2007; Popovic and Ney, 2004; Oflazer and El-Kahlout, 2007).

Hybrid methods exploit that a term or a named entity can be translated in various ways across languages (Shao and Ng, 2004; Feng et al., 2004; Lu and Zhao, 2006). For instance, person names are usually *translated by transliteration* (i.e., words exhibiting pronunciation similarities across languages, are likely to be mutual translations) while technical terms are likely to be *translated by meaning* (i.e., the same semantic units are used to generate the translation of the term in the target language). The resulting hybrid systems were reported to perform at least as well as existing SMT systems (Feng et al., 2004).

Lepage and Denoual (2005) presented an analogical learning machine translation system as part of the IWSLT task (Eck and Hori, 2005) that requires no training process and it is able to achieve state-of-the art performance. The core method of their system models relationships between sequences of characters, e.g., sentences, phrases or words, across languages using *proportional analogies*, i.e., $[a : b = c : d]$, "a is to b as c is to d", and is able to solve unknown *analogical equations*, i.e., $[x : y = z : ?]$ (Lepage, 1998). Analogical learning has been proven effective in translating unseen words (Langlais and Patry, 2007). Furthermore, analogical learning is reported to achieve a better precision but a lower recall than a phrase-based machine translation system when translating medical terms (Langlais et al., 2009).

3 Methodology

Let $e^m = (e_1, \cdots, e_m)$ be an English term consisting of m translation units and $f^n = (f_1, \cdots, f_n)$ a French or Chinese term consisting of n units. As translation units, we consider character grams. We define a function $f : (e^m, f^n) \longrightarrow \{0, 1\}$:

$$f(e^m, f^n) = \begin{cases} 1, & \text{if } e^m \text{ translates into } f^n \\ 0, & \text{otherwise} \end{cases}$$

The function can be learned by training a *Random Forest (RF)* classifier[1]. Let N be the number of training instances, $|\Omega|$ the total number of features, i.e. the number of dimensions of the feature space, $|\tau|$ a predefined number of random decision trees and $|\phi|$ a predefined number of random features. An RF classifier is defined as a collection of fully grown decision tree classifiers, $\delta_i(X)$ (Breiman, 2001):

$$RF = \{\delta_1(X), \cdots, \delta_\tau(X)\}, \; X = (e^m, ch^n) \quad (1)$$

A pair of terms is classified as a *translation* pair if the majority of the trees is voting for this class label. Let $I(\delta_i(X))$ be the vote of the ith tree in the forest and $av_{j\in\{0,1\}}$ the average number of votes for class labels 0 (*translation*) and 1 (*non-translation*). The function f of τ decision trees can be written as the majority function:

$$\begin{aligned} f(e^m, ch^n) &= \text{Maj}\,(I(\delta_1(X)), \cdots, I(\delta_\tau(X))) \\ &= \left\lfloor \frac{1}{2} \frac{\sum_1^\tau I(\delta_i(X)) + 1/2(-1)^r}{\tau} \right\rfloor \end{aligned} \quad (2)$$

[1]The WEKA implementation (Hall et al., 2009) of RF was used for all experiments of this paper.

The majority function returns 1 if the majority of $I(\delta_i(X))$ is 1, or returns 0 if the majority of $I(\delta_i(X))$ is 0. Adding or subtracting $1/2$ controls whether a tie is resolved towards 1 or 0, respectively. In RF ties are resolved randomly. To represent this, the negative unit (-1) is raised to a randomly chosen positive integer $r \in \mathbb{N}^+$.

We tuned the RF classifier using 140 random trees and $|\phi| = \log_2|\Omega| + 1$ features as suggested in Breiman (Breiman, 2001).
The RF mechanism that triggers term construction rules across languages lies in the decision trees. A RF grows a decision tree by selecting the most informative feature, i.e. corresponding to the lowest entropy, out of ϕ random features. For each selected feature, a node is created and this process is repeated for all ϕ random features of the unprunned decision trees. In other words, the process starts with the most informative feature and builds association rules between all random features. These are the construction rules that we are interested in. Figure 1 illustrates a path in one of the decision trees of an RF classifier taken from the experiments we conducted on the English-Chinese dataset. In only one of thousands of branches of the *forest*, the classifier is able to partially trigger the construction rule of *kinase*, a type of enzyme, between English and Chinese. The translation rule correctly associates the English n-grams *kin* and *as* with their Chinese translation 激酶. In addition, the translation rule contains both positive and negative associations between features. The English n-grams *ing* and *or* are negatively correlated with the term *kinase*.

3.1 Feature Engineering

Each pair of terms is represented as a feature vector of character n-grams. We further define two types of character n-gram features, namely *first order* and *second order*. First order character n-grams are boolean features that designate the occurrence of a corresponding character gram of predefined length in the input term. These features are monolingual, extracted separately from the source and target term. The RF classifier is shown to benefit from only monolingual features and achieves the best observed performance. In contrast, SVMs were shown not to perform well using the *first order* feature space because they cannot directly associate the source with the target character grams. To enhance the performance of SVMs, we constructed a *second order* feature space that contains associations between *first order* features. A *second order* feature is a tuple of a source and a target character gram that co-occur in one or more translation pairs. Table 2 illustrates an example. *Second order* character n-grams are multilingual features and are defined over true translation pairs. For this reason, we extract *second order* features from the training data only.
In all experiments, the features were sorted in decreasing order of frequency of occurrence. We trained a RF and two SVM classifiers, namely linear-SVM and RBF-SVM, using a gradually increasing number of features, always starting from the top of the list. SMT frameworks cannot be trained on an increasing number of features because each training instance needs to correspond to at least one known translation unit (i.e., first order features). Therefore, GIZA++ is trained on the complete set of translation units.

4 Experiments

In this section, we discuss the employed datasets of biomedical terms in English-French and English-Chinese and three baseline methods. We compare and discuss RF and SVMs trained on the *first order* and *second order* features. Finally, we report results of all classification methods evaluated on the same datasets.

4.1 Datasets

For our experiments, we used an online bilingual dictionary[2] for English-Chinese terms and the UMLS metathesaurus[3] for English-French terms. The former contains $31,700$ entries while the latter is a much larger dictionary containing $84,000$ entries. For training, we used the same number of instances for both language pairs (i.e., $21,000$ entries) in order not to bias the performance towards the larger English-French dataset. The remaining instances were used for testing (i.e., $10,7000$ and $63,000$ English-Chinese and English-French respectively). In the case where a source term corresponded to more that one target terms according to the seed dictionary, we randomly selected only one translation. Negative instances were created by randomly matching non-translation pairs of terms. Since we are dealing with a balanced clas-

[2]www2.chkd.cnki.net/kns50/
[3]nlm.nih.gov/research/umls

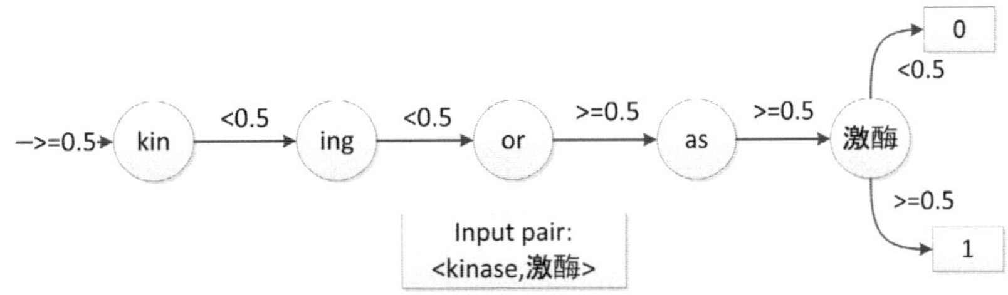

Figure 1: Example of a term construction rule as a branch in a decision tree.

Input pair of English-French terms : $(e_1, e_2, e_3, f_1, f_2, f_3)$		
English first order	French first order	Second order
$\phi_1(e_1, e_2)$	$\phi_1(f_1, f_2)$	$\phi_1(e_1e_2, f_1f_2)$, $\phi_1(e_1e_2, f_2f_3)$
$\phi_1(e_2, e_3)$	$\phi_1(f_2, f_3)$	$\phi_1(e_2e_3, f_1f_2)$, $\phi_1(e_2e_3, f_2f_3)$

Table 2: Example of first and second order features using a predefined n-gram size of 2.

sification problem, we created as many negative instances as the positive ones in all our datasets. In all experiments we performed a 3-fold cross-validation.

4.2 Baselines

We evaluated RF against three classification methods, namely SVMs, GIZA++ and a Levenshtein distance-based classifier.

SVMs coordinate a hyperplane in the hyperspace defined by the features to best separate the positive and negative instances, i.e. aligned from non-aligned pairs. In contrast to RF, SVMs do not support building association rules between features, i.e., translation units, which in our task seems to be a deficiency. SVMs produce one final association rule, i.e. the *classification boundary* which separates positive from negative examples. Its ability to distinguish aligned from non-aligned pair of terms depends on how separable the two clusters are. We evaluated several settings for the SVM classifier. Apart from the default linear kernel function, we applied a radial basis function, i.e. RBF-SVM. RBF-SVM uses the *kernel trick* to project the instances in a higher dimensional space to better separate the two clusters. While tuning the SVM's classification cost *C*, we observed optimal performance for a value of 100. Secondly, we seeded the association rules of translation units to the SVM classifier by creating a *second order* feature space, discussed in detail in section 3.1. We employed the *LIBSVM* implementation (Chang and Lin, 2011) of SVMs using both the linear and RBF kernels.

The second baseline method is GIZA++, an open source implementation of the 5 IBM-models (Brown et al., 1993). GIZA++ is traditionally trained on a bilingual, parallel corpus of aligned sentences and estimates the probability $P(s|t)$ of a source translation unit (typically a word), s, given a target unit t. To apply GIZA++ on our dataset, we consider the list of terms as parallel sentences. GIZA++, trained on a list of terms, estimates the alignment probability of English-Chinese and English-French textual units, i.e. character n-grams. Each entry i, j in the *translation table* is the probability $P(s_i|t_j)$, where s_i and t_j are the source and target character n-grams in row i and column j, respectively. Further details about training a SMT toolkit for aligning technical terms can be found in (Tsunakawa et al., 2008; Freitag and Khadivi, 2007; Wu et al., 2008). After training GIZA++ we estimate the posterior probability $P(cf^n|e^m)$ that a test, Chinese or French term $cf^n = \{cf_1, \cdots, cf_n\}$ is aligned with a given English term $e^m = \{e_1, \cdots, e_m\}$ as follows:

$$p(cf^n|e^m) = n^{-m} \sum_{i=1}^{n} \sum_{j=1}^{m} P(cf_i|e_j) \quad (3)$$

A threshold ξ was defined to classify a pair of terms into *translations* or *non-translations*:

$$f(e^m, cf^n) = \begin{cases} 1, & \text{if } p(cf^n|e^m) \geq \xi \\ 0, & \text{otherwise} \end{cases} \quad (4)$$

We experimented with different values of ξ (*greedy search*) and we selected a value that maximizes classification performance.

In order to estimate how phonetically similar the two language pairs are, we employed a third base-

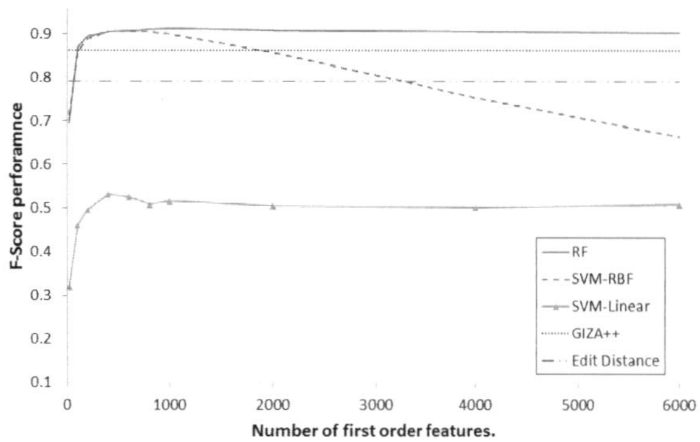

(a) English-French dataset

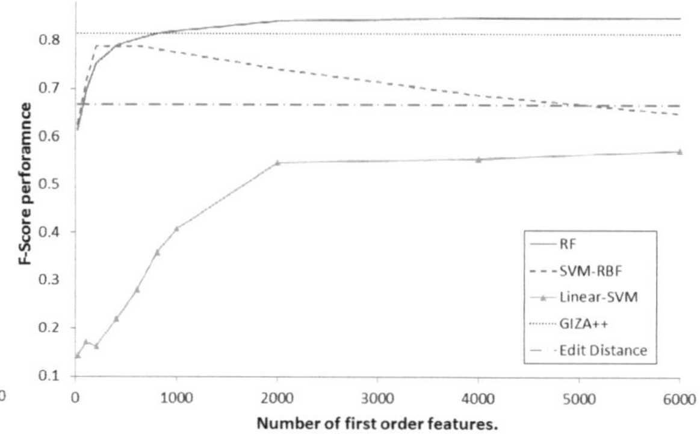

(b) English-Chinese dataset

Figure 2: F-Score of the RF and SVM, GIZA++ and Levenshtein distance-based classifier on the *first order* dataset

line method that uses the *Edit/Levenshtein distance* of pairs of terms to classify instances as translations or not. The Levenshtein distance is defined as the minimum edit operations, i.e., insertion, deletions and substitution, required to transform one sequence of characters to another. We cannot directly calculate the Levenshtein distance between English-Chinese pairs of terms since the two languages are using different scripts. Therefore, before we applied the Levenshtein distance-based classifier, we converted the Chinese terms to their *pinyin* form, i.e., Romanization system of Chinese characters. As with GIZA++, we selected a threshold ξ that maximizes the performance of the classifier.

4.3 Results

We hypothesise that a RF classifier is able to form association paths between first order features. We also have the theoretical intuition that SVM classifiers are not able to form such association paths. As a result, we expect limited performance on the first order feature set, because it does not contain any associations among character grams.

Figure 2 shows the F-Score achieved by RF, linear-SVM, RBF-SVM, GIZA++ and Levenshtein/Edit distance-based classifier on the English-French and English-Chinese datasets. RF and SVMs are trained on an increasing number of features. The behaviour of the classifiers is approximately the same in both datasets. Performance is greater on the English-French dataset since English is more similar to French than to Chinese.

We also observe that linear-SVM and RBF-SVM do not behave consistently. RBF-SVM's performance quickly climbs to a maximum and afterwards it declines while linear-SVM's performance is constantly increasing until it balances to a very high error rate, almost corresponding to random classification. The linear-SVM classifier performs poorly using *first order* features only, indicating that this feature space is *non-linearly* separable, i.e. there exists no hyperplane that separates *translation* from *non-translation* instances. Contrary, RBF-SVM is able to construct a higher dimensional space by applying the *kernel trick* so as to take full advantage of a small number of frequent and informative *first order* features. In this higher dimensional space of few but informative first order features, the RBF-SVM classifier coordinates a hyperplane that effectively separates positive from negative instances. However, increasing the number of features introduces noise that affects the performance.

The RF is able to profit from larger sets of *first order* features; thus, its performance is continuously increasing until it stabilises at $6,000$ features. The branches of the decision trees are shown to manage features correctly to construct most of the translation rules. Increasing the size of the feature space minimises the classification error, because more translation rules that generalize well on unseen data are constructed.

The bilingual dictionary that we use for our experiments contains heterogeneous biomedical terms of diverse semantic categories. For example, our data-set contains common medical terms such as *Intellectual Products* (e.g. *Pain Management, prise en charge de la douleur,* 控制疼痛) or complex biological concepts such as *Enzymes* (e.g. *homogentisate 1,2-dioxygenase,*

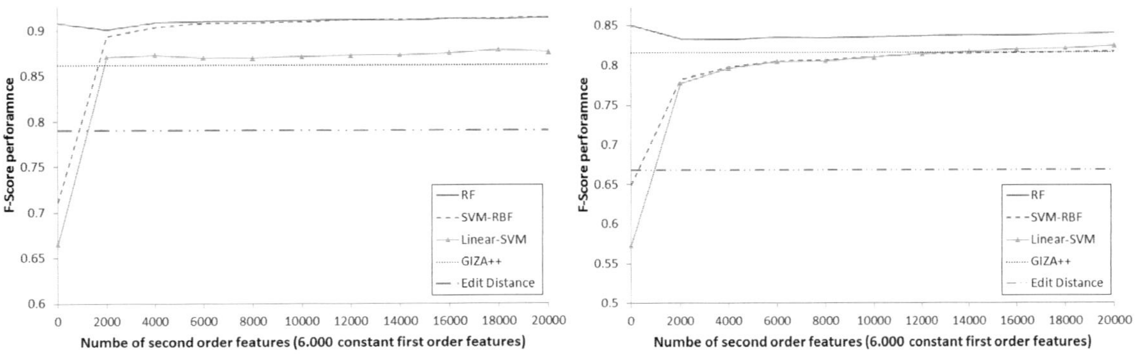

(a) English-French dataset

(b) English-Chinese dataset

Figure 3: F-Score of the RF and SVM, GIZA++ and Levenshtein distance-based classifier on the *second order* dataset

	English-French pairs			English-Chinese pairs		
	P	R	F_1	P	R	F_1
GIZA++	0.901	0.826	0.862	0.907	0.742	0.816
Levenshtein Distance	0.762	0.821	0.791	0.501	**0.990**	0.668
$SVM\text{-}RBF_{second\text{-}order}$	0.946	0.884	0.914	0.750	0.899	0.818
$Linear\text{-}SVM_{second\text{-}order}$	0.866	**0.887**	0.8763	0.765	0.893	0.824
$RF_{first\text{-}order}$	**0.962**	0.874	**0.916**	0.779	0.940	**0.851**

Table 3: Best observed performance of RF, SVM and GIZA++ and Levenshtein Distance

acide homogentisique-oxydase, 尿黑酸*1,2*-双氧酶). Therefore, we would expect poor performance of the supervised methods using only a small portion of the total set of *first order* features due to the high diversity of the terms. For example the morpheme *ache/ mal/* 痛 is more frequent in *Disease or Syndrome* named entities rather than *Enzyme* named entities. However, the results indicate that RF can generalize well on heterogeneous terms. Figure 2 shows that the RF classifier outperforms SMT based methods, using only 1000 features.

The Levenshtein distance-based classifier performs considerably better in the English-French dataset than in English-Chinese. In fact, its best performance for the English-Chinese dataset is achieved when classifying every pair of terms as a translation, i.e. 100% recall but 50% precision.

In a second experiment, we attempted to explore whether the performance of SVMs can be improved by providing cross-language association features. We employed the *second order* feature set discussed in subsection 3.1. We used a constant number of $6,000$ *first order* features, the number of features that achieved maximum F-Score for RF in the previous experiment. Besides these *first order* features, we added an increasing number of *second order* ones. Figure 3 shows the F-Score curves of the RF, linear-SVM, RBF-SVM, GIZA++ and Levenshtein distance using this feature space.

We observe that *second order* features improved the performance of both SVMs considerably. In contrast to the previous experiment, the two SVMs present consistent bevaviour. Interestingly, the performance of the RF slightly decreased when using a small number of *second order* features. A possible explanation of this behaviour is that the *second order* associative features added noise, since the RF had already formed the association rules from *first order* features. In addition, for m English and n Chinese or French *first order* features there were $m \times n$ possible combinations of *second order* features as explained in Subsection 3.1. Hence, there was a large number of *second order* features that we excluded from the training process. Consequently, decision tree branches were populated with incomplete association rules while the RF was able to form these associations automatically. Nevertheless, as more *second order* features were added, more association rules were explored and the RF performance increased. Table 3 summarises the highest performance achieved by the RF, SVMs, GIZA++ and Levenshtein distance all trained and tested on the same dataset. The resulting performance of the RF compared with GIZA++ is statistically significant ($p < 0.0001$) in all experiments. Comparing the RF with the SVMs, we note that in the English-French dataset, the performance of the SVM-RBF is approximately the same with the performance of our proposed method. However, this comes with a cost. Firstly, SVMs can possibly achieve a comparable performance to the RF when using multilingual, second order features. In contrast, our experiments show that RF benefit from monolingual, first order features only. Secondly, SVMs need a large number of additional multilingual features, (6.000 second order features or more) to perform similarly to RF. As a consequence, the resulting models of the SVM classifiers are more complex. We measured the average time needed by the two classifiers to decide for a single pair of terms. The RF is approximately 30 times faster than SVMs (on average 0.010 and 0.292 seconds, respectively). Finally, in the English-Chinese dataset the RF performed significantly better than both SVMs.

5 Discussion And Future Work

In this paper, we presented a novel classification method that uses *Random Forest (RF)* to recognise translations of biomedical terms across languages. Our approach is based on the hypothesis that in many languages, there exist some rules for combining textual units, e.g. n-grams, to form biomedical terms. Based on this assumption, we defined a *first order* feature space of character grams and demonstrated that an RF classifier is able to discover such cross language translation rules for terms. We experimented with two diverse language pairs: English-French and English-Chinese. In the former case, pairs of terms exhibit high phonetic similarity while in the latter case they do not. Our results showed that the proposed method performs robustly in both cases and achieves a significantly better performance than GIZA++. We also evaluated *Support Vector Machines (SVM)* classifiers on the same *first order* feature space and showed that they fail to form translation rules in both language pairs, possibly because it cannot associate *first order* features with each other successfully. We attempted to boost the performance of the SVM classifier by adding association evidence of textual units to the features. We extracted *second order* features from the training data and we defined a new feature set consisting of both *first order* and *second order* features. In this feature space, the performance of the SVMs improved significantly.

In addition to this, we observe from the reported experiments that RF achieves a better F-Score performance than GIZA++ in all datasets. Nonetheless, GIZA++ presents a better precision (but lower recall) in one dataset, i.e., English/Chinese. Based on this observation we plan to investigate the performance of a hybrid system combining RF with MT approaches.

One trivial approach to apply the proposed method for compiling large-scale bilingual dictionaries of terms from comparable corpora would be to directly classify all possible pairs of terms into *translations* or *non-translations*. However, in comparable corpora, the size of the search space is quadratic to the input data. Therefore, the classification task is much more challenging since the distribution of positive and negative instances is highly skewed. To cope with the vast search space of comparable corpora, we plan to incorporate context-based approaches with the RF classification method. Context-based approaches, such as *distributional vector similarity* (Fung and McKeown, 1997; Rapp, 1995; Koehn and Knight, 2002; Haghighi et al., 2008), can be used to limit the number of candidate translations by filtering out pairs of terms with low contextual similarity.

Finally, the proposed method can be also used to *online* augment the *phrase table* of *Statistical Machine Translation (SMT)* in order to better handle the *Out-of-Vocabulary* problem i.e. inability to translate textual units that consist of one or more words and do not occur in the training data (Habash, 2008).

Acknowledgements

The work described in this paper is partially funded by the European Community's Seventh Framework Program (FP7/2007-2013) under grant agreement no. 318736 (OSSMETER).

References

Y. Al-Onaizan and K. Knight. 2002. Translating named entities using monolingual and bilingual resources. In *Proceedings of the 40th Annual Meeting on Association for Computational Linguistics*, pages 400–408. Association for Computational Linguistics.

L. Ballesteros and W.B. Croft. 1997. Phrasal translation and query expansion techniques for cross-language information retrieval. In *ACM SIGIR Forum*, volume 31, pages 84–91. ACM.

L. Breiman. 2001. Random forests. *Machine learning*, 45(1):5–32.

P.F. Brown, V.J.D. Pietra, S.A.D. Pietra, and R.L. Mercer. 1993. The mathematics of statistical machine translation: Parameter estimation. *Computational linguistics*, 19(2):263–311.

C.C. Chang and C.J. Lin. 2011. Libsvm: a library for support vector machines. *ACM Transactions on Intelligent Systems and Technology (TIST)*, 2(3):27.

X.W. Chen and M. Liu. 2005. Prediction of protein–protein interactions using random decision forest framework. *Bioinformatics*, 21(24):4394–4400.

R. Díaz-Uriarte and S.A. De Andres. 2006. Gene selection and classification of microarray data using random forest. *BMC bioinformatics*, 7(1):3.

Matthias Eck and Chiori Hori. 2005. Overview of the iwslt 2005 evaluation campaign. In *Proc. of the International Workshop on Spoken Language Translation*, pages 1–22.

D. Feng, Y. Lv, and M. Zhou. 2004. A new approach for english-chinese named entity alignment. In *Empirical Methods in Natural Language Processing*, pages 372–379.

D. Freitag and S. Khadivi. 2007. A sequence alignment model based on the averaged perceptron. In *Conference on Empirical methods in Natural Language Processing*, pages 238–247.

P. Fung and K. McKeown. 1997. A technical word- and term-translation aid using noisy parallel corpora across language groups. *Machine Translation*, 12(1):53–87.

N. Habash. 2008. Four techniques for online handling of out-of-vocabulary words in arabic-english statistical machine translation. In *Proceedings of the 46th Annual Meeting of the Association for Computational Linguistics on Human Language Technologies: Short Papers*, pages 57–60. Association for Computational Linguistics.

A. Haghighi, P. Liang, T. Berg-Kirkpatrick, and D. Klein. 2008. Learning bilingual lexicons from monolingual corpora. *Proceedings of ACL-08: HLT*, pages 771–779.

M. Hall, E. Frank, G. Holmes, B. Pfahringer, P. Reutemann, and I.H. Witten. 2009. The weka data mining software: an update. *ACM SIGKDD Explorations Newsletter*, 11(1):10–18.

F. Huang and S. Vogel. 2002. Improved named entity translation and bilingual named entity extraction. In *International Conference on Multimodal Interaction*, pages 253–258. IEEE.

P. Jiang, H. Wu, W. Wang, W. Ma, X. Sun, and Z. Lu. 2007. Mipred: classification of real and pseudo microrna precursors using random forest prediction model with combined features. *Nucleic acids research*, 35(suppl 2):W339–W344.

D. Klein, J. Smarr, H. Nguyen, and C.D. Manning. 2003. Named entity recognition with character-level models. In *Proceedings of the seventh conference on Natural language learning at HLT-NAACL*, pages 180–183. Association for Computational Linguistics.

A. Klementiev and D. Roth. 2006. Weakly supervised named entity transliteration and discovery from multilingual comparable corpora. In *Proceedings of the 21st International Conference on Computational Linguistics and the 44th annual meeting of the Association for Computational Linguistics*, pages 817–824. Association for Computational Linguistics.

P. Koehn and K. Knight. 2002. Learning a translation lexicon from monolingual corpora. In *Proceedings of the ACL-02 workshop on Unsupervised lexical acquisition-Volume 9*, pages 9–16. Association for Computational Linguistics.

P. Koehn, H. Hoang, A. Birch, C. Callison-Burch, M. Federico, N. Bertoldi, B. Cowan, W. Shen, C. Moran, R. Zens, et al. 2007. Moses: Open source toolkit for statistical machine translation. In *Proceedings of the 45th Annual Meeting of the ACL on Interactive Poster and Demonstration Sessions*, pages 177–180. Association for Computational Linguistics.

Philippe Langlais and Alexandre Patry. 2007. Translating unknown words by analogical learning. In *Proceedings of EMNLP-CoNLL*, pages 877–886.

Philippe Langlais, François Yvon, and Pierre Zweigenbaum. 2009. Improvements in analogical learning: application to translating multi-terms of the medical domain. In *Proceedings of the 12th Conference of the European Chapter of the Association for Computational Linguistics*, pages 487–495. Association for Computational Linguistics.

Yves Lepage. 1998. Solving analogies on words: an algorithm. In *Proceedings of the 17th international conference on Computational linguistics-Volume 1*, pages 728–734. Association for Computational Linguistics.

M. Lu and J. Zhao. 2006. Multi-feature based chinese-english named entity extraction from comparable corpora. pages 131–141.

R.D. Nielsen and S. Pradhan. 2004. Mixing weak learners in semantic parsing. In *Empirical Methods in Natural Language Processing*.

F.J. Och and H. Ney. 2003. A systematic comparison of various statistical alignment models. *Computational linguistics*, 29(1):19–51.

K. Oflazer and I.D. El-Kahlout. 2007. Exploring different representational units in english-to-turkish statistical machine translation. In *Proceedings of the Second Workshop on Statistical Machine Translation*, pages 25–32. Association for Computational Linguistics.

Maja Popovic and Hermann Ney. 2004. Towards the Use of Word Stems and Suffixes for Statistical Machine Translation. In *4th International Conference on Language Resources and Evaluation (LREC)*, pages 1585–1588, Lisbon,Portugal.

J. Pustejovsky, J. Castano, B. Cochran, M. Kotecki, and M. Morrell. 2001. Automatic extraction of acronym-meaning pairs from medline databases. *Studies in health technology and informatics*, (1):371–375.

R. Rapp. 1995. Identifying word translations in non-parallel texts. In *Proceedings of the 33rd annual meeting on Association for Computational Linguistics*, pages 320–322. Association for Computational Linguistics.

L. Shao and H.T. Ng. 2004. Mining new word translations from comparable corpora. In *Proceedings of the 20th international conference on Computational Linguistics*, page 618. Association for Computational Linguistics.

R. Sproat and T. Emerson. 2003. The first international chinese word segmentation bakeoff. In *Proceedings of the second SIGHAN workshop on Chinese language processing-Volume 17*, pages 133–143. Association for Computational Linguistics.

Efstathios Stamatatos. 2006. Ensemble-based author identification using character n-grams. In *In Proc. of the 3rd Int. Workshop on Textbased Information Retrieval*, pages 41–46.

V. Svetnik, A. Liaw, C. Tong, J.C. Culberson, R.P. Sheridan, and B.P. Feuston. 2003. Random forest: a classification and regression tool for compound classification and qsar modeling. *Journal of chemical information and computer sciences*, 43(6):1947–1958.

T. Tsunakawa, N. Okazaki, and J. Tsujii. 2008. Building bilingual lexicons using lexical translation probabilities via pivot languages. In *Proceedings of the Sixth International Conference on Language Resources and Evaluation (LREC'08)*, Marrakech, Morocco, may.

S. Virpioja, J.J. Väyrynen, M. Creutz, and M. Sadeniemi. 2007. Morphology-aware statistical machine translation based on morphs induced in an unsupervised manner. *Machine Translation Summit XI*, 2007:491–498.

X. Wu, N. Okazaki, T. Tsunakawa, and J. Tsujii. 2008. Improving English-to-Chinese Translation for Technical Terms Using Morphological Information. In *AMTA-2008. MT at work: Proceedings of the Eighth Conference of the Association for Machine Translation in the Americas*, pages 202–211, Waikiki, Hawai'i, October.

P. Xu and F. Jelinek. 2004. Random forests in language modeling. In *Empirical Methods in Natural Language Processing*, pages 325–332. Association for Computational Linguistics.

Comparing Multilingual Comparable Articles Based On Opinions

Motaz Saad **David Langlois** **Kamel Smaïli**
Speech Group, LORIA
INRIA, Villers-lès-Nancy, F-54600, France
Université de Lorraine, LORIA, UMR 7503, Villers-lès-Nancy, F-54600, France
CNRS, LORIA, UMR 7503, Villers-lès-Nancy, F-54600, France
{firstName.lastName}@loria.fr

Abstract

Multilingual sentiment analysis attracts increased attention as the massive growth of multilingual web contents. This conducts to study opinions across different languages by comparing the underlying messages written by different people having different opinions. In this paper, we propose Sentiment based Comparability Measures (SCM) to compare opinions in multilingual comparable articles without translating source/target into the same language. This will allow media trackers (journalists) to automatically detect public opinion split across huge multilingual web contents. To develop SCM, we need either to get or to build parallel sentiment corpora. Because this kind of corpora are not available, we decided to build them. For that, we propose a new method to automatically label parallel corpora with sentiment classes. Then we use the extracted parallel sentiment corpora to develop multilingual sentiment analysis system. Experimental results show that, the proposed measure can capture differences in terms of opinions. The results also show that comparable articles variate in their objectivity and positivity.

1 Introduction

We can distinguish two kinds of sentiments analysis depending on monolingual or multilingual articles.

In the following, as in (Pang and Lee, 2008), the terms Sentiment Analysis (SA) and Opinion Mining (OM) are used as synonyms. Mining opinions is to identify the subjectivity and/or the polarity of a given text at article or sentence level. Subjectivity identification is to classify the text into subjective or objective, while polarity identification is to classify the text into negative or positive.

Popular methods for monolingual sentiment analysis are based on lexicon and corpus. Lexicon based methods use string matching techniques between texts and annotated lexicons. The most common sentiment lexicons for English language are WordNet-Affect (Valitutti, 2004) and SentiWordNet (Esuli and Sebastiani, 2006), which are extensions of WordNet. Additionally, SenticNet (Cambria et al., 2010) is a knowledge-base extension of aforementioned lexicons. On the other hand, corpus based approach is popular for sentiment analysis (Pang and Lee, 2008). It uses corpora and machine learning algorithms to build sentiment classification systems. For example, Pang *et al.* used polarity (Pang et al., 2002) and subjectivity (Pang and Lee, 2004) English corpora to train machine learning algorithms to build sentiment classifiers. These resources have been adapted to other languages by many researchers as we will see in the following.

Multilingual sentiments analysis becomes a reality because of the massive growth of multilingual web contents. In this case, sentiment analysis identifies sentiments across multiple languages instead of one language. This can be done by creating sentiment resources for new languages by translating existing English resources (lexicons/corpora) into the target language, or by translating target text into English, then pass the translated text to English models for sentiment analysis (Rushdi-Saleh et al., 2011; Bautin et al., 2008; Denecke, 2008; Ghorbel, 2012). However, (Brooke et al., 2009) reported that creating new resources to build sentiment models from scratch works better than using the approach based on machine translation.

As we see in the previous discussion, works on multilingual sentiment analysis just try to identify sentiments across multiple languages. However, it is worthy to compare opinions about a given topic in several languages, not just to identify these opinions. If people from different cultures wrote an article about political/societal topics, they may judge these topics differently according to their cultures. In fact, detecting disagreement of opinions in multiple languages is a promising research area. So, our goal is to enable media trackers (journalists) to automatically detect the split of public opinions about a given topic across multiple languages. To the best of our knowledge, there are no work in the literature that serve our goal, therefore, we propose to develop automatic measures that compare opinions in multilingual comparable articles. These comparability measures will be the core of our goal which is building multilingual automatic journalist review system.

For that, we propose a Sentiment based Comparability Measures (SCM) which identify sentiments, score them and compare them across multilingual documents. Therefore, we need to identify and score sentiments in multiple languages. Namely, SCM needs a multilingual sentiment analysis system to identify and score sentiments. To build this system, we need parallel sentiment corpora from different topics. Unfortunately, we do not have such corpora, we only have English sentiment corpus. So, we propose in Section 2 a new method to build parallel sentiment corpora. We start from English sentiment corpora (movie reviews domain), then use it to build sentiment classifier for English language and then label a new parallel English/target corpora which is different from the movie one. In section 3, we use the obtained parallel sentiment corpora to build a multilingual sentiment analysis system which is used to develop SCM, then we use SCM to compare multilingual comparable articles in terms of opinions. The advantage of this idea is that we do not need to translate corpora/lexicons to analyse multilingual text.

The rest of this article is organized as follows, Section 2 describes our method to build parallel sentiment corpora, Section 3 presents our proposed sentiment based comparability measures (SCM) and experimental results conducted on corpora. Finally, we state the conclusions.

2 Sentiment Corpora Extraction

As we introduced earlier, we need parallel corpora to build the sentiment comparability measure. Therefore, we present in this section a method to annotate parallel corpora with sentiment labels. This method can be applied on any English/target language pairs. In this work, we label English/Arabic parallel sentences. The idea is to use an English sentiment classifier to label each English sentence in the new parallel corpora, then we can assign the same label to the target (Arabic) sentence, because sentences are parallel and convey the same opinions.

The widely used approach to build a classifier is to build a Naive Bayes model using n-grams linguistic features (Pang et al., 2002; Dave et al., 2003; Pang and Lee, 2004; Kim and Hovy, 2004; Cui et al., 2006; Tan et al., 2009). So, we use this method on bigrams extracted from English sentiment corpora of movie reviews. These corpora are manually labelled with subjectivity and polarity labels. Each review in the collection is represented as a vector composed of bigram occurrences. Then, each vector is feed to Naive Bayes classifier with corresponding class label for training. Naive Bayes classifies the vector to the highest probable class. Our objective in this paper is to compare opinions, this is why we used this traditional method for building the sentiment classifier.

The parallel corpora, that we annotate, cover variant topics (newspapers, UN resolutions, and transcribed talks), and are available in many languages. The newspapers are collection of parallel articles from AFP, ANN, ASB, and provided by LDC[1]. UN corpora[2] is a collection of United Nations General Assembly Resolutions. Transcribed talks are collection of multilingual transcriptions from TED provided by WIT3[3].

Figure 1 illustrates our method and Table 1 describes corpora denoted in the figure. The mentioned corpora are: *senti-corp*, *parallel*, and *new-senti-corp*. *senti-corp* represents the monolingual (English) manually labelled, *parallel* represents parallel corpora in variant topics, and *new-senti-corp* represents the extracted corpora. Corpora sizes are presented in Tables 2 and 3. Table 2 presents the number of reviews of *senti-corp* with

[1]LDC - Linguistic Data Consortium: ldc.upenn.edu

[2]Corpora of the United Nations: uncorpora.org

[3]WIT3 Web Inventory of Transcribed and Translated Talks wit3.fbk.eu

respect to sentiment classes, and Table 3 presents the number of sentences of parallel corpora.

Table 1: Corpora description

Corpora	Description
senti-corp	Monolingual manually labelled sentiment corpus (polarity or subjectivity)
senti-corp-p1	Part 1 of senti-corp (90%): used to build classification models which are used for labelling task
senti-corp-p2	Part 2 of senti-corp (10%): This is the (test corpus) which is used to test the extracted corpora
parallel	Multilingual parallel corpora
parallel-p1	Part 1 of the parallel corpora (90%): to be labelled automatically
parallel-p2	Part 2 of the parallel corpora (10%): to be used to evaluate SCM
new-senti-corp	Multilingual automatically labelled sentiment corpus

Table 2: *Senti-cor*p size (number of reviews)

Class	senti-corp-p1	senti-corp-p2
subjective	4500	500
objective	4500	500
negative	900	100
positive	900	100

Table 3: *Parallel* Corpora size

Corpus	# of sentences
parallel-p1	364K
parallel-p2	40K

The following steps describe the method we propose:

1. Split *senti-corp* into two parts: *senti-corp-p1* is 90%, and *senti-corp-p2* is 10%.

2. Use *senti-corp-p1* to train a Naive Bayes classifier to build a monolingual sentiment model.

3. Split the parallel corpora into two parts: *parallel-p1* is 90%, and *parallel-p2* is 10%.

4. Using the sentiment classification model obtained in step 2, classify and label English sentences of *parallel-p1* and assign the same sentiment class to the corresponding Arabic sentences.

5. Refine and filter sentences which are labelled in step 4. The filtering process keeps only sentences that have high sentiment score. Then, we obtain *new-senti-corp* which is Arabic/English parallel sentiment labelled corpora in different domains.

6. Use the English part of *new-senti-corp* which is obtained in step 5 to train a Naive Bayes classifier.

7. Evaluate the classifier built in step 6 on *senti-corp-p2*. If the classification accuracy is accepted, then continues, otherwise, try other corpora and/or models.

This method is independent of the the sentiment class labels. So, it can be applied for subjectivity or polarity corpus.

Tables 4 and 5 present the experimental results of steps 4 and 5 of the Figure 1. Table 4 shows the statistical information of sentiment scores of the labelled corpora, where Rate is the class label distribution (percentage) with respect to the whole dataset. μ, σ, Min, and Max are the mean, standard deviation, minimum, and maximum values of sentiment scores respectively. For subjectivity labels, 54% and 46% of sentences are labelled as subjective and objective respectively. For polarity labels, 58% and 42% of sentences are labelled as negative and positive respectively. Table 5 presents the frequency table of intervals of sentiment scores of the labelled sentences. We can see from Table 5 that most of sentences have high sentiment scores (from 0.9 to 1.0). To extract high quality labelled sentences, we keep only sentences with score greater than 0.8.

In order to evaluate the quality of the extracted corpora (step 7 in Figure 1), we need first to build a sentiment classifier based on this corpora and then evaluate the accuracy of this classifier. The detail of this process is given bellow:

1. Train a Naive Bayes classifier on the parallel sentiment corpora *new-senti-corp*.

2. Test the obtained classifiers on the manually labelled corpus *senti-corp-p2*.

Figure 1: Approach for parallel sentiment corpora extraction and evaluation

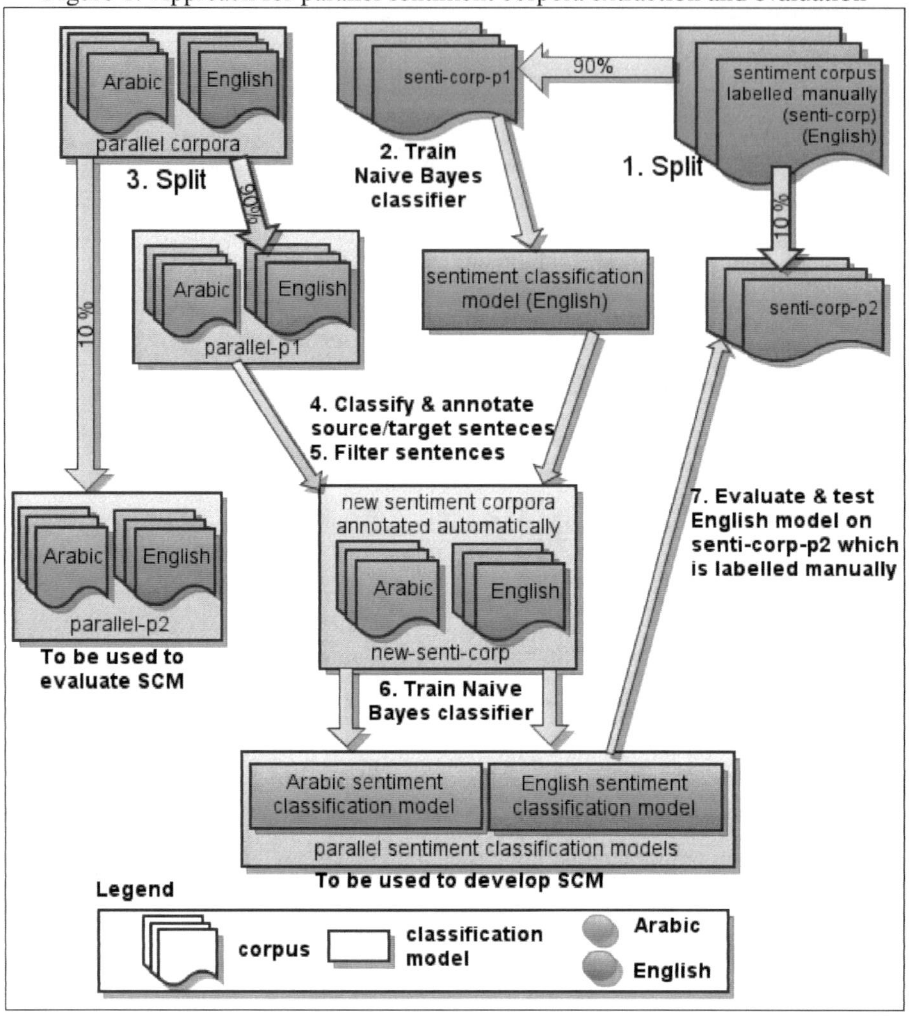

Table 4: Sentiment classes statistics for labelled sentences scores of *parallel-p1* corpora

Label	Count	Rate	μ	σ	Min	Max
subjective	231,180	54%	0.93	0.11	0.60	1.00
objective	197,981	46%	0.93	0.11	0.60	1.00
negative	219,070	58%	0.84	0.12	0.60	0.99
positive	159,396	42%	0.83	0.12	0.60	1.0

Table 5: Frequency table of sentiment scores intervals of labelled sentences of *parallel-p1* corpora

Label	[0.6,0.7)	[0.7,0.8)	[0.8,0.9)	[0.9,1]
subjective	6.1%	9.0%	11.9%	73.0%
objective	6.8%	8.1%	10.8%	74.3%
negative	17.7%	18.0%	21.6%	42.7%
positive	20.4%	20.8%	21.7%	37.2%

In the following, *senti-corp-p2* is the test corpus. The evaluation is presented in Table 6. The metrics include classification accuracy, and F-measures. F-neg, F-pos, F-sub, and F-obj are the F-measures for negative, positive, subjective, and objective classes respectively. For subjectiv-

Table 6: Evaluation of extracted corpus (step 7)

Subjectivity		Polarity	
Accuracy	0.765	Accuracy	0.720
F-sub	0.717	F-neg	0.754
F-obj	0.799	F-pos	0.674

ity test, the classifier achieved 76.5% of accuracy and an average of 75.8% of f-measure. For polarity test, the classifier leads to 72% of accuracy and an average of 71% of F-measure.

We wanted to compare these results with others works in sentiment classification, but unfortunately the used corpora are not the same. Anyway, these results are only indicative for us, because our objective is not to propose a new method for automatic sentiment classification, but to build a sentiment based comparability measure.

Now, we obtained English/Arabic parallel sentiment corpora in multiple topics. We use these corpora to develop sentiment based comparability measures that will be described in the next section.

Notice that at the beginning the only available sentiment corpus was a collection of movie reviews in English language, with the proposed method, we got multilingual sentiment corpora of different topics. Furthermore, using this method, one can obtain sentiment corpus for under-resourced languages. The advantage of the parallel corpora is to build sentiment classifiers that can be used to develop sentiment based comparability measures.

3 Sentiment Based Comparability Measures

As we stated in the introduction, there are no work in the literature that serve our goal, which is to compare multilingual articles in terms opinions. Therefore, we propose to develop automatic measures that compare opinions in multilingual comparable articles.

In the previous section, we built a parallel sentiment corpora where both source and its corresponding sentence have the same sentiment label. In this section, we compare multilingual comparable articles in terms of sentiments. Obviously, in this case we do not have the same sentiment labels since articles are comparable and not parallel. So, we develop Sentiment based Comparability Measures (SCM) which measure the differences of opinions in multilingual corpora. For that, we use the achieved parallel sentiment corpora *new-senti-corp* to build multilingual sentiment analysis systems, using the same method as in Section 2.

The idea is to identify and score sentiments in the source and target comparable articles and provide these information to SCM to compare their opinions. In the following, we describe how to compute SCM for comparable articles based on average score of all sentences.

We use formula 1 which is derived from Naive Bayes to compute opinion score and assign the corresponding label:

$$classify(S) = \underset{c}{argmax} P(c) \prod_{k=1}^{n} P(f_k|c) \quad (1)$$

where S is a sentence, f_k are the features of S, $c \in \{o, \bar{o}\}$ for subjectivity and $c \in \{p, \bar{p}\}$ for polarity, where o is objective, $\bar{o}$ is subjective, p is positive, $\bar{p}$ is negative.

An article may contain some sentences belonging to the subjective class, and others belonging to the objective class (idem for positive and negative). So, for a given pair of comparable articles, SCM has three parameters d_x, d_y, c, where d_x, d_y are the source and the target articles respectively, and c is the class label. This score is calculated as follows:

$$SCM(d_x, d_y, c) = \left| \frac{\sum\limits_{C(S_x)=c} P(S_x|c)}{N_x} - \frac{\sum\limits_{C(S_y)=c} P(S_y|c)}{N_y} \right| \quad (2)$$

Where $S_x \in d_x$, $S_y \in d_y$, and $\sum\limits_{C(S_x)=c} P(S_x|c)$ and $\sum\limits_{C(S_y)=c} P(S_y|c)$ are the sum of probabilities for all source and target sentences respectively that belong to class c. N_x and N_y are the number of source and target sentences respectively that belong to the class c. Formally speaking, for a given pair of documents d_x, d_y, we have four measures: $SCM(d_x, d_y, o)$, $SCM(d_x, d_y, \bar{o})$ for subjectivity, and $SCM(d_x, d_y, p)$, $SCM(d_x, d_y, \bar{p})$ for polarity.

In our experiments, we calculate SCM for pair of articles in parallel and comparable corpora. Calculating SCM for parallel corpora could be very surprising, but we did it in order to show that for this kind of corpora, the proposed measure should be better than the one achieved for comparable corpora.

Table 7: Comparable corpora information

	AFEWC		eNews	
	English	Arabic	English	Arabic
Articles	40290	40290	34442	34442
Sentences	4.8M	1.2M	744K	622K
Average #sentences/article	119	30	21	17
Average #words/article	2266	548	198	161
Words	91.3M	22M	6.8M	5.5M
Vocabulary	2.8M	1.5M	232K	373K

Table 8: Average Sentiment Based Comparability Measures (SCM)

Corpora		$SCM(d_x, d_y, \bar{o})$	$SCM(d_x, d_y, o)$	$SCM(d_x, d_y, \bar{p})$	$SCM(d_x, d_y, p)$
parallel-p2	AFP	0.02	0.02	0.1	0.12
	ANN	0.05	0.06	0.1	0.1
	ASB	0.07	0.1	0.12	0.14
	TED	0.06	0.06	0.08	0.07
	UN	0.05	0.02	0.07	0.08
Comparable	ENews	0.07	0.15	0.11	0.15
	AFEWC	0.11	0.19	0.11	0.16

The comparable corpora that we use for our experiments are AFEWC and eNews which were collected and aligned at article level (Saad et al., 2013). Each pair of comparable articles is related to the same topic. AFEWC corpus is collected from Wikipedia and eNews is collected from Euronews website. Table 7 presents the number of articles, sentences, average sentences per article, average words per article, words, and vocabulary of these corpora.

Table 8 presents the experimental results of SCM computed using formula 2. SCM is computed for the source and target articles for parallel corpora *parallel-p2* and comparable corpora (AFEWC and eNews). We note that SCM for AFP, ANN, ASB, TED, and UN corpora are small because they are parallel. This shows that the proposed measure is well adapted to capture the similarity between parallel articles. Indeed, they have the same sentiments. On the other hand, SCM become larger for comparable corpora, because the concerned articles do not necessary have the same sentiments. The only exception to what have been claimed is that the subjectivity SCM for eNews comparable corpora is similar to the one of ASB which is parallel corpora. In contrast, the objectivity SCM is larger (0.15) for eNews, that means pair of articles in eNews corpora have similar subjective but different objective sentiments. In other words, source and target are considered similar in terms of subjectivity but different in terms of objectivity (idem for negative and positive). Consequently, comparable articles do not necessary have the same opinions. Additionally, we note that the SCM for AFEWC corpora are the largest in comparison to the others, this is maybe because Wikipedia has been written by many different contributors from different cultures.

4 Conclusions

We presented a new method for comparing multilingual sentiments through comparable articles without the need of translating source/target articles into the same language. Our results showed that it is possible now for media trackers to automatically detect difference in public opinions across huge multilingual web contents. The results showed that the comparable articles variate in their objectivity and positivity. To develop our system, we required parallel sentiment corpora. So, we presented in this paper an original method to build parallel sentiment corpora. We started from an English movie corpus annotated in terms of sentiments, we trained NB classier to classify an English text concerning topics different from movie, and then we deduced the sentiment labels of the the corresponding target parallel text by assigning the same labels. This method is interesting because it allows us to produce several parallel sentiment corpora concerning different topics. We built SCM using these parallel sentiment corpora, then, SCM identifies sentiments, scores them and compares them across multilingual documents. In the future works, we will elaborate our journalist review system by developing a multilingual comparability measure that can handle semantics and integrate it with the sentiment based measure.

References

M. Bautin, L. Vijayarenu, and S. Skiena. 2008. International sentiment analysis for news and blogs. In *Proceedings of the International Conference on Weblogs and Social Media (ICWSM)*.

J. Brooke, M. Tofiloski, and M. Taboada. 2009. Cross-linguistic sentiment analysis: From english to spanish. In *International Conference RANLP*, pages 50–54.

E. Cambria, R. Speer, C. Havasi, and A. Hussain. 2010. Senticnet: A publicly available semantic resource for opinion mining. *Artificial Intelligence*, pages 14–18.

H. Cui, V. Mittal, and M. Datar. 2006. Comparative experiments on sentiment classification for online product reviews. In *proceedings of the 21st national conference on Artificial intelligence - Volume 2*, AAAI'06, pages 1265–1270. AAAI Press.

K. Dave, S. Lawrence, and D. M. Pennock. 2003. Mining the peanut gallery: opinion extraction and semantic classification of product reviews. In *Proceedings of the 12th international conference on World Wide Web*, WWW '03, pages 519–528, New York, NY, USA. ACM.

K. Denecke. 2008. Using sentiwordnet for multilingual sentiment analysis. In *Data Engineering Workshop, 2008. ICDEW 2008. IEEE 24th International Conference on*, pages 507–512.

A. Esuli and F. Sebastiani. 2006. Sentiwordnet: A publicly available lexical resource for opinion mining. In *In Proceedings of the 5th Conference on Language Resources and Evaluation*, pages 417–422.

H. Ghorbel. 2012. Experiments in cross-lingual sentiment analysis in discussion forums. In K. Aberer, A. Flache, W. Jager, L. Liu, J. Tang, and C. Guret, editors, *Social Informatics*, volume 7710 of *Lecture Notes in Computer Science*, pages 138–151. Springer Berlin Heidelberg.

S.-M. Kim and E. Hovy. 2004. Determining the sentiment of opinions. In *Proceedings of the 20th international conference on Computational Linguistics*, COLING '04, Stroudsburg, PA, USA. Association for Computational Linguistics.

B. Pang and L. Lee. 2004. A sentimental education: Sentiment analysis using subjectivity summarization based on minimum cuts. In *Proceedings of the 42nd Annual Meeting on Association for Computational Linguistics*, page 271. Association for Computational Linguistics.

B. Pang and L. Lee. 2008. Opinion mining and sentiment analysis. *Found. Trends Inf. Retr.*, 2(1-2):1–135, January.

B. Pang, L. Lee, and S. Vaithyanathan. 2002. Thumbs up?: sentiment classification using machine learning techniques. In *Proceedings of the ACL-02 conference on Empirical methods in natural language processing-Volume 10*, pages 79–86. Association for Computational Linguistics.

M. Rushdi-Saleh, M. T. Martín-Valdivia, L. A. Ureña López, and J. M. Perea-Ortega. 2011. Bilingual experiments with an arabic-english corpus for opinion mining. In *Proceedings of the International Conference Recent Advances in Natural Language Processing 2011*, pages 740–745, Hissar, Bulgaria, September. RANLP 2011 Organising Committee.

M. Saad, D. Langlois, and K. Smaïli. 2013. Extracting comparable articles from wikipedia and measuring their comparabilities. In *V International Conference on Corpus Linguistics*. University of Alicante, Spain.

S. Tan, X. Cheng, Y. Wang, and H. Xu. 2009. Adapting naive bayes to domain adaptation for sentiment analysis. In *Advances in Information Retrieval*, pages 337–349. Springer.

R. Valitutti. 2004. Wordnet-affect: an affective extension of wordnet. In *In Proceedings of the 4th International Conference on Language Resources and Evaluation*, pages 1083–1086.

Mining for Domain-specific Parallel Text from Wikipedia

Magdalena Plamadă, Martin Volk
Institute of Computational Linguistics, University of Zurich
Binzmühlestrasse 14, 8050 Zurich
{plamada, volk}@cl.uzh.ch

Abstract

Previous attempts in extracting parallel data from Wikipedia were restricted by the monotonicity constraint of the alignment algorithm used for matching possible candidates. This paper proposes a method for exploiting Wikipedia articles without worrying about the position of the sentences in the text. The algorithm ranks the candidate sentence pairs by means of a customized metric, which combines different similarity criteria. Moreover, we limit the search space to a specific topical domain, since our final goal is to use the extracted data in a domain-specific Statistical Machine Translation (SMT) setting. The precision estimates show that the extracted sentence pairs are clearly semantically equivalent. The SMT experiments, however, show that the extracted data is not refined enough to improve a strong in-domain SMT system. Nevertheless, it is good enough to boost the performance of an out-of-domain system trained on sizable amounts of data.

1 Introduction

A high-quality Statistical Machine Translation (SMT) system can only be built with large quantities of parallel texts. Moreover, systems specialized in specific domains require in-domain training data. A well-known problem of SMT systems is that existing parallel corpora cover a small percentage of the possible language pairs and very few domains. We therefore need a language-independent approach for discovering parallel sentences in the available multilingual resources.

This idea was explored intensively in the last decade with different text sources, generically called comparable corpora, such as news feeds, encyclopedias or even the entire Web. The first approaches focused merely on news corpora and were either based on IBM alignment models (Zhao and Vogel, 2002; Fung and Cheung, 2004) or employing machine learning techniques (Munteanu and Marcu, 2005; Abdul Rauf and Schwenk, 2011).

The multilingual Wikipedia is another source of comparable texts, not yet thoroughly explored. Adafre and de Rijke (2006) describe two methods for identifying parallel sentences across it based on monolingual sentence similarity (MT and respectively, lexicon based). Fung et al. (2010) approach the problem by combining recall- and precision-oriented methods for sentence alignment, such as the DK-vec algorithm or algorithms based on cosine similarities. Both approaches have achieved good results in terms of precision and recall.

However, we are interested in real application scenarios, such as SMT systems. The following approaches report significant performance improvements when using the extracted data as training material for SMT: Smith et al. (2010) use a maximum entropy-based classifier with various feature functions (e.g. alignment coverage, word fertility, translation probability, distortion). Ştefănescu et al. (2012) propose an algorithm based on cross-lingual information retrieval, which also considers similarity features equivalent to the ones mentioned in the previous paper.

The presented approaches extract general purpose sentences, but we are interested in a specific topical domain. We have previously tackled the problem (Plamada and Volk, 2012) and encountered two major bottlenecks: the alignment algorithm for matching possible candidates and the similarity metric used to compare them. To our knowledge, existing sentence alignment algorithms (including the one we have employed in the first place) have a monotonic order constraint, meaning that crossing alignments are not allowed. But this phenomenon occurs often in Wikipedia, because its articles in different languages are edited independently, without respecting any guidelines. Moreover, the string-based comparison metric proved to be unreliable for identifying parallel sentences.

In this paper we propose an improved approach for selecting parallel sentences in Wikipedia articles which considers all possible sentence pairs, regardless of their position in the text. The selection will be made by means of a more informed similarity metric, which rates different aspects concerning the correspondences between two sentences. Although the approach is language and domain-independent, the present paper reports results obtained through querying the German and French Wikipedia for Alpine texts (i.e. mountaineering reports, hiking recommendations, articles on the biology and the geology of mountainous regions). Moreover, we report preliminary results regarding the use of the extracted corpus for SMT training.

2 Finding candidate articles

The general architecture of our parallel sentence extraction process is shown in Figure 1. We applied the approach only to the language pair German-French, as these are the languages we have expertise in. In the project Domain-specific Statistical Machine Translation[1] we have built an SMT system for the Alpine domain and for this language pair. The training data comes from the Text+Berg corpus[2], which contains the digitized publications of the Swiss Alpine Club (SAC) from 1864 until 2011, in German and French. This SMT system will generate the automatic translations required in the extraction process.

The input consists of German and French Wikipedia dumps[3], available in the MediaWiki format [4]. Therefore our workflow requires a preprocessing step, where the MediaWiki contents are transformed to XML and then to raw text. Preprocessing is based on existing tools, such as WikiPrep[5], but further customization is needed in order to correctly convert localized MediaWiki elements (namespaces, templates, date and number formats etc.). We then identify Wikipedia articles

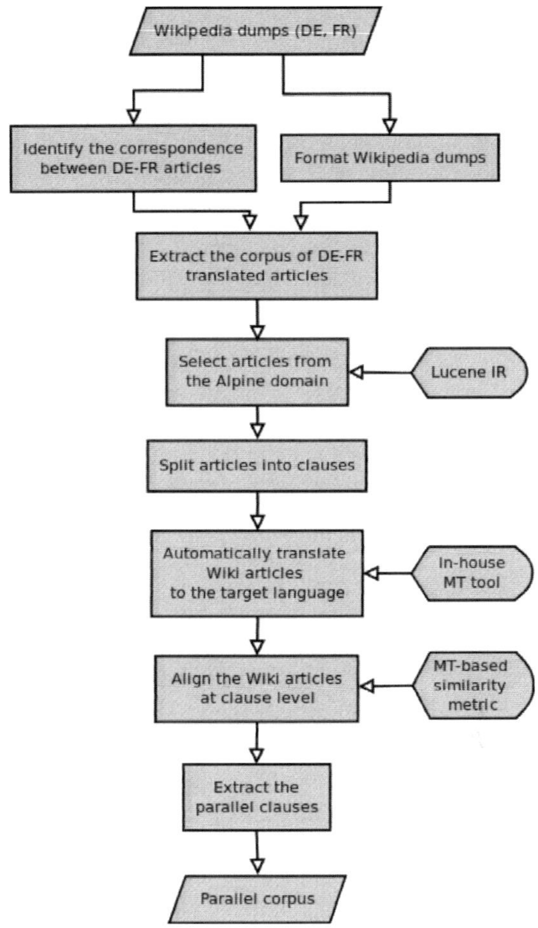

Figure 1: The extraction workflow

available in both languages by means of the interlanguage links provided by Wikipedia itself. This reliable information is a good basis for the extraction workflow, since we do not have to worry about the document alignment.

Upon completion of this step, we have extracted a bilingual corpus of approximately 400 000 articles per language. The corpus is subsequently used for information retrieval (IR) queries aiming to identify the articles belonging to the Alpine domain. The input queries contain the 100 most frequent mountaineering keywords in the Text+Berg corpus (e.g. *Alp, Gipfel, Berg, Route* in German and *montagne, sommet, voie, cabane* in French). This filter reduces the search space to 40 000 articles. Although we have refined our search terms by discarding the ones occurring frequently in other text types (e.g. *meter, day, year, end*), we were not able to avoid a small percentage of false positives. Once we extract the Alpine comparable corpus, we proceed to the extraction of

[1] http://www.cl.uzh.ch/research_en.html
[2] See www.textberg.ch
[3] Accessed in September 2011
[4] http://www.mediawiki.org/wiki/MediaWiki
[5] http://sourceforge.net/projects/wikiprep/

parallel sentences, which will be thoroughly discussed in the following section. See (Plamada and Volk, 2012) for more details about the extraction pipeline.

3 Finding parallel segments in Wikipedia articles

The analysis of our previous results brought into attention many "parallel" sentence pairs of different lengths, meaning that the shared translated content does not span over the whole sentence. As an example, consider the following sentences which have been retrieved by the extraction pipeline. Although they both contain information about the valleys connected by the Turini pass, the German sentence contains a fragment about its position, which has not been translated into French.

DE: Der Pass liegt in der äusseren, besiedelten Zone des Nationalpark Mercantour und stellt den Übergang zwischen dem Tal der Bévéra und dem Tal der Vésubie dar.

FR: Le col de Turini relie la vallée de la Vésubie à la vallée de la Bévéra.

If this sentence pair would be used for MT training, it would most probably confuse the system, because noisy word alignments are to be expected. Our solution to this problem is to split the sentences into smaller entities (e.g. clauses) and then to find the alignments on this granularity level. The clause boundary detection is performed independently for German and French, respectively, following the approach developed by Volk (2001). The general idea is to split the sentences into clauses containing a single full verb.

Our alignment algorithm, unlike previous approaches, ignores the position of the clauses in the texts. Although Wikipedia articles are divided into sections, their structure is not synchronized across the language variants, since articles are edited independently. We have encountered, for example, cases where one section in the French article was included in the general introduction of the German article. If we would have considered sections boundaries as anchor points, we would have missed useful clause pairs. We therefore decided to use an exhaustive matching algorithm, in order to cover all possible combinations.

For the sake of simplicity, we reduce the problem to a monolingual alignment task by using an intermediary machine translation of the source article. We decided that German articles should always be considered the source because we expect a better automatic translation quality from German to French. The translation is performed by our inhouse SMT system trained on Alpine texts. The algorithm generates all possible clause pairs between the automatic translation and the targeted article and computes for each of them a similarity score. Subsequently it reduces the search space by keeping only the 3 best-scoring alignment candidates for each clause. Finally the algorithm returns the alignment pair which maximizes the similarity score and complies with the injectivity constraint. In the end we filter the results by allowing only clause pairs above the set threshold.

We defined our similarity measure as a weighted sum of feature functions, which returns values in the range [0,1]. The similarity score models two comparison criteria:

- **METEOR score**
  We used the METEOR similarity metric because, unlike other string-based metrics (e.g. BLEU (Papineni et al., 2002)), it considers not only exact matches, but also word stems, synonyms, and paraphrases (Denkowski and Lavie, 2011). Suppose that we compute the similarity between the following sentences in French: *j' aimerais bien vous voir* and *je voudrais vous voir* (both meaning *I would like to see you*). BLEU, which is a string-based metric, would assign a similarity score of 52.5. This value could hardly be considered reliable, given that the sentence *ta voiture vous voir* (paired with the first sentence) would get the same BLEU score, although the latter sentence (EN: your car see you) is obviously nonsense. On the other hand, METEOR would return a score of 90.3 for the original sentence pair, since it can appreciate that the two pronouns (*je* and *j'*) are both variations of the first person singular in French and that the predicates convey the same meaning.

- **Number of aligned content words**
  However, METEOR scores can also be misleading, since they rely on automatic word alignments. Two sentences are likely to receive a high similarity score when they share many aligned words. However, the alignments are not always reliable. We often saw

sentence pairs with a decent Meteor score where only some determiners, punctuation signs or simple word collocations (e.g. *de la montagne* (EN: of the mountain)) were matched. As an illustration, consider the following sentence pair and its corresponding alignment:

Hyp: les armoiries , le désir de la ville de breslau par ferdinand i. le 12 mars 1530 a

Ref: le 19 juin 1990 , le conseil municipal rétablit le blason original de la ville

```
2-4 3-5 5-12 6-13 7-14 13-0
```

Although the sentences are obviously not semantically equivalent (a fact also suggested by the sparse word alignments), the pair receives a METEOR score of 0.23. We decided to compensate for this by counting only the aligned pairs which link content words and dividing them by the total number of words in the longest sentence from the considered pair. In the example above, only one valid alignment (7-14) can be identified, therefore the sentence pair will get a partial score of 1/18. In this manner we can ensure the decrease of the initial similarity score.

Additionally, we have defined a token ratio feature to penalize the sentence length differences. Although a length penalty is already included in the METEOR score, we still found false candidate pairs with exceedingly different lengths. Therefore we decided to use this criterion as a selection filter rather than including it in the similarity function, in order to increase the chances of other candidates with similar length. Even if no other candidate will pass all the filters, at least we expect the precision to increase, since we will have one false positive less.

The final formula for the similarity score between two clauses *src* in the source language and, respectively *trg* in the target language is:

$$score(src, trg) = w_1 * s_1 + (1 - w_1) * s_2 \quad (1)$$

where s_1 represents the METEOR score and s_2 the alignment score.

The weights, as well as the final threshold are tuned to maximize the correlation with human judgments. We modeled the task as a minimization problem, where the function value increases by 1 for each correctly selected clause pair and decreases by 1 for each wrong pair. The solution (consisting of the individual weights and the threshold) is found using a brute force approach, for which we employed the `scipy.optimize` package from Python. The training set consists of an article with 1300 clause pairs, 25 of which are parallel and the rest non-parallel. We chose this distribution of the useful/not useful clauses because this corresponds to the real distribution observed in Wikipedia articles. In the best configuration, we retrieve 23 good clause pairs and 1 wrong. This corresponds to a precision of 95% and a recall of 92% on this small test set.

However, we can influence the quantity of extracted parallel clauses by manually adjusting the final filter threshold. Figure 2 depicts the size variations of the resulting corpus at different thresholds, where the relative frequency is represented on a logarithmic scale. We notice that the rate of decrease is linear in the log scale of the number of extracted clause pairs. We start at a similarity score of 0.2 because the pairs below this threshold are too noisy. The data between 0.2 and 0.3 is already mixed, as it will be shown in the following sections. However, since this data segment contains approximately twice as much data as the summed superior ones, we decided to include it in the corpus.

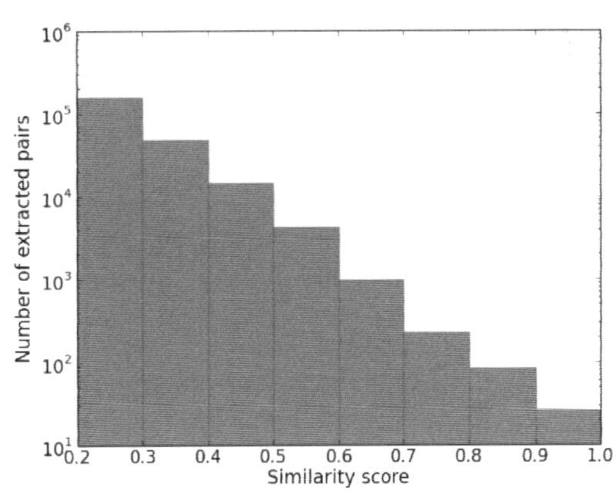

Figure 2: The distribution of the extracted clause pairs at different thresholds

Table 1 presents German-French clause pairs with their corresponding similarity scores. On the top we can find rather short clauses (up to 10 words) with perfectly aligned words. One expects that the decrease of the values implies that

Nr.	French clause	German clause	Score
1	mcnish écrit dans son journal :	mcnish schrieb in sein tagebuch :	1.0
2	son journal n' a pas été retrouvé	sein tagebuch wurde nie gefunden	0.950
3	elle travailla pendant plusieurs semaines avec lui	während mehrerer wochen arbeitete sie mit ihm zusammen	0.840
4	en 1783, il fait une première tentative infructueuse avec marc théodore bourrit	paccard startete 1783 zusammen mit marc theodore bourrit einen ersten, erfolglosen besteigungsversuch	0.717
5	en 1962, les bavarois toni kinshofer, siegfried löw et anderl mannhardt réussirent pour la première fois l' ascension par la face du diamir	1962 durchstiegen die bayern toni kinshofer, siegfried löw und anderl mannhardt erstmals die diamir-flanke	0.623
6	le 19 août 1828 il tenta, avec les deux guides jakob leuthold et johann wahren l' ascension du finsteraarhorn	august 1828 versuchte er zusammen mit den beiden bergführern jakob leuthold und johann währen das finsteraarhorn zu besteigen	0.519
7	le parc protège le mont robson, le plus haut sommet des rocheuses canadiennes	das 2248 km^2 große schutzgebiet erstreckt sich um den 3954 m hohen mount robson, dem höchsten berg der kanadischen rocky mountains	0.470
8	la plupart des édifices volcaniques du haut eifel sont des dômes isolés plus ou moins aplatis	die meisten der vulkanbauten der hocheifel sind als isolierte kuppen vereinzelt oder in reihen der mehr oder minder flachen hochfläche aufgesetzt	0.379
9	le site, candidat au patrimoine mondial, se compose d' esplanades-autels faits de pierres	die stätte, ein kandidat für das unesco-welterbe, besteht aus altarplattformen aus steinen und erde, gestützt auf einer unterirdischen konstruktion aus bemalten ton-pfeilern	0.259
10	qu' un cas mineur ayant un effet limité sur la santé	wie sich diese substanzen auf die gesundheit auswirken,	0.200

Table 1: Examples of extracted clause pairs

the clauses contain less or even no translated fragments. A manual inspection of the extracted pairs showed that this is not always the case. We have found clause pairs with almost perfect 1-1 word correspondences and a similarity score of only 0.51. The "low" score is due to the fact that we are comparing human language to automatic translations, which are not perfect.

On the other hand, a comparable score can be achieved by a pair in which one of the clauses contains some extra information (e.g. pair number 7). The extra parts in the German variant (*2248 km^2 große* - EN: with an area of 2248 km^2; *3954 m hohen* - EN: 3954 m high) cannot be separated by means of clause boundary detection, since they don't contain any verbs. This finding would motivate the idea of splitting the phrases into subsentential segments (linguistically motivated or not) and aligning the segments, similar to what Munteanu (2006) proposed. Nevertheless, we consider this pair a good candidate for the parallel corpus.

Pair number 8 has the same coordinates (i.e. an extra tail in the German variant), yet it receives a lower score, which might disqualify it for the final list, if we only look at the numbers. In this case, the low score is caused by the German compounds (*Vulkanbauten, Hocheifel*), which are unknown to the SMT system, therefore they are left untranslated and cannot be aligned. However, we argue that this clause pair should also be part of the extracted corpus.

Score range	Average sentence length	
	German	French
[0.9 – 1.0]	4	4.26
[0.8 – 0.9)	4.87	5.04
[0.7 – 0.8)	6.47	6.65
[0.6 – 0.7)	10.78	10.71
[0.5 – 0.6)	12.09	11.51
[0.4 – 0.5)	11.91	11.80
[0.3 – 0.4)	11.28	11.22
[0.2 – 0.3)	11.22	11.01

Table 2: The average sentence length for different score ranges

The last pair is definitely a bad candidate for a parallel corpus, since the clauses do not convey the same meaning, although they share many words (*avoir un effet - auswirken, sur la santé - auf die Gesundheit*). A subsentential approach would allow us to extract the useful segments in this case, as well. There are, of course, pairs with similar scores and poorer quality, therefore 0.2 is the lowest threshold which can provide useful candidate pairs. At the other end of the scale, we consider pairs above 0.4 as parallel and everything below as comparable. As a general rule, a high threshold ensures a high accuracy of the extraction pipeline.

Table 2 presents the average length (number of tokens) of the extracted clauses for different ranges of the similarity score. We notice that the best ranked clauses tend to be very short, whereas the last ranked are longer, as the examples in table 1 confirm. However, the average length over the whole extracted corpus is below 10 words, a small value compared to the results reported on Wikipedia articles by Ştefănescu and Ion (2013). This finding is due to the fact that we are aligning clauses instead of whole sentences.

We expected the German sentences to be usually shorter than the French ones (or at least have a similar number of words), since they are more likely to contain compounds. This fact is confirmed by the first part of the table. A turnaround occurs in the range (0.5,0.6), where the German sentences become slightly longer than the French ones, since they tend to contain extra information (see also table 1).

4 Experiments and Results

The conducted experiments have focused only on the extraction of parallel clauses and their use in a SMT scenario. For this purpose, we have used as input the articles selected and preprocessed in the previous development phase (Plamada and Volk, 2012). Specifically, the data set consists of 39 000 parallel articles with approximately 6 million German clauses and 2.7 million French ones. We were able to extract 225 000 parallel clause pairs out of them, by setting the final filter threshold to 0.2. This means that roughly 4% of the German clauses have an French equivalent (and 8% when reporting to the French clauses), figures comparable to our previous results on a different sized data set. However, the quality of the extracted data is higher than in our previous approaches.

To evaluate the quality of the parallel data extracted, we manually checked a set of 200 automatically aligned clauses with similarity scores above 0.25. For this test set, 39% of the extracted data represent perfect translations, 26% are translations with an extra segment (e.g. a noun phrase) on one side and 35% represent misalignments. However, given the high degree of parallelism between the clauses from the middle class, we consider them as true positives, achieving a precision of 65%. Furthermore, 40% of the false positives have been introduced by matching proper names, 32% contain matching subsentential segments (word sequences longer than 3 words) and 27% represent failures in the alignment process.

4.1 SMT Experiments

In addition to the manual evaluation discussed in the previous subsection, we have run preliminary investigations with regard to the usefulness of the extracted corpus for SMT. In this evaluation scenario, we use only pairs with a similarity score above 0.35. The results discussed in this section refer only to the translation direction German-French. The SMT systems are trained with the Moses toolkit (Koehn et al., 2007), according to the WMT 2011 guidelines[6]. The translation performance was measured using the BLEU evaluation metric on a single reference translation. We also report statistical significance scores, in order to indicate the validity of the comparisons between the MT systems (Riezler and Maxwell, 2005). We consider the BLEU score difference significant if the computed p-value is below 0.05.

We compare two baseline MT systems and several systems with different model mixtures (trans-

[6]http://www.statmt.org/wmt11/baseline.html

lation models, language models or both). The first baseline system is an in-domain one, trained on the Text+Berg corpus and is the same used for the automatic translations required in the extraction step (see section 3). The second system is purely out-of-domain and it is trained on Europarl, a collection of parliamentary proceedings (Koehn, 2005). The development set and the test set contain in-domain data, held out from the Text+Berg corpus. Table 3 lists the sizes of the data sets used for the SMT experiments.

Data set	Sentences	DE Words	FR Words
SAC	220 000	4 200 000	4 700 000
Europarl	1 680 000	37 000 000	43 000 000
Wikipedia	120 000	1 000 000	1 000 000
Dev set	1424	30 000	33 000
Test set	991	19 000	21 000

Table 3: The size of the German-French data sets

Our first intuition was to add the extracted sentences to the existing in-domain training corpus and to evaluate the performance of the system. In the second scenario, we added the extracted data to an SMT system for which no in-domain parallel data was available. For this purpose, we experimented with different combinations of the models involved in the translation process, namely the German-French translation model (responsible for the translation variants) and the French language model (ensures the fluency of the output). Besides of the models trained on the parallel data available in each of the data sets, we also built combined models with optimized weights for each of the involved data sets. The optimization was performed with the tools provided by Sennrich (2012) as part of the Moses toolkit. We also want to compare several language models, some trained on the individual data sets, others obtained by linearly interpolating different data sets, all optimized for minimal perplexity on the in-domain development set. The results are summarized in table 4.

A first remark is that an out-of-domain language model (LM) adapted with in-domain data (extracted from Wikipedia and/or SAC data) significantly improves on top of a baseline system trained with out-of-domain texts (Europarl, EP) with up to 1.7 BLEU points. And this improvement can be achieved with only a small quantity of additional data compared to the size of the original training data (120k or 220k versus 1680k sentence pairs). When replacing the out-of-domain

Translation model	Language model	BLEU score
Europarl TM	EP LM	9.45
Europarl TM	EP+Wiki LM	10.39
EP+Wiki TM	EP+Wiki LM	10.37
Europarl TM	EP+Wiki+SAC LM	11.22
EP+Wiki TM	EP+Wiki+SAC LM	11.74
EP+WMix TM	EP+Wiki+SAC LM	10.40
SAC TM	SAC LM	16.71
SAC+Wiki TM	SAC+Wiki LM	16.51
SAC+WMix TM	SAC+Wiki LM	16.37

Table 4: SMT results for German-French

translation model with a combined one (including the Wikipedia data set) and keeping only the adapted language models, we can observe two tendencies. In the first case (using a combination of out-of-domain and Wikipedia-data for the language model), the BLEU score remains approximately at the same level (10.37-10.39), the difference not being statistically significant (p-value = 0.387).

The addition of quality in-domain data for the LM from the previous configuration brings an improvement of 0.5 BLEU points on top of the best Europarl system (11.22 BLEU points). Given that all other factors are kept constant, this improvement can be attributed to the additional translation model (TM) trained on Wikipedia data. Moreover, the statistical significance tests confirm that the improved system performs better than the previous one (p-value = 0.005). To demonstrate that these results are not accidental, we replaced the Wikipedia extracted sentences with a random combination thereof (referred to as WMix) and retrained the system. Under these circumstances, the performance of the system dropped to 10.40 BLEU points. These findings demonstrate the effect of a small in-domain data set on the performance of an out-of-domain system trained on big amounts of data. If the data is of good quality, it can improve the performance of the system, otherwise it significantly deteriorates it.

We notice that the performance of a strong in-domain baseline system (SAC) cannot be heavily influenced (either positively or negatively) by translation and language model mixtures combining existing in-domain data with Wikipedia data. In terms of BLEU points, the mixture models trained with "good" Wikipedia data cause a performance drop of 0.2, but the significance test shows that the difference is not statistically significant (p-value = 0.08). On the other hand, the TM including shuffled Wikipedia sentences causes a performance drop of 0.34 BLEU points, which is statistically significant (p-value = 0.013). We can conclude that the quantity of the data is not the decisive factor for the performance change, but rather the quality of the data. The Wikipedia extracted data set maintains the good performance, whereas a random mixture of the Wikipedia data set causes a performance decrease. Therefore the focus of future work should be on obtaining high quality data, regardless of its amount.

5 Conclusions and Outlook

In this paper we presented a method for extracting domain-specific parallel data from Wikipedia articles. Based on previous experiments, we focus on clause level alignments rather than on full-sentence extraction methods. Moreover, the ranking of the candidates is based on a metric combining different similarity criteria, which we defined ourselves. The precision estimates show that the extracted sentence pairs are clearly semantically equivalent. The SMT experiments, however, show that the extracted data is not refined enough to improve a strong in-domain SMT system. Nevertheless, it is good enough to overtake an out-of-domain system trained on 10 times bigger amounts of data.

Since our extraction system is merely a prototype, there are several ways to improve its performance, including better filtering for in-domain articles, finer grained alignment and more sophisticated similarity metrics. For example, the selection of domain-specific articles can be improved by means of an additional filter based on Wikipedia categories. The accuracy of the extraction procedure can be improved by means of a more informed similarity metric, weighting more feature functions. Moreover, we can bypass the manual choice of thresholds by employing a classifier (e.g. SVM^{light} (Joachims, 2002)). Additionally, we could try to align even shorter sentence fragments (not necessarily linguistically motivated).

We are confident that Wikipedia can be seen as a useful resource for SMT, but further investigation is needed in order to find the best method to exploit the extracted data in a SMT scenario. For this purpose, quality data should be preferred over sizable data. We would therefore like to experiment with different ratio combinations of the data sets (Wikipedia extracted and in-domain data) until we find a combination which outperforms our in-domain baseline system.

References

Sadaf Abdul Rauf and Holger Schwenk. 2011. Parallel sentence generation from comparable corpora for improved SMT. *Machine Translation*, 25:341–375.

Sisay Fissaha Adafre and Maarten de Rijke. 2006. Finding similar sentences across multiple languages in Wikipedia. *Proceedings of the 11th Conference of the European Chapter of the Association for Computational Linguistics*, pages 62–69.

Michael Denkowski and Alon Lavie. 2011. Meteor 1.3: Automatic metric for reliable optimization and evaluation of machine translation systems. In *Proceedings of the EMNLP 2011 Workshop on Statistical Machine Translation*.

Pascale Fung and Percy Cheung. 2004. Mining very-non-parallel corpora: Parallel sentence and lexicon extraction via bootstrapping and EM. In *Proceedings of EMNLP*.

Pascale Fung, Emmanuel Prochasson, and Simon Shi. 2010. Trillions of comparable documents. In *Proceedings of the the 3rd workshop on Building and Using Comparable Corpora (BUCC'10)*, Malta.

Thorsten Joachims. 2002. *Learning to classify text using Support Vector Machines*. Kluwer Academic Publishers.

Philipp Koehn, Hieu Hoang, Alexandra Birch, Chris Callison-Burch, Marcello Federico, Nicola Bertoldi, Brooke Cowan, Wade Shen, Christine Moran, Richard Zens, Chris Dyer, Ondřej Bojar, Alexandra Constantin, and Evan Herbst. 2007. Moses: open source toolkit for statistical machine translation. In *Proceedings of the 45th Annual Meeting of the ACL on Interactive Poster and Demonstration Sessions*, ACL '07, pages 177–180.

Philipp Koehn. 2005. Europarl: A parallel corpus for statistical machine translation. In *Machine Translation Summit X*, pages 79–86.

Dragos Stefan Munteanu and Daniel Marcu. 2005. Improving machine translation performance by exploiting non-parallel corpora. *Computational Linguistics*, 31:477–504, December.

Dragos Stefan Munteanu. 2006. *Exploiting comparable corpora*. Ph.D. thesis, University Of Southern California.

Kishore Papineni, Salim Roukos, Todd Ward, and Wei-Jing Zhu. 2002. BLEU: a method for automatic evaluation of machine translation. In *Proceedings of the 40th Annual Meeting on Association for Computational Linguistics*, ACL '02, pages 311–318, Stroudsburg, PA, USA. Association for Computational Linguistics.

Magdalena Plamada and Martin Volk. 2012. Towards a Wikipedia-extracted alpine corpus. In *Proceedings of the Fifth Workshop on Building and Using Comparable Corpora*, Istanbul, May.

Stefan Riezler and John T. Maxwell. 2005. On some pitfalls in automatic evaluation and significance testing for MT. In *Proceedings of the ACL Workshop on Intrinsic and Extrinsic Evaluation Measures for Machine Translation and/or Summarization*, pages 57–64, Ann Arbor, Michigan, June. Association for Computational Linguistics.

Rico Sennrich. 2012. Perplexity minimization for translation model domain adaptation in statistical machine translation. In *Proceedings of the 13th Conference of the European Chapter of the Association for Computational Linguistics*, pages 539–549, Avignon, France. Association For Computational Linguistics.

Jason Smith, Chris Quirk, and Kristina Toutanova. 2010. Extracting parallel sentences from comparable corpora using document level alignment. In *Human Language Technologies: The 2010 Annual Conference of the North American Chapter of the Association for Computational Linguistics*, pages 403–411, Stroudsburg, PA, USA. Association for Computational Linguistics.

Dan Ştefănescu and Radu Ion. 2013. Parallel-Wiki: A collection of parallel sentences extracted from Wikipedia. In *Proceedings of the 14th Conference on Intelligent Text Processing and Computational Linguistics (CICLing 2013).*

Dan Ştefănescu, Radu Ion, and Sabine Hunsicker. 2012. Hybrid parallel sentence mining from comparable corpora. In Mauro Cettolo, Marcello Federico, Lucia Specia, and AndyEditors Way, editors, *Proceedings of the 16th Conference of the European Association for Machine Translation EAMT 2012*, pages 137–144.

Martin Volk. 2001. *The automatic resolution of prepositional phrase - attachment ambiguities in German.* Habilitation thesis, University of Zurich.

Bing Zhao and Stephan Vogel. 2002. Adaptive parallel sentences mining from web bilingual news collection. In *Proceedings of the 2002 IEEE International Conference on Data Mining*, ICDM '02, pages 745–748, Washington, DC, USA. IEEE Computer Society.

Gathering and Generating Paraphrases from Twitter with Application to Normalization

Wei Xu[+] Alan Ritter[^] Ralph Grishman[+]
[+]New York University, New York, NY, USA
{xuwei, grishman}@cs.nyu.edu
[^]University of Washington, Seattle, WA, USA
aritter@cs.washington.edu

Abstract

We present a new and unique paraphrase resource, which contains meaning-preserving transformations between informal user-generated text. Sentential paraphrases are extracted from a comparable corpus of temporally and topically related messages on Twitter which often express semantically identical information through distinct surface forms. We demonstrate the utility of this new resource on the task of paraphrasing and normalizing noisy text, showing improvement over several state-of-the-art paraphrase and normalization systems [1].

1 Introduction

Social media services provide a massive amount of valuable information and demand NLP tools specifically developed to accommodate their noisy style. So far not much success has been reported on a key NLP technology on social media data: paraphrasing. Paraphrases are alternative ways to express the same meaning in the same language and commonly employed to improve the performance of many other NLP applications (Madnani and Dorr, 2010). In the case of Twitter, Petrović et al. (2012) showed improvements on first story detection by using paraphrases extracted from WordNet.

Learning paraphrases from tweets could be especially beneficial. First, the high level of information redundancy in Twitter provides a good opportunity to collect many different expressions. Second, tweets contain many kinds of paraphrases not available elsewhere including typos, abbreviations, ungrammatical expressions and slang, which can be particularly valuable for many applications, such as phrase-based text normalization (Kaufmann and Kalita, 2010) and correction of writing mistakes (Gamon et al., 2008), given the difficulty of acquiring annotated data. Paraphrase models that are derived from microblog data could be useful to improve other NLP tasks on noisy user-generated text and help users to interpret a large range of up-to-date abbreviations (e.g. dlt → Doritos Locos Taco) and native expressions (e.g. oh my god → {oh my goodness | oh my gosh | oh my gawd | oh my jesus}) etc.

This paper presents the first investigation into automatically collecting a large paraphrase corpus of tweets, which can be used for building paraphrase systems adapted to Twitter using techniques from statistical machine translation (SMT). We show experimental results demonstrating the benefits of an in-domain parallel corpus when paraphrasing tweets. In addition, our paraphrase models can be applied to the task of normalizing noisy text where we show improvements over the state-of-the-art.

Relevant previous work has extracted sentence-level paraphrases from news corpora (Dolan et al., 2004; Barzilay and Lee, 2003; Quirk et al., 2004). Paraphrases gathered from noisy user-generated text on Twitter have unique characteristics which make this comparable corpus a valuable new resource for mining sentence-level paraphrases. Twitter also has much less context than news articles and much more diverse content, thus posing new challenges to control the noise in mining paraphrases while retaining the desired superficial dissimilarity.

2 Related Work

There are several key strands of related work, including previous work on gathering parallel monolingual text from topically clustered news articles, normalizing noisy Twitter text using word-based

[1] Our Twitter paraphrase models are available online at https://github.com/cocoxu/twitterparaphrase/

models, and applying out-of-domain paraphrase systems to improve NLP tasks in Twitter.

On the observation of the lack of a large paraphrase corpus, Chen and Dolan (2011) have resorted to crowdsourcing to collect paraphrases by asking multiple independent users for descriptions of the same short video. As we show in §5, however, this data is very different from Twitter, so paraphrase systems trained on in-domain Twitter paraphrases tend to perform much better.

The task of paraphrasing tweets is also related to previous work on normalizing noisy Twitter text (Han and Baldwin, 2011; Han et al., 2012; Liu et al., 2012). Most previous work on normalization has applied word-based models. While there are challenges in applying Twitter paraphrase systems to the task of normalization, access to parallel text allows us to make phrase-based transformations to the input string rather than relying on word-to-word mappings (for more details see §4).

Also relevant is recent work on collecting bilingual parallel data from Twitter (Jehl et al., 2012; Ling et al., 2013). In contrast, we focus on monolingual paraphrases rather than multilingual translations.

Finally we highlight recent work on applying out-of-domain paraphrase systems to improve performance at first story detection in Twitter (Petrović et al., 2012). By building better paraphrase models adapted to Twitter, it should be possible to improve performance at such tasks, which benefit from paraphrasing Tweets.

3 Gathering A Parallel Tweet Corpus

There is a huge amount of redundant information on Twitter. When significant events take place in the world, many people go to Twitter to share, comment and discuss them. Among tweets on the same topic, many will convey similar meaning using widely divergent expressions. Whereas researchers have exploited multiple news reports about the same event for paraphrase acquisition (Dolan et al., 2004), Twitter contains more variety in terms of both language forms and types of events, and requires different treatment due to its unique characteristics.

As described in §3.1, our approach first identifies tweets which refer to the same popular event as those which mention a unique named entity and date, then aligns tweets within each event to construct a parallel corpus. To generate paraphrases, we apply a typical phrase-based statistical MT pipeline, performing word alignment on the parallel data using GIZA++ (Och and Ney, 2003), then extracting phrase pairs and performing decoding uses Moses (Koehn et al., 2007).

3.1 Extracting Events from Tweets

As a first step towards extracting paraphrases from popular events discussed on Twitter, we need a way to identify Tweets which mention the same event. To do this we follow previous work by Ritter et al. (2012), extracting named entities and resolving temporal expressions (for example "tomorrow" or "on Wednesday"). Because tweets are compact and self-contained, those which mention the same named entity and date are likely to reference the same event. We also employ a statistical significance test to measure strength of association between each named entity and date, and thereby identify important events discussed widely among users with a specific focus, such as the release of a new iPhone as opposed to individual users discussing everyday events involving their phones. By gathering tweets based on popular real-world events, we can efficiently extract pairwise paraphrases within a small group of closely related tweets, rather than exploring every pair of tweets in a large corpus. By discarding frequent but insignificant events, such as "I like my iPhone" and "I like broke my iPhone", we can reduce noise and encourage diversity of paraphrases by requiring less lexical overlap. Example events identified using this procedure are presented in Table 1.

3.2 Extracting Paraphrases Within Events

Twitter users are likely to express the same meaning in relation to an important event, however not every pair of tweets mentioning the same event will have the same meaning. People may have opposite opinions and complicated events such as presidential elections can have many aspects. To build a useful monolingual paraphrase corpus, we need some additional filtering to prevent unrelated sentence pairs.

If two tweets mention the same event and also share many words in common, they are very likely to be paraphrases. We use the Jaccard distance metric (Jaccard, 1912) to identify pairs of sentences within an event that are similar at the lexical level. Since tweets are extremely short with little context and include a broad range of topics, using only surface similarity is prone to unrelated sen-

Entity/Date	Example Tweets
Obama 11/6/2012	Vote for Obama on November 6th!
	OBAMA is #winning his 2nd term on November 6th 2012.
	November 6th we will re-elect Obama!!
James Bond 11/9/2012	Bought movie tickets to see James Bond tomorrow. I'm a big #007 fan!
	Who wants to go with me and see that new James Bond movie tomorrow?
	I wanna go see James Bond tomorrow
North Korea 12/29/2012	North Korea Announces December 29 Launch Date for Rocket
	Pyongyang reschedules launch to December 29 due to 'technical deficiency'
	North Korea to extend rocket launch period to December 29

Table 1: Example sentences taken from automatically identified significant events extracted from Twitter. Because many users express similar information when mentioning these events, there are many opportunities for paraphrase.

tence pairs. The average sentence length is only 11.9 words in our Twitter corpus, compared to 18.6 words in newswire (Dolan et al., 2004) which also contains additional document-level information. Even after filtering tweets with both their event cluster and lexical overlap, some unrelated sentence pairs remain in the parallel corpus. For example, names of two separate music venues in the same city might be mismatched together if they happen to have concerts on the same night that people tweeted using a canonical phrasing like "I am going to a concert at ______ in Austin tonight".

4 Paraphrasing Tweets for Normalization

Paraphrase models built from grammatical text are not appropriate for the task of normalizing noisy text. However, the unique characteristics of the Twitter data allow our paraphrase models to include both normal and noisy language and consequently translate between them. Our models have a tendency to normalize because correct spellings and grammar are most frequently used,[2] but there is still danger of introducing noise. For the purposes of normalization, we therefore biased our models using a language model built using text taken from the New York Times which is used to represent grammatical English.

Previous work on microblog normalization is mostly limited to word-level adaptation or out-of-domain annotated data. Our phrase-based models fill the gap left by previous studies by exploiting a large, automatically curated, in-domain paraphrase corpus.

Lexical normalization (Han and Baldwin, 2011) only considers transforming an out-of-vocabulary (OOV) word to its standard form, i.e. in-vocabulary (IV) word. Beyond word-to-word conversions, our phrase-based model is also able to handle the following types of errors without requiring any annotated data:

Error type	Ill form	Standard form
1-to-many	everytime	every time
incorrect IVs	can't want for	can't wait for
grammar	I'm going a movie	I'm going to a movie
ambiguities	4	4 / 4th / for / four

Kaufmann and Kalita (2010) explored machine translation techniques for the normalization task using an SMS corpus which was manually annotated with grammatical paraphrases. Microblogs, however, contain a much broader range of content than SMS and have no in-domain annotated data available. In addition, the ability to gather paraphrases *automatically* opens up the possibility to build normalization models from orders of magnitude more data, and also to produce up-to-date normalization models which capture new abbreviations and slang as they are invented.

5 Experiments

We evaluate our system and several baselines at the task of paraphrasing Tweets using previously developed automatic evaluation metrics which have been shown to have high correlation with human judgments (Chen and Dolan, 2011).

[2]Even though misspellings and grammatical errors are quite common, there is much more variety and less agreement.

In addition, because no previous work has evaluated these metrics in the context of noisy Twitter data, we perform a human evaluation in which annotators are asked to choose which system generates the best paraphrase. Finally we evaluate our phrase-based normalization system against a state-of-the-art word-based normalizer developed for Twitter (Han et al., 2012).

5.1 Paraphrasing Tweets

5.1.1 Data

Our paraphrase dataset is distilled from a large corpus of tweets gathered over a one-year period spanning November 2011 to October 2012 using the Twitter Streaming API. Following Ritter et al. (2012), we grouped together all tweets which mention the same named entity (recognized using a Twitter specific name entity tagger[3]) and a reference to the same unique calendar date (resolved using a temporal expression processor (Mani and Wilson, 2000)). Then we applied a statistical significance test (the G test) to rank the events, which considers the corpus frequency of the named entity, the number of times the date has been mentioned, and the number of tweets which mention both together. Altogether we collected more than 3 million tweets from the 50 top events of each day according to the p-value from the statistical test, with an average of 229 tweets per event cluster.

Each of these tweets was passed through a Twitter tokenizer[4] and a simple sentence splitter, which also removes emoticons, URLs and most of the hashtags and usernames. Hashtags and usernames that were in the middle of sentences and might be part of the text were kept. Within each event cluster, redundant and short sentences (less than 3 words) were filtered out, and the remaining sentences were paired together if their Jaccard similarity was no less than 0.5. This resulted in a parallel corpus consisting of 4,008,946 sentence pairs with 800,728 unique sentences.

We then trained paraphrase models by applying a typical phrase-based statistical MT pipeline on the parallel data, which uses GIZA++ for word alignment and Moses for extracting phrase pairs, training and decoding. We use a language model trained on the 3 million collected tweets in the decoding process. The parameters are tuned over development data and the exact configuration are released together with the phrase table for system replication.

Sentence alignment in comparable corpora is more difficult than between direct translations (Moore, 2002), and Twitter's noisy style, short context and broad range of content present additional complications. Our automatically constructed parallel corpus contains some proportion of unrelated sentence pairs and therefore does result in some unreasonable paraphrases. We prune out unlikely phrase pairs using a technique proposed by Johnson et al. (2007) with their recommended setting, which is based on the significance testing of phrase pair co-occurrence in the parallel corpus (Moore, 2004). We further prevent unreasonable translations by adding additional entries to the phrase table to ensure every phrase has an option to remain unchanged during paraphrasing and normalization. Without these noise reduction steps, our system will produce paraphrases with serious errors (e.g. change a person's last name) for 100 out of 200 test tweets in the evaluation in §5.1.5.

At the same time, it is also important to promote lexical dissimilarity in the paraphrase task. Following Ritter et. al. (2011) we add a lexical similarity penalty to each phrase pair in our system, in addition to the four basic components (translation model, distortion model, language model and word penalty) in SMT.

5.1.2 Evaluation Details

The beauty of lexical similarity penalty is that it gives control over the degree of paraphrasing by adjusting its weight versus the other components. Thus we can plot a BLEU-PINC curve to express the tradeoff between semantic adequacy and lexical dissimilarity with the input, where BLUE (Papineni et al., 2002) and PINC (Chen and Dolan, 2011) are previously proposed automatic evaluation metrics to measure respectively the two criteria of paraphrase quality.

To compute these automatic evaluation metrics, we manually prepared a dataset of gold paraphrases by tracking the trending topics on Twitter[5] and gathering groups of paraphrases in November 2012. In total 20 sets of sentences were collected and each set contains 5 different sentences that express the same meaning. Each sentence is used

[3] https://github.com/aritter/twitter_nlp

[4] https://github.com/brendano/tweetmotif

[5] https://support.twitter.com/articles/101125-faqs-about-twitter-s-trends

Input	Output
Hostess is going outta biz	hostess is going out of business
REPUBLICAN IMMIGRATION REFORM IS A THING NOW	gop imigration law is a thing now
Freedom Writers will always be one of my fav movies	freedom writers will forever be one of my favorite movies
sources confirm that Phil Jackson has cancelled all weekend plans and upcoming guest appearances, will meet with LAL front office	source confirms that phil jackson has canceled all weekend plans , upcomin guest appearances and will meet with lakers front office

Table 2: Example paraphrases generated by our system on the test data.

once as input while other 4 sentences in the same set serve as reference translation for automatic evaluation of semantic adequacy using BLEU.

5.1.3 Baselines

We consider two state-of-the-art paraphrase systems as baselines, both of which are trained on parallel corpora of aligned sentences. The first one is trained on a large-scale corpus gathered by asking users of Amazon's Mechanical Turk Service (Snow et al., 2008) to write a one-sentence description of a short video clip (Chen and Dolan, 2011). We combined a phrase table and distortion table extracted from this parallel corpus with the same Twitter language model, applying the Moses decoder to generate paraphrases. The additional noise removal steps described in §5.1.1 were found helpful for this model during development and were therefore applied. The second baseline uses the Microsoft Research paraphrase tables that are automatically extracted from news articles in combination with the Twitter language model.[6]

5.1.4 Results

Figure 1 compares our system against both baselines, varying the lexical similarity penalty for each system to generate BLEU-PINC curves. Our system trained on automatically gathered in-domain Twitter paraphrases achieves higher BLEU at equivalent PINC for the entire length of the curves. Table 2 shows some sample outputs of our system on real Twitter data.

One novel feature of our approach, compared to previous work on paraphrasing, is that it captures many slang terms, acronyms, abbreviations and misspellings that are otherwise hard to learn.

[6]No distortion table or noisy removal process is applied because the parallel corpus is not available.

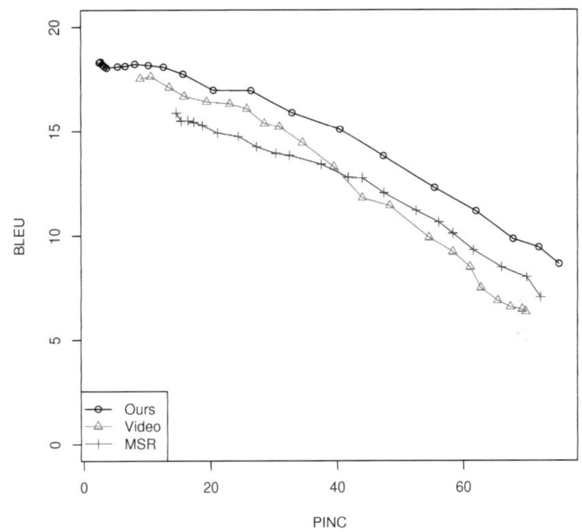

Figure 1: Results from automatic paraphrase evaluation. PINC measures n-gram dissimilarity from the source sentence, whereas BLEU roughly measures n-gram similarity to the reference paraphrases.

Several examples are shown in table 3. The rich semantic redundancy in Twitter helps generate a large variety of typical paraphrases as well (see an example in table 4).

5.1.5 Human Evaluation

In addition to automatic evaluation, we also performed a human evaluation in which annotators were asked to pick which system generated the best paraphrase. We used the same dataset of 200 tweets gathered for the automatic evaluation and generated paraphrases using the 3 systems in Figure 1 with the highest BLEU which achieve a PINC of at least 40. The human annotators were then asked to pick which of the 3 systems generated the best paraphrase using the criteria that it should be both different from the original and also

Input	Top-ranked Outputs
amped	pumped
lemme kno	let me know
bb	bigbang, big brother
snl	nbcsnl, saturday night live
apply 4 tix	apply for tickets, ask for tickets, applying for tickets
the boys	one direction (a band, whose members are often referred as "the boys"), they, the boy, the gys, the lads, my boys, the direction (can be used to refer to the band "one direction"), the onedirection, our boys, our guys
oh my god	oh my gosh, omfg, thank the lord, omg, oh my lord, thank you god, oh my jesus, oh god
can't wait	cant wait, cant wait, cannot wait, i cannot wait, so excited, cnt wait, i have to wait, i can'wait, ready, so ready, so pumped, seriously can'wait, really can't wait

Table 3: Example paraphrases of noisy phrases and slang commonly found on Twitter

Input	Top-ranked Outputs
who want to get a beer	wants to get a beer, so who wants to get a beer, who wants to go get a beer, who wants to get beer, who want to get a beer, trying to get a beer, who wants to buy a beer, who wants to get a drink, who wants to get a rootbeer, who trying to get a beer, who wants to have a beer, who wants to order a beer, i want to get a beer, who wants to get me a beer, who else wants to get a beer, who wants to win a beer, anyone wants to get a beer, who wanted to get a beer, who wants to a beer, someone to get a beer, who wants to receive a beer, someone wants to get a beer

Table 4: Example paraphrases of a given sentence "who want to get a beer"

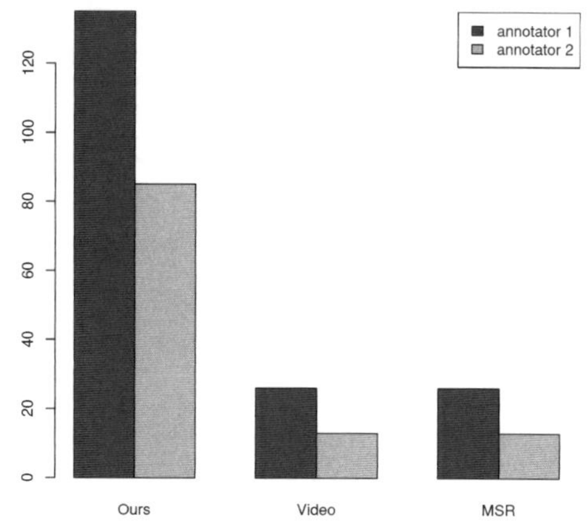

Figure 2: Number of paraphrases (200 in total) preferred by the annotators for each system

capture as much of the original meaning as possible. The annotators were asked to abstain from picking one as the best in cases where there were no changes to the input, or where the resulting paraphrases totally lost the meaning.

Figure 2 displays the number of times each annotator picked each system's output as the best. Annotator 2 was somewhat more conservative than annotator 1, choosing to abstain more frequently and leading to lower overall frequencies, however in both cases we see a clear advantage from paraphrasing using in-domain models. As a measure of inter-rater agreement, we computed Cohen's Kappa between the annotators judgment as to whether the Twitter-trained system's output best. The value of Cohen's Kappa in this case was 0.525.

5.2 Phrase-Based Normalization

Because Twitter contains both normal and noisy language, with appropriate tuning, our models have the capability to translate between these two styles, e.g. paraphrasing into noisy style or normalizing into standard language. Here we demonstrate its capability to normalize tweets at the sentence-level.

5.2.1 Baselines

Much effort has been devoted recently for developing normalization dictionaries for Microblogs. One of the most competitive dictionaries available today is HB-dict+GHM-dict+S-dict used by Han et al. (2012), which combines a manually-constructed Internet slang dictionary , a small (Gouws et al., 2011) and a large automatically-derived dictionary based on distributional and string similarity. We evaluate two baselines using this large dictionary consisting of 41181 words; following Han et. al. (2012), one is a simple dictionary look up. The other baseline uses the machinery of statistical machine translation using this dictionary as a phrase table in combination with Twitter and NYT language models.

5.2.2 System Details

Our base normalization system is the same as the paraphrase model described in §5.1.1, except that the distortion model is turned off to exclude reordering. We tuned the system towards correct spelling and grammar by adding a language model built from all New York Times articles written in 2008. We also filtered out the phrase pairs which map from in-vocabulary to out-of-vocabulary words. In addition, we integrated the dictionaries by linear combination to increase the coverage of phrase-based SMT model (Bisazza et al., 2011).

5.2.3 Evaluation Details

We adopt the normalization dataset of Han and Baldwin (2011), which was initially annotated for the token-level normalization task, and which we augmented with sentence-level annotations. It contains 549 English messages sampled from Twitter API from August to October, 2010.

5.2.4 Results

Normalization results are presented in figure 5. Using only our phrase table extracted from Twitter events we achieve poorer performance than the state-of-the-art dictionary baseline, however we find that by combining the normalization dictionary of Han et. al. (2012) with our automatically constructed phrase-table we are able to combine the high coverage of the normalization dictionary with the ability to perform phrase-level normalizations (e.g. "outta" → "out of" and examples in §4) achieving both higher PINC and BLEU than the systems which rely exclusively on word-level mappings. Our phrase table also contains many words that are not covered by the dictionary (e.g. "pts" → "points", "noms" → "nominations").

	BLEU	PINC
No-Change	60.00	0.0
SMT+TwitterLM	62.54	5.78
SMT+TwitterNYTLM	65.72	9.23
Dictionary	75.07	22.10
Dicionary+TwitterNYTLM	75.12	20.26
SMT+Dictionary+TwitterNYTLM	77.44	25.33

Table 5: Normalization performance

6 Conclusions

We have presented the first approach to gathering parallel monolingual text from Twitter, and built the first in-domain models for paraphrasing tweets. By paraphrasing using models trained on in-domain data we showed significant performance improvements over state-of-the-art out-of-domain paraphrase systems as demonstrated through automatic and human evaluations. We showed that because tweets include both normal and noisy language, paraphrase systems built from Twitter can be fruitfully applied to the task of normalizing noisy text, covering phrase-based normalizations not handled by previous dictionary-based normalization systems. We also make our Twitter-tuned paraphrase models publicly available. For future work, we consider developing additional methods to improve the accuracy of tweet clustering and paraphrase pair selection.

Acknowledgments

This research was supported in part by NSF grant IIS-0803481, ONR grant N00014-08-1-0431, and DARPA contract FA8750- 09-C-0179.

References

Regina Barzilay and Lillian Lee. 2003. Learning to paraphrase: an unsupervised approach using multiple-sequence alignment. In *Proceedings of the 2003 Conference of the North American Chapter of the Association for Computational Linguistics on Human Language Technology - Volume 1*, NAACL '03.

Arianna Bisazza, Nick Ruiz, and Marcello Federico. 2011. Fill-up versus interpolation methods for phrase-based smt adaptation. In *International Workshop on Spoken Language Translation (IWSLT), San Francisco, CA.*

David L. Chen and William B. Dolan. 2011. Collecting highly parallel data for paraphrase evaluation. In *Proceedings of the 49th Annual Meeting of the Association for Computational Linguistics (ACL-2011)*, Portland, OR, June.

Bill Dolan, Chris Quirk, and Chris Brockett. 2004. Unsupervised construction of large paraphrase corpora: Exploiting massively parallel news sources. In *Proceedings of Coling 2004*.

Michael Gamon, Jianfeng Gao, Chris Brockett, Alexander Klementiev, William B. Dolan, Dmitriy Belenko, and Lucy Vanderwende. 2008. Using contextual speller techniques and language modeling for esl error correction. *IJCNLP*.

S. Gouws, D. Hovy, and D. Metzler. 2011. Unsupervised mining of lexical variants from noisy text. In *Proceedings of the First workshop on Unsupervised Learning in NLP*, pages 82–90. Association for Computational Linguistics.

Bo Han and Timothy Baldwin. 2011. Lexical normalisation of short text messages: Makn sens a# twitter. In *Proceedings of the 49th Annual Meeting of the Association for Computational Linguistics: Human Language Technologies*, volume 1, pages 368–378.

Bo Han, Paul Cook, and Timothy Baldwin. 2012. Automatically constructing a normalisation dictionary for microblogs. In *Proceedings of the 2012 Joint Conference on Empirical Methods in Natural Language Processing and Computational Natural Language Learning*, pages 421–432, Stroudsburg, PA, USA.

P. Jaccard. 1912. The distribution of the flora in the alpine zone. *New Phytologist*, 11(2):37–50.

Laura Jehl, Felix Hieber, and Stefan Riezler. 2012. Twitter translation using translation-based cross-lingual retrieval. In *Proceedings of the Seventh Workshop on Statistical Machine Translation*, pages 410–421. Association for Computational Linguistics.

J.H. Johnson, J. Martin, G. Foster, and R. Kuhn. 2007. Improving translation quality by discarding most of the phrasetable.

Max Kaufmann and Jugal Kalita. 2010. Syntactic normalization of twitter messages. In *International Conference on Natural Language Processing, Kharagpur, India.*

Philipp Koehn, Hieu Hoang, Alexandra Birch, Chris Callison-Burch, Marcello Federico, Nicola Bertoldi, Brooke Cowan, Wade Shen, Christine Moran, Richard Zens, Chris Dyer, Ondřej Bojar, Alexandra Constantin, and Evan Herbst. 2007. Moses: open source toolkit for statistical machine translation. In *Proceedings of the 45th Annual Meeting of the ACL on Interactive Poster and Demonstration Sessions*.

Wang Ling, Guang Xiang, Chris Dyer, Alan Black, and Isabel Trancoso. 2013. Microblogs as parallel corpora. In *Proceedings of the 51st Annual Meeting of the Association for Computational Linguistics*.

Fei Liu, Fuliang Weng, and Xiao Jiang. 2012. A broadcoverage normalization system for social media language. In *Proceedings of the 50th Annual Meeting of the Association for Computational Linguistics (ACL 2012), Jeju, Republic of Korea.*

Nitin Madnani and Bonnie J. Dorr. 2010. Generating phrasal and sentential paraphrases: A survey of data-driven methods. *Comput. Linguist.*

Inderjeet Mani and George Wilson. 2000. Robust temporal processing of news. In *Proceedings of the 38th Annual Meeting on Association for Computational Linguistics*, ACL '00, pages 69–76, Stroudsburg, PA, USA. Association for Computational Linguistics.

Robert C. Moore. 2002. Fast and accurate sentence alignment of bilingual corpora. In *Proceedings of the 5th Conference of the Association for Machine Translation in the Americas on Machine Translation: From Research to Real Users*, AMTA '02.

Robert C. Moore. 2004. On log-likelihood-ratios and the significance of rare events. In *Proceedings of the 2004 Conference on Empirical Methods in Natural Language Processing*, pages 333–340.

Franz Josef Och and Hermann Ney. 2003. A systematic comparison of various statistical alignment models. *Comput. Linguist.*

Kishore Papineni, Salim Roukos, Todd Ward, and Wei-Jing Zhu. 2002. Bleu: a method for automatic evaluation of machine translation. In *Proceedings of the 40th Annual Meeting on Association for Computational Linguistics*.

Saša Petrović, Miles Osborne, and Victor Lavrenko. 2012. Using paraphrases for improving first story detection in news and twitter.

Chris Quirk, Chris Brockett, and William Dolan. 2004. Monolingual machine translation for paraphrase generation. In *Proceedings of EMNLP 2004*.

Alan Ritter, Colin Cherry, and William B. Dolan. 2011. Data-driven response generation in social media. In *Proceedings of the Conference on Empirical Methods in Natural Language Processing*.

Alan Ritter, Mausam, Oren Etzioni, and Sam Clark. 2012. Open domain event extraction from twitter. In *KDD*, pages 1104–1112. ACM.

Rion Snow, Brendan O'Connor, Daniel Jurafsky, and Andrew Y. Ng. 2008. Cheap and fast—but is it good?: evaluating non-expert annotations for natural language tasks. In *Proceedings of the Conference on Empirical Methods in Natural Language Processing*, EMNLP '08.

Learning Comparable Corpora from Latent Semantic Analysis Simplified Document Space

Ekaterina Stambolieva
euroscript Luxembourg S.à. r.l.
55, rue de Luxembourg, L-8077
Luxembourg
ekaterina.stambolieva@euroscript.lu

Abstract

Focusing on a systematic Latent Semantic Analysis (LSA) and Machine Learning (ML) approach, this research contributes to the development of a methodology for the automatic compilation of comparable collections of documents. Its originality lies within the delineation of relevant comparability characteristics of similar documents in line with an established definition of comparable corpora. These innovative characteristics are used to build a LSA vector-based representation of the texts. In accordance with this new reduced in dimensionality document space, an unsupervised machine learning algorithm gathers similar texts into comparable clusters. On a monolingual collection of less than 100 documents, the proposed approach assigns comparable documents to different comparable corpora with high confidence.

1 Introduction

The problem of collecting comparable corpora is challenging and yet enchanting. Many can benefit from the availability of such corpora as translation professionals, machine learning researchers and computational linguistics specialists. Yet there is not an even consent about the notion covered by the term comparable corpora. The degree of similarity between comparable corpora documents has not been formalized strictly and leaves space for different interpretations of similarity, contributing to abundant text collections of similar and semi-similar documents. The current research endeavors to contribute to an approach, which assembles a collection of comparable documents that are closely related to each other on the basis of a strict definition of comparable corpora. The proposed approach incorporates originally a Latent Semantic Analysis technique in order to match similar concepts instead of words thus contributing to better automatic learning of comparability between documents.

2 Comparable Corpora Definition

Maia (2003) discusses the characteristics of comparable corpora. Nevertheless, the adopted definition of comparable corpora in this study is given by McEnery (2003):

> "Comparable corpora are corpora where series of monolingual corpora are collected for a range of languages, preferably using the same sampling and frame and with similar balance and representativeness, to enable the study of those languages in contrast."

McEnery (2003) characterizes comparable corpora as "corpora where series of monolingual corpora are collected for the range of languages". In the views of McEnery (2003), a monolingual corpus is a corpus that is not collected for a range of languages, but instead the documents selected are written in one language. In the context of the current research, a comparable corpus, a sublanguage corpus, can be constructed from documents in one language under the condition they are compliant with the preferred guidelines provided by McEnery (2003). These preferred guidelines are similar sampling frame, balance and representativeness.

A document feature corresponding to text sampling is explicated taking into consideration the domain and genre of the documents. Additionally, similar terminology vocabulary insures genre correspondence. Therefore, the same sampling scheme in collecting documents is evaluated considering domain and genre and viewed as document features.

Language is rapidly changing and evolving throughout the years (Crystal 2001). As a result, restricting the time period a document has been published increases the chances of it being comparable to another one written during the same time frame. When events are reported in the newspaper domain, their date of publication is strong similarity evidence and is used as a filter between weakly comparable and non-comparable text articles (Skadiņa et al. 2010a).

The question of how representativeness of a corpus is decided upon is answered in different ways depending on the specific corpus purpose. For the purposes of this research, a corpus is considered representative when corresponding texts are similar in size. As reported by Manning and Schűtze (1999), a balanced corpus is one, which is assembled "as to give each subtype of text a share of the corpus that is proportional to some predetermined criterion of importance".
Skadina et al. (2010b) present a good summary of the advantages of exploiting comparable corpora. It is discussed that "they can draw on much richer, more available and more diverse sources which are produced every day (e.g. multilingual news feeds) and are available on the Web in large quantities for many languages and domains." (Skadina et al. 2010b).

3 Related Work

The most closely-related to machine learning work that mines comparable corpora is that by Sharoff (2010). His research incorporates intelligent self-learning techniques to the compilation of comparable documents. Unlike other researchers that experiment with Cross-Lingual Information Retrieval (CLIR) techniques as in Tao and Zhai (2005), Sharoff (2010) estimates the document collection's internal subgroup system in search for structure. The possible structure and grouping of a set of documents is most easily defined by ranked words that are representative for the subsets in the collection. Sharoff's approach relies heavily on keywords and keyword estimation. One thing Sharoff (2010) does not elaborate on in details is the definition of a comparable corpus. A possible reason for that is that unsupervised machine learning approaches produce related sets of documents in an environment where the selection process is automated and not supervised by any linguistically-dependent rules.

What is written by Goeuriot et al. (2009) is also an influential and relevant material to the current research. Their paper is on the compilation of comparable corpora in a specialized domain with a focus on English and Japanese. The article is significant for the reason the authors investigate ways of building comparable corpora using machine learning classification algorithms, namely Support Vector Machine and C4.5. The experimental setup in the work of Goeuriot et al. (2009) relies on manually labeled data, which is then fed to the machine learning algorithm core. The paper by Goeuriot et al. (2009) is directed towards building a tool to automatically compile comparable corpora in a predefined set of documents and languages. The text comparability characteristics extracted, which allow comparison between the documents, are external and internal to the textual data. Goeuriot et al. (2009) emphasize on selecting ways to automatic recognition of useful features similar texts have and experiment with these features to test and predict their reliability. The comparability of the documents defined by them is on three levels - type of discourse, topic and domain, focusing on locutive, ellocutive and allocutive act labels.

Bekavac et al. (2004) discuss the grounds of a methodology describing similarity comparison of under-resourced monolingual corpora. Contrary to other methodologies that exploit seed words or seed texts as a basis for search, the researchers have at their disposal two monolingual documents sets from which they aim to mine comparable documents. The advantage of their approach is that it is applicable to texts collection written in one language for the reason that they are easily mined and compiled from the available textual resources nowadays. The concept behind their research is to align comparable documents that are found in pre-collected different monolingual corpora. Content features are used to test the degree to which two texts are similar to each other in the sense of sharing the same information and common words. These features, composition features, need to be representative for the texts. The composition features, extracted from the data, monitor the size, the format and the time span of the documents.

Clustering based on semantic keyword extraction is performed by Finkelstein et al. (2001). This approach is relevant to the current research as it suggests a different methodology of feeding texts to machine learning algorithms. The researchers aim to generate new content based on input user queries by using context – "a body of words surrounding a user-selected phrase" (Finkelstein et al. 2001). They emphasise on the significance of using context when developing Natural Language Processing (NLP) applications. The keyword extraction algorithm presented relies on a precisely-designed clustering algorithm, different than k-means, to recursively clean clustering results and present refined statistical output.

With regards to evaluation metrics of comparable corpora, one of the main focuses of the ACCURAT Project (Skadina et al. 2010b) is to design metrics of comparability estimation between texts. The ACCURAT researchers (Skadina et al. 2010b) concentrate on the development of comparable corpora criteria for different texts and different types of parallelism between the texts. Saralegi et al. (2008) suggest measures based on distribution of topics or time with regards to publication dates. Kilgariff (2001) aims to measure the level of comparability between two collections of documents. He focuses additionally on the shortcoming of known corpus similarity metrics. He discusses evaluation methods for corpus comparability measures, which are based on Spearman rank correlation coefficient, perplexity and cross-entropy, χ^2 and others. To his knowledge, the χ^2 test performs the best when comparing two sets of documents. It is important to note that the approach adopted by Kilgariff (2001) relies on words and n-gram sequence features. Not only does he regard the texts as bag-of-words, but also he incorporates n-gram characteristics in his evaluation metric analysis.

Mining word similarity techniques are discussed in the work of Deerwester et al. (1990); Baeza-Yates and Ribeiro-Netto (1999); and Dagan, Lee and Pereira (1999). Deerwester et al. (1990) incorporate LSA as a technique to identify word relatedness. LSA "identifies a number of most prominent dimensions in the data, which are assumed to correspond to 'latent concepts'." (Radinsky et al. 2011). Radinsky et al. (2011) indicate that LSA vector space models are "difficult to interpret". Consequently, the current research focuses not only on the incorporation of LSA to mapping content, but also of the employment of a machine learning technique to group projected into the two-dimensional space documents into similar clusters. Baeza-Yates and Ribeiro-Netto (1999), as Sharoff (2009) and Goeuriot et al. (2010), consider texts as bag-of-words as the least complex word similarity approaches can be incorporated. Mapping distributional similarity, Lee (1999) opts for similar word co-occurrence probability estimation improvement. Dagan et al. (1999) also aim for better estimation of word co-occurrence likelihood not based on empirical methods, but instead relying on distributional similarity for the generation of language models. WordNet-based and distributional-similarity comparisons of word similarity are presented in Agirre et al. (2009). They suggest different views of word relatedness comparison – bag-of-words, context windows and syntactic dependency approaches. They describe their findings as yielding best results on known test sets. What is important to be remarked is that their methodology requires minor fine-tuning in order to give good results on cross-lingual word similarity.

4 Methodology

The novelty of our approach is the incorporation of the Latent Semantic Analysis technique, which matches concepts, or information units, from one document to another instead of approximating word similarity. LSA expects and constructs a new vector-based representation of the documents to be compared. A concept holds not only textual, but also morphological information about each word present in the texts. By employing LSA, the document space is projected into the two-dimensional space in correspondence with the latent relationships between the words in the texts. In the two-dimensional space, clusters of similar documents are compiled together using a simple, but powerful unsupervised machine learning algorithm, k-means clustering. Clustering evaluation metrics such as precision, recall and purity are employed towards automatic evaluation and analysis of the resulting comparable corpora.

In order to compile comparable corpora with the current settings, a set of pre-collected documents is needed. From this set of documents, two to five comparable corpora are identified and texts with similar topics, domains and features are assigned to relevant comparable corpora.

LSA has its known limitations. It acknowledges documents as bags-of-words and mines the latent relationships between the words in the bags-of-words. Working with information units overcomes this limitation of LSA. The information units contain additional linguistic information about the syntactic and morphological relationships between words, therefore forming concepts of these words. The order of the words, or the information units, is not imperative, therefore it is not controlled by the methodology.

LSA allows words to have only one meaning thus restricting the robustness of the natural languages. This limitation is tackled by suggesting different word sense candidates for words and constructing a separate information unit for each promoted word sense.

5 Data Feature Selection

The innovation of the discussed research approach lays in its basic concept of perceiving texts as bags of interrelated concepts. The surface-form words found in the texts are enriched with linguistic information that furnishes better matching procedure of the concepts lying within the texts for comparison.

Unlike previous work, which regards documents as bags-of-words (Sharoff 2009, Goeuriot et al. 2010) the methodology treats documents as collections of concepts, each concept containing comparable textual information. The concepts are represented by information units. The process of recognizing such units happens at document level, where each document is viewed as a separate text with its own context. Each information unit is defined as the inseparable pair of lemma and its context-dependent part-of-speech (POS) tag. A lemmatization technique is applied to transform the texts into linguistically-simplified versions of the originals, where each word (infected or not) is substituted by its corresponding lexeme.

As stated before, the information units incorporate POS output. A POS tagger is used to process the texts before linguistically-simplifying it using lemmatization techniques. The idea of enriching the words by POS information is not new to the research of Natural Language Processing, but it is new for the research of compiling comparable corpora. By identifying the POS information of a sentence, lexical ambiguity is reduced. The accompanying POS tag to each lemma assists the disambiguation of the information units. For example, *run* as being the action of walking fast has a verb POS tag opposed to *run* as the period of some event happening has a noun POS tag. In this example, the POS tag provides the needed information for disambiguating the two different meanings of a word. In the current research scenario, the POS tagging module[1] emulates the results of a basic Word Sense Disambiguation technique.

Furthermore, the input set of documents is transformed into a set of lists of information units as described, where a single list of units corresponds to a single document. When compared, the units are matched for correspondence both based on the lemma's lexical category in the sentence and its base form.

Another feature, which helps build context related concepts, is the identification of Noun Phrases (NP) in the texts. Noun Phrase recognition is imperative since it further develops the simple word sense disambiguation method. Some words to have a different meaning when occurring in a chain of words such as a noun phrase. Unlike the proposed by Su and Babych (2012) approach to NP recognition, NPs are identified following linguistically-derived rules, which represent common constructions of the language under consideration. When a NP is identified, it is listed as a new information unit with a corresponding *NP* POS tag. All POS annotations as well as lemma information of its constituent words are removed from the documents' list of information units.

6 Experiments

6.1 Experimental Corpus

A pre-collected corpus of documents, part of the NPs for Events (NP4E) corpus (Hasler et al. 2006), is used for experimenting. The NP4E corpus is collected for the special purpose of extracting coreference resolution in English. Nevertheless, the structure and the organization of the corpus are suitable for the needs of acquisition of a test corpus for the current study. The NP4E corpus contains five different groups of news articles based on topic gathered from the Reuters. The news articles are collected in the time frame

[1] TreeTagger http://www.ims.uni-stuttgart.de/projekte/corplex/TreeTagger/

of two years – 1996 and 1997 (Rose, Stevenson and Whitehead 2002). Four of the five NP4E news article groups are used to compile an experimental corpus containing roughly 40000 words or 520 words per text. The chosen experimental collection consists of sub-corpora that have documents comparable to the others in their sub-corpora based on domain. The domain of these comparable corpora is terrorism, and the four distinct topics are connected with terrorism, bombing and suicide respectively for events in Israel, Tajikistan, China and Peru. In total, the experimental corpus consists of 77 newswire articles. The distribution of the documents in this selected corpus is 20 on Israel topic, 19 on Tajikistan topic, 19 for China topic and 19 on Peru topic. These sub-corpora are referred to as Israel (I), Tajikistan (T), China (C) and Peru (P) onwards.

6.2 Experimental Set-up

The experimental set-up is structured as a chain of two simple procedures. They are respectively an experimental setup data selection and experimental setup clustering distribution.

6.2.1 Data Selection Frame

The data selection frame describes how document features are selected. The documents are afterwards preprocessed in order to extract all underlying text features and binary vectors are constructed to represent each separate document. The document features on focus consist of all identified information units enriched with the noun phrases that were recognized in the texts. The binary vectors then are used as an input to the LSA algorithm.

6.2.2 Cluster Distribution

The number of resulting clusters, or comparable corpora, should be set in advance for unsupervised machine learning algorithms. An experiments with *k*, *k* is in the range of 2 to 5, are conducted. Testing with number of clusters greater or equal to two comes logical. In the case of expecting two resulting clusters, the methodology groups all similar documents in one comparable corpus, and withdraws the non-similar documents to the second collection. When *k* is chosen to be 2 or 3, the resulting comparable corpora tend to be weakly-comparable (Skadiņa et al. 2010a) for the reason the algorithms are forced to gather documents with four distinct topics into only two or three comparable collections. It is interesting to analyze the research methodology's performance in the case four output comparable corpora are expected, meaning when the learning algorithm is asked to suggest four comparable sets of documents.

To evaluate clustering performance in terms of forcing the system to split the document collection into more comparable corpora than present, *k* equals to 5 is also used in the experiments. Consequently, the number of clusters varies between 2 and 5.

6.2.3 Evaluation Metrics

Three metrics are chosen to evaluate results - the standard precision and recall, and additionally - purity. Precision shows how many documents in the resulting collections are identified correctly as comparable to the majority of documents on a specific topic in the cluster. For example, when 16 out of 19 documents are recognized to be comparable to each other, the precision of this clustering result is 0.84. Recall shows how many false negatives are identified as comparable to a certain topic-related collection of texts. The false negatives are the documents on a different topic, which the machine learning algorithm falsely lists to be comparable to documents on another topic. When 21 documents are grouped in one similarity cluster, 19 of them being on a related topic, 3 of them being on another topic, the recall of the learning performance is 0.86.

Purity is an evaluation metric used to estimate the purity of the resulting clusters (Figure 1.). A cluster is recognized as pure when it contains a number of documents with the same label (meaning they are listed to be comparable to each other by a human evaluator) and as less as possible documents that have a different label from the dominant label (Manning et al. 2008):

$$Purity = \frac{(nom_{cluster\ 1} + .. + nom_{cluster\ k})}{no_{clusters}}$$

Figure 1. Purity score formula

where $nom_{cluster\ i}$ is the number of the majority class members in each resulting cluster *i*, and $no_{clustrers}$ is the number of resulting clusters, or *k*. As Manning et al. (2008) warn "High purity is easy to achieve when the number of clusters is large - in particular, purity is 1 if each document gets its own cluster". The number of clusters for the current research is not big. Nonetheless, the results are evaluated based on two other metrics.

The other metrics for measuring the comparability between documents that are chosen for exploitation in the current research, are Mutual Infromation (MI) and Normalized Mutual Infroamtion (NMI). The formula for NMI is as follows and shown in Figure 2.:

$$NMI(\Omega, C) = \frac{MI(\Omega, C)}{(H(\Omega) + H(C))/2}$$

Figure 2. NMI score formula

MI is explained in details in Kalgariff (2001) and (Manning et al. 2008). Manning et al. (2008) discuss additionally the formula for the entropy H, and NMI. Ω is the group of clusters addressed in the experiments, and *C* is the group of labels – namely the different characteristics of the comparable corpora.

In the current scenario, no human evaluation is performed. Rather than that the corpus is predesigned in a way to contain four different comparable corpora that need not to be manually labeled

6.3 Evaluation

Results are obtained after conducting different set-up experiments. One set-up focuses on evaluating comparable corpus collection having as an input part of the experimental corpus. This part contains documents on two out of the four different topics. The two-topic collections are compiled by combining all combinations possible of two topic-based sets together from the four distinct topic sub-corpora. In this experimental scenario, the total of different corpora for evaluation is 6 (according to the combination's formula $\binom{4}{2}$) - Peru and China, Peru and Tajikistan, Peru and Israel, Tajikistan and China, Tajikistan and Israel, China and Israel. Table 1 shows the results of running LSA with k-means clustering on the discussed sub-groups. As seen on Table 1. the learning algorithm performance is excellent when the number of comparable corpora that are expected is greater than two. When three or more comparable clusters are elected, each similar by topic document is grouped with all other documents that are comparable to it in the same resulting comparable corpus. In the case of expecting three comparable corpora with Precision and Recall equal to 1.0, one of these corpora contains all documents of two different sub-corpora and the rest contain all documents of one of the predefined experimental sub-corpora. In the case of expecting five comparable corpora with Precision and Recall equal to 1.0, one sub-corpus is split into two comparable clusters, these clusters containing documents on the same topic. What is interesting in this experimental set-up are the results the learning algorithm obtains when it aims to produce only two comparable clusters. For three of the test sets - China and Israel, Peru and China and Tajikistan and Israel, grouping of documents on different topics into the same similar collection is seen. The lowest results obtained are for the test set Tajikistan and Israel, where 3 of the 19 documents on an Israel topic are grouped together with the texts on the Tajikistan topic. The reason behind this automatic learning confusion originates from the fact the Tajikistan and Israel topic documents contain many similar concepts, which make good clustering harder to achieve.

The purity of the resulting corpora is very high, above 0.9, indicating that comparable documents are identified correctly with high relevance. The only exception is the results on the Tajikistan and Israel test set with purity 0.56. This exception occurs because of poor clustering results, which have been discussed.

Sub-corpus	Topic	Precision				Recall				Purity
		2Cl	**3Cl**	**4Cl**	**5Cl**	**2Cl**	**3Cl**	**4Cl**	**5Cl**	
P	Peru	0.84	1	1	1	1	1	1	1	0.921
C	China	1	1	1	1	0.86	1	1	1	
P	Peru	0.84	1	1	1	1	1	1	1	0.921
T	Tajikistan	1	1	1	1	0.86	1	1	1	
P	Peru	1	1	1	1	1	1	1	1	1.00
I	Israel	1	1	1	1	1	1	1	1	
T	Tajikistan	1	1	1	1	1	1	1	1	1.00
C	China	1	1	1	1	1	1	1	1	
T	Tajikistan	1	1	1	1	0.52	1	1	1	0.56
I	Israel	0.15	1	1	1	1	1	1	1	
C	China	0.86	1	1	1	1	1	1	1	0.923
I	Israel	1	1	1	1	0.85	1	1	1	

Table 1. Clustering results for test sets of combinations of two topic sub-corpora
(*n*Cl pointing to the numbers of clusters identified)

Another set-up focuses on the analysis and evaluation of the results on clusters containing documents on three of the four different topics. The same way as the two-topic collections are constructed, combining three topic sub-corpora into one results in the development of the input for the LSA and k-means clustering algorithms. In this experimental scenario, a total of 4 distinct input collections are compiled -Tajikistan, Israel and China; Tajikistan, Israel and Peru; Peru, China and Israel; and Tajikistan, China and Peru.

The results of the learning comparable corpora from them are listed in Table 2. As it can be easily seen, the clustering performance is impeccable. Therefore, providing more documents, more data features, helps identifying better similar documents applying the proposed research approach.

Table 3. Shows the clustering results when all texts of the experimental corpus are suggested as an input. The algorithms once more do not have problems collecting the similar documents into comparable corpora with high precision and recall.

MI and NMI are computed only for the results presented in Table 1. The reasoning behind is that Table 2. And Table 3. show perfect clustering results of comparable corpora obtained on the whole set of input documents described in Section 6.1.

The results of the comparable texts grouping are estimated using a clustering quality trade-off metric, NMI. Table 4. shows the NMI results of the clustering performance on the two-topic collections described in the first experimental set-up at the beginning of Section 6.3.

Sub-corpus	Topic	Precision				Recall				Purity
		2Cl	**3Cl**	**4CL**	**5Cl**	**2Cl**	**3Cl**	**4Cl**	**5Cl**	
T	Tajikistan	1	1	1	1	1	1	1	1	
I	Israel	1	1	1	1	1	1	1	1	1.00
C	China	1	1	1	1	1	1	1	1	
T	Tajikistan	1	1	1	1	1	1	1	1	
I	Israel	1	1	1	1	1	1	1	1	1.00
P	Peru	1	1	1	1	1	1	1	1	
P	Peru	1	1	1	1	1	1	1	1	
C	China	1	1	1	1	1	1	1	1	1.00
I	Israel	1	1	1	1	1	1	1	1	
T	Tajikistan	1	1	1	1	1	1	1	1	
C	China	1	1	1	1	1	1	1	1	1.00
P	Peru	1	1	1	1	1	1	1	1	

Table 2. Clustering results for test sets of combinations of three topic sub-corpora

	Precision				Recall				Purity
	2cl	**3cl**	**4cL**	**5cl**	**2cl**	**3cl**	**4cl**	**5cl**	
T	1	1	1	1	1	1	1	1	
C	1	1	1	1	1	1	1	1	1.00
I	1	1	1	1	1	1	1	1	
P	1	1	1	1	1	1	1	1	

Table 3. Clustering results on the whole experimental corpus

	Mutual Information	**H(Ω)**	**H(C)**	**NMI**
	2CL	**2CL**	**2CL**	**2Cl**
Peru China	0.6866	0.9927	1	0.6916
Peru Tajikistan	0.6866	0.9927	1	0.6916
Peru Israel	1.0230	1.0074	1.0074	0.9522
Tajikistan China	1	1	1	1
Tajikistan Israel	0.0844	0.3912	1.0074	0.1262
China Israel	0.6855	0.9744	1.0074	0.6917

Table 4. MI and NMI scores results for test sets of combinations of two topic sub-corpora

Consequently, the results shown on Table 4. are obtained with respects to the precision, recall and purity scores presented in Table 1. The NMI score is evidence of the identified comparable corpora quality. As seen on Table 4., the lowest NMI score correspond to the clustering results on the Peru- and China- topic texts. As shown on Table 1., the proposed approach is not confident when grouping the Peru- and China- topic texts into comparable collections. The results of the NMI metric shown on Table 4. only confirm this conclusion. The best results obtained according to the NMI score are NMI is dependent on the mutual information and the entropy the texts to be clustered share. MI is a metric, which estimates how the amount of information presented in the documents affect the clustering output. When the MI score is low, as in the example of grouping the Tajikistan- and Israel- topic texts, the information contained in the documents does not contribute to highly-comparable clusters of corpora. When the MI score obtained is high, as in the Tajikistan- and China- topic documents experiment, the information in these documents is a strong evidence of the text relatedness. Table 4. lists the intermediate calculations of the entropy based on the available labels H(C) and the resulting clusters H(Ω).

7 Remarks

The problems identified in the current methodology are classified into two different groups: text processing resources errors and clustering output errors. The processing resources are taken as off-the-shelf modules and the development focus of the study in not concentrating on improving their performance. The second type of errors is the clustering errors. Their size can be reduced by improving the performance of the text preprocessing resources. Additionally, enhanced clustering output evaluation metrics can reveal learning algorithm's weaknesses and suggest ways for improvement.

8 Future Work

More can be done in the future to improve the proposed methodology. One idea for further investigation is experimenting with larger collections of data. The results on the experimental corpus are promising, but the document collection is not big and contains less than 80 texts. It would be interesting to experiment with corpora that consist of hundreds of documents to test clustering performance. Additionally, a new experimental collection of documents is being compiled. It contains psycholinguistics texts both in Spanish and English. As the collection of this document set is still in progress, the results obtained on it are not presented in the current paper. These results will be reported in future work publications.

Furthermore, a new translation equivalent source can be added. In the case of compiling specialized collections of comparable documents, a specialized bilingual or multilingual dictionary can prove to be a valuable resource. An untested interesting experimental setup can be investigating the resulting clustering performance when more than 50% or more of the most relevant lemmas (with noun phrases) are selected as document features. A Named Entity Recognizer (NER) and a synonymy suggestion module have the possibility to serve as good text processing resources and further improve grouping outcomes. In connection with NER, it is interesting additionally to investigate if the test corpus contains local names, which make clustering better easier. Lastly, potential source for further development is the automatic recognition of diasystematic text features, such as diachronic, diatopic or diatechnic information.

Clustering results of comparable corpora are obtained when the document characteristics are filtered by best keyword estimation metric - TF.BM25, explained in Pérez-Iglesias et al. (2009). The results show decrease in good clustering performance. A future work aspect is to investigate the cause this lower performance.

9 Conclusion

An innovative approach to the problem of compilation of comparable corpora is described. The approach suggests guidelines to textual characteristics selection scheme. Additionally, the approach incorporates LSA and unsupervised ML techniques. Different evaluation metrics, such as precision, purity and normalized mutual information, are employed to estimate comparable corpus clustering results. These metrics show good results when evaluating comparable clusters from a predefined set of less than 100 documents. The methodology suggested is applied for monolingual selection of documents; nonetheless it is readily extendable to more languages.

References

Agirre, Eneko, Alfonseca, Enrique, Hall, Keith, Kravalova, Jana, Paşca, Marius and Soroa, Aitor.2009. A study of Similarity and Relatedness Using Distributional and WordNet-based approaches. In *NAACL '09*, pages 19-27.

Baeza-Yates, Ricardo and Ribeiro-Neto, Betrhier. 1999. *Modern Infromation Retieval*, Addison Wesley.

Bekavac, Božo, Osenova, Petya, Simov, Kiril and Tadic, Marco. 2004. Making Monolingual Corpora Comparable: a Case Study of Bulgarian and Croatian. In *Proceedings of LREC2004*, pages 1187-1190, Lisbon.

Crystal, David. 2001. *Language and the Internet*. Cambidge University, Press. Cambidge.UK, pages 91-93.

Dagan, Igo, Lee, Lillian and Pereira, Fernando. 1999. Similarity-based models of word co-occurrence probabilities. *Machine Learning*. 34(1-3), pages 43-69.

Deerwester, Scott, Dumais, Susan, Furnas, George, Landauer, Thomas and Harshman, Richard. 1990. Indexing by latent semantic analysis. *Journal of the Americal Society for Information Science*. 41(6), pages 391-407.

Finkelstein, Lev, Gabrilovich, Evgeniy, Matias, Yossi, Rivlin, Ehud, Solan, Zach, Wolfman, Gadi and Ruppin, Eytan. 2001. Placing Search in Context: The Concept Revisited. In *WWW'01*, pages 406-414.

Goeuriot, Lorraine, Emmanuel Morin and Béatrice Daille. 2009. Compilation of specialized comparable corpora in French and Japanese. In *Proceedings of the 2nd workshop on Building and Using Comparable Corpora: from Parallel to Non-parallel Corpora*, August 06, 2009, Suntec, Singapore.

Hasler, Laura, Constantin Orasan and Karin Naumann. 2006. NPs for Events: Experiments in Conference Annotation. In *Proceedings of the 5th edition of the International Conference on Language Resources and Evaluation (LREC2006)*, pages 1167-1172, 24-26 May 2006, Genoa, Italy.

Ion, Radu, Dan Tufiş, Tiberiu Boroş, Ru Ceauşu and Dan Ştefănescu. 2010. On-line Compilation of Comparable Corpora and Their Evaluation. In *Proceedingds of the 7th International Conference of Formal Approaches to South Slavic and Balkan Languages (FASSBL7)*, pages 29-34, Dubrovnic, Croatia.

Kilgarriff, Adam. 2001. Comparing corpora. *International Journal of Corpus Lingusitics*, 6(1), pages 97-133.

Lee, Lillian. 1999. Measures of distributional similarity. *Proceedings of ACL 1999*, pages 25-32.

Maia, Belinda. 2003. What are Comparable Corpora? *Electronic resource:* http://web.letras.up.pt/bhsmaia/belinda/pubs/CL2003%20workshop.doc.

Manning, Christopher D. and Hinrich Schűtze. 1999. *Introduction to Information Retrieval*. Cambridge University Press, Cambridge, UK.

Manning, Christopher D., Prabhakan Raghavan, and Hinrich Schűtze. 2008. *Introduction to Information Retrieval*, Cambridge University Press, pages 356-358.

McEnery, Tony. 2003. Corpus Linguistics. In Ruslan Mitkov, editor, *The Handbook of Computational Lingustics*. Oxford University Press, Oxford, UK, pages 448-464.

Radinsky, Kira, Agichtein, Eugene, Gabrilovich, Evgeniy and Markovitch, Shaul. 2011. A word at a time: Computing Word Relatedness using Temporal Semantic Analysis. In *WWW'11*, pages 337-346.

Pérez-Iglesias, Joaquín, Pérez-Agüera, José, Fresno, Víctor and Feinstein, Yuval. 2009. Integrating the probabilistic model BM25/BM25F into Lucene. In *CoRR, abs/0911.5046*.

Rose, Tony, Mark Stevenson and Miles Whitehead. 2002. The Reuters Corpus Volume 1 – from Yesterday's News to Tomorrow's Language Resource. In *Proceedings of LREC2002*, pages 827-833.

Sarageli, Xabier., San Vincente, Inaki, Gurrutxaga. Antton 2002.Automatic Extraction of bilingual terms from comparable corpora in a popular science domain. In *Proceedings of the workshop on Comparable Corpora, LREC'08*.

Sharoff, Serge. 2010. Analysing similarities and differences between corpora. In *Proceedings of the 7th Conference of Language Technologies (Jezikovne Tehnologije)*, pages 5-11, Ljubljiana. Slovenia.

Skadiņa, Inguna, Ahmet Aker, Voula Giouli, Dan Tufis, Robert Gaizauskas, Madara Mieriņa and Nikos Mastropavlos. 2010a. A Collection of Comparable Corpora for Under-Resourced Languages. In Inguna Skadiņa and Dan Tufis, editors, *Human Language Technologies. The Baltic Perspective. Proceedings of the 4th International Conference Baltic HLT 2010*, pages 161-168.

Skadiņa, Inguna, Vasiljeiv, Andrejs, Skadiņš, Raivis, Gaizauskas, Robert, Tufiş, Dan and Gornostay, Tatiana. 2010b. Analysis and Evaluation of Compoarable Corpora for Under Resourced Areas of Machine Translation. In *Proceedings of the 3rd Workshop on Building and Using Comparable Corpora. Applications of Parallel and Comparable Corpora in Natural Language PEngineering and the Humanities*, pages 6-14.

Su, Fangzhoung and Bogdan Babych. 2012. Measuring Comparability of Documents in Non-Parallel Corpora for Efficient Extraction of (Semi-)Parallel Translation Equivalents. In *Proceedings of the Joint Workshop on Exploiting Synergies between Information Retrieval and Machine Translation (ESIRMT) and Hybrid Approaches to Machine Translation (HyTra)*, pages 10-19, Avignon, France.

Tao, Tao and Cheng Xiang Zhai. 2005. Mining Comparable Bilingual Text Corpora for Cross-Language Information Integration. In *Proceedings of the eleventh ACM SIGKDD international conference on Knowledge discovery in data mining*, pages 691-696.

Finding More Bilingual Webpages with High Credibility via Link Analysis

Chengzhi Zhang*
Nanjing University of Science and Technology
Nanjing, China

Xuchen Yao†
Johns Hopkins University
Baltimore, MD, USA

Chunyu Kit
City University of Hong Kong, Hong Kong SAR, China

Abstract

This paper presents an efficient approach to finding more bilingual webpage pairs with high credibility via link analysis, using little prior knowledge or heuristics. It extends from a previous algorithm that takes the number of bilingual URL pairs that a key (i.e., a URL pairing pattern) can match as the objective function to search for the best set of keys yielding the greatest number of webpage pairs within targeted bilingual websites. Enhanced algorithms are proposed to match more bilingual webpages following the credibility based on statistical analysis of the link relationship of the seed websites available. With about 12,800 seed websites as test set, the enhanced algorithms improve precision over baseline by more than 5%, from 94.06% to 99.40%, and hence find above 20% more true bilingual URL pairs, illustrating that significantly more bilingual webpages with high credibility can be mined with the help of the link analysis.

1 Introduction

Parallel corpora of bilingual text (bitext) are indispensable language resources for many data-driven tasks of natural language processing, such as statistical machine translation (Brown et al., 1990), cross-language information retrieval (Davis and Dunning, 1995; Oard, 1997), and bilingual lexical acquisition (Gale and Church, 1991; Melamed, 1997; Jiang et al., 2009), to name but a few. A general way to develop such corpora from web texts starts from exploring the structure of known bilingual websites, which are usually organized by their web masters in a way to facilitate both navigation and maintenance (Nie, 2010). The most common strategy is to create a parallel structure in terms of URL hierarchies, exploiting some known naming conventions for webpages of corresponding languages (Huang and Tilley, 2001; Nie, 2010). Following available structures and naming conventions, researchers have been exploring various means to mine parallel corpora from the web and a good number of such systems have demonstrated the feasibility and practicality in automatic acquisition of parallel corpora from bilingual and/or multilingual web sites, e.g., STRAND (Resnik, 1998; Resnik, 1999; Resnik and Smith, 2003), BITS (Ma and Liberman, 1999), PTMiner (Chen and Nie, 2000), PTI (Chen et al., 2004), WPDE (Zhang et al., 2006), the DOM tree alignment model (Shi et al., 2006), PagePairGetter (YE et al., 2008) and Bitextor (Esplà-Gomis and Forcada, 2010).

Most of these systems are run in three steps: first, bilingual websites are identified and crawled; second, pairs of parallel webpages are extracted; and finally, the extracted pairs are validated (Kit and Ng, 2007). Among them, prior knowledge about parallel webpages, mostly in the form of ad hoc heuristics for identifying webpage languages or pre-defined patterns for matching or computing similarity between webpages, is commonly used for webpage pair extraction (Chen and Nie, 2000; Resnik and Smith, 2003; Zhang et al., 2006; Shi et al., 2006; Yulia and Shuly, 2010; Tomás et al., 2008). Specifically, these systems exploit search engines and heuristics across webpage anchors to locate candidate bilingual websites and then identify webpage pairs based on pre-defined URL matching patterns. However, ad hoc heuristics cannot exhaust all possible patterns. Many webpages do not even have any language label in their anchors, not to mention many untrustworthy labels. Also, using a limited set of pre-

*Performed while a research associate at City University of Hong Kong.

†Performed while a visiting student at City University of Hong Kong.

defined URL patterns inevitably means to give up all reachable bilingual webpages that fall outside their coverage.

Addressing such weaknesses of the previous approaches, we instead present an efficient bilingual web mining system based on analyzing link relationship of websites without resorting to prior ad hoc knowledge. This approach extends, on top of re-engineering, the previous work of Kit and Ng (2007). It aims at (1) further advancing the idea of finding bilingual webpages via automatic discovery of non-ad-hoc bilingual URL pairing patterns, (2) applying the found pairing patterns to dig out more bilingual webpage pairs, especially those involving a deep webpage unaccessible by web crawling, (3) discovering more bilingual websites (and then more bilingual webpages) with high credibility via statistical analysis of bilingual URL patterns and link relationship of available seed websites. The results from our experiments on $12,800$ seed websites show that the proposed algorithms can find considerably more bilingual webpage pairs on top of the baseline, achieving a significant improvement of pairing precision by more than 5%.

2 Algorithm

This section first introduces the idea of unsupervised detection of bilingual URL pairing patterns (§2.1) and then continues to formulate the use of the detected patterns to explore more websites, including deep webpages (§2.2), and those not included in our initial website list (§2.3).

2.1 Bilingual URL Pattern Detection

Our current research is conducted on top of the re-implementation of the intelligent web agent to automatically identify bilingual URL pairing patterns as described in Kit and Ng (2007). The underlying assumption for this approach is that rather than random matching, parallel webpages have static pairing patterns assigned by web masters for engineering purpose and these patterns are put in use to match as many pairs of URLs as possible within the same domain. Given a URL u from the set U of URLs of the same domain, the web agent goes through the set $U-\{u\}$ of all other URLs and finds among them all those that differ from u by a single token[1] – a token is naturally separated by a special set of characters including slash /, dot ., hyphen -, and underscore _ in a URL. Then, the single-token difference of a candidate URL pairs is taken as a candidate of URL paring pattern, and all candidate patterns are put in competition against each other in a way to allow a stronger one (that matches more candidate URL pairs) to win over a weaker one (that matches fewer). For instance, the candidate pattern `<en, zh>` can be detected from the following candidate URL pair:

www.legco.gov.hk/yr99-00/en/fc/esc/e0.htm
www.legco.gov.hk/yr99-00/zh/fc/esc/e0.htm

The re-implementation has achieved a number of improvements on the original algorithm through re-engineering, including the following major ones.

1. It is enhanced from token-based to character-based URL matching. Thus, more general patterns, such as `<e, c>`, can be aggregated from a number of weaker ones like `<1e, 1c>`, `<2e, 2c>`, ..., etc., many of which may otherwise fail to survive the competition.
2. The original algorithm is speeded up from $O(|U|^2)$ to $O(|U|)$ time, by building inverted indices for URLs and establishing constant lookup time for shortest matching URL strings.[2]
3. The language detection component has been expanded from bilingual to multi-lingual and hence had the capacity to practically handle multilingual websites such as those from EU and UN.

When detected URL patterns are used to match URLs in a web domain for identifying bilingual webpages, noisy patterns (most of which are presumably weak keys) would better be filtered out. A straightforward strategy to do this is by thresholding the credibility of a pattern, which can be defined as

$$C(p, w) = \frac{N(p, w)}{|w|}.$$

where $N(p, w)$ is the number of webpages matched into pairs by pattern p within website w, and $|w|$ the size of w in number of webpages. Note that this is the *local* credibility of a key with respect to a certain website w. Empirically, Kit and

[1] If language identification has been done on webpages, it only needs to go through all URLs of the other language.

[2] Achieved by utilizing SecondString `http://secondstring.sf.net/`

Ng (2007) set a threshold of 0.1 to rule out weak noisy keys.

Some patterns happen to generalize across domains. The *global* credibility of such a pattern p is thus computed by summing over all websites involved, in a way that each webpage matched by p is counted in respect to the local credibility of p in the respective website:

$$C(p) = \sum_{w} C(p, w)\, N(p, w).$$

Interestingly, it is observed that many weak keys ruled out by the threshold 0.1 are in fact good patterns with a nice global credibility value. In practice, it is important to "rescue" a local weak key with strong global credibility. A common practice is to do it straightforwardly with a global credibility threshold, e.g., $C(p) > 500$ as for the current work.

Finally, the bilingual credibility of a website is defined as

$$C(w) = \max_{p} C(p, w).$$

It will be used to measure the bilingual degree of a website in a later phase of our work, for which an assumption is that bilingual websites tend to link with other bilingual websites.

2.2 Deep Webpage Recovery

Some websites contain webpages that cannot be crawled by search engines. These webpages do not "exist" until they are created dynamically as the result of a specific search, mostly triggered by JavaScript or Flash actions. This kind of webpages as a whole is called *deep web*. Specifically, we are interested in the case where webpages in one language are visible but their counterparts in the other language are hidden. A very chance that we may have to unearth these deep hidden webpages is that their URLs follow some common naming conventions for convenience of pairing with their visible counterparts.

Thus for each of those URLs still missing a paired URL after the URL matching using our bilingual URL pattern collection, a candidate URL will be automatically generated with each applicable pattern in the collection for a trial to access its possibly hidden counterpart. If found, then mark them as a candidate pair. For example, the pattern `<english,tc_chi>` is found applicable to the first URL in Table 1 and accordingly generates the second as a candidate link to its English counterpart, which turns out to be a valid page.

2.3 Incremental Bilingual Website Exploration

Starting with a seed bilingual website list of size N, bilingual URL pairing patterns are first mined, and then used to reach out for other bilingual websites. The assumption for this phase of work is that bilingual websites are more likely to be referenced by other bilingual websites. Accordingly, a weighted version of PageRank is formulated for prediction.

Firstly, outgoing links and PageRank are used as baselines. *Linkout*(w) is the total number of outgoing links from website w, and the PageRank of w is defined as (Brin and Page, 1998):

$$\mathit{PageRank}(w) = \frac{r}{N} + (1-r) \sum_{w \in M(w)} \frac{\mathit{PageRank}(w)}{\mathit{Linkout}(w)},$$

where $M(w)$ is the set of websites that link to w in the seed set of N bilingual websites, and $r \in [0, 1]$ a damping factor empirically set to 0.15. Initially, the *PageRank* value of w is 1. In order to reduce time and space cost, both *Linkout*(w) and *PageRank*(w) are computed only in terms of the relationship of bilingual websites in the seed set.

The *WeightedPageRank*(w) is defined as the *PageRank*(w) weighted by w's credibility $C(w)$. To reach out for a related website s outside the initial seed set of websites, our approach first finds the set $R(s)$ of seed websites that have outgoing links to s, and then computes the sum of these three values over each outgoing link, namely, $\sum_w \mathit{Linkout}(w)$, $\sum_w \mathit{PageRank}(w)$, and $\sum_w \mathit{WeightedPageRank}(w)$ for each $w \in R(s)$, for the purpose of measuring how "likely" s is bilingual. An illustration of link relationship of this kind is presented in Figure 1.

In practice, the exploration of related websites can be combined with bilingual URL pattern detection to literately harvest both bilingual websites and URL patterns, e.g., through the following procedure:

1. Starting from a seed set of websites as the current set, detect bilingual URL patterns and then use them to identify their bilingual webpages.
2. Select the top K linked websites from the seed set according to either $\sum \mathit{Linkout}$, $\sum \mathit{PageRank}$, or $\sum \mathit{WeightedPageRank}$.

(1)	http://www.fehd.gov.hk/`tc_chi`/LLB_web/cagenda_20070904.htm
(2)	http://www.fehd.gov.hk/`english`/LLB_web/cagenda_20070904.htm

Table 1: Illustration of URL generation for a deep webpage

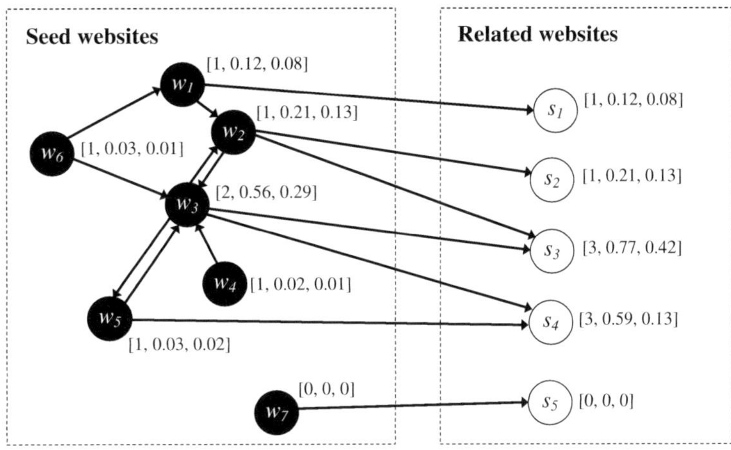

Figure 1: Illustration of link relationship of seed websites and related websites, with associated $\sum$*Linkout*, $\sum$*PageRank* and $\sum$*WeightedPageRank* in square brackets and with arrows to indicate outgoing links from a seed website to others.

3. Add the top K selected websites to the current set, and repeat the above steps for desired iterations.

3 Evaluation

The implementation of our method results in PupSniffer,[3] a Java-based tool that has been released for free. A series of experiments were conducted with it to investigate the performance of the proposed method on about $12,800$ seed websites. A web interface was also implemented for evaluating the candidate bilingual webpage pairs identified by our system.

3.1 Seed Websites

The initial seed websites were collected from two resources, namely

- Hong Kong Website Directory[4] and
- Hong Kong World Wide Web Database.[5]

After the removal of invalid ones, $12,800$ websites were finally acquired as our seed set.[6]

3.2 URL Pattern Detection and Deep Webpage Recovery

The enhanced algorithm described in Section 2.1 above was ran to extract credible URL patterns. In general, the extracted patterns are valid as long as the threshold is not too low – it is set to $C(p, w) > 0.1$ in our experiments. A number of strongest patterns found are presented in Table 2 for demonstration. Most of them, especially <`en,tc`> and <`eng,chi`>, are very intuitive patterns. A full list of URL pairing patterns detected in our experiments is also available.[7] Particularly interesting is that all these patterns were identified in an unsupervised fashion without any manual heuristics.

Using these patterns, the original algorithm retrieved about $290K$ candidate bilingual webpage pairs. By the simple trick of rescuing weak local patterns with the global credibility threshold $C(p) > 500$, $10K$ more webpage pairs were further found. Additionally, other $16K$ webpage pairs were dug out from deep webpages by automatically generating paired webpages with the aid of identified URL patterns.

[3] `http://code.google.com/p/pupsniffer`

[4] `http://www.852.com`

[5] `http://www.cuhk.edu.hk/hkwww.htm`

[6] `http://mega.ctl.cityu.edu.hk/~czhang22/pupsniffer-eval/Data/All_Seed_Websites_List.txt`

[7] `http://mega.ctl.cityu.edu.hk/~czhang22/pupsniffer-eval/Data/Pattern_Credibility_LargeThan100.txt`

Pattern	$C(p)$
`<en,tc>`	13997.36
`<eng,tc>`	12869.56
`<english,tc_chi>`	11436.12
`<english,chinese>`	11032.46
`<eng,chi>`	7824.86

Table 2: Top 5 patterns with their global credibility values.

Method	Pairs	Precision
Kit and Ng (2007)	290,247	94.06%
Weak key rescue	10,015	89.27%
Deep page recovery	15,825	95.02%
Incremental exploration	37,491	99.40%
Total	348,058	94.72%
True pair increment	55,674	20.76%

Table 3: Number of bilingual webpage pairs found and their precision from sampled evaluation.

3.3 Website Exploration

To go beyond the original 12,800 websites, the incremental algorithm described in Section 2.3 was run for one iteration to find outside bilingual websites directly linked from the seeds. The top 500 of them, ranked by $\sum$*Linkout*, $\sum$*PageRank* and $\sum$*WeightedPageRank*, respectively, were manually checked by five students, giving the curves of the total number of true bilingual websites and overall precision per top N websites as plotted in Figure 2. These results show that almost 50% of the top 500 related outside websites ranked by $\sum$*WeightedPageRank* are true bilingual websites. A higher precision indicates more bilingual webpage pairs correctly matched by the URL patterns in use.

After one iteration of the incremental algorithm, $37K$ more candidate bilingual webpage pairs were found in the related outside websites, besides the $290K$ by the original algorithm. Table 3 presents the number of webpage pairs identified by each algorithm with a respective precision drawn from random sampling. These results suggest that our proposed enhancement is able to harvest above 20% more bilingual webpage pairs without degrading the overall precision. Error analysis shows that around 80% of errors were due to mistakes in language identification for webpages. For instance, some Japanese webpages were mistakenly recognized as Chinese ones.

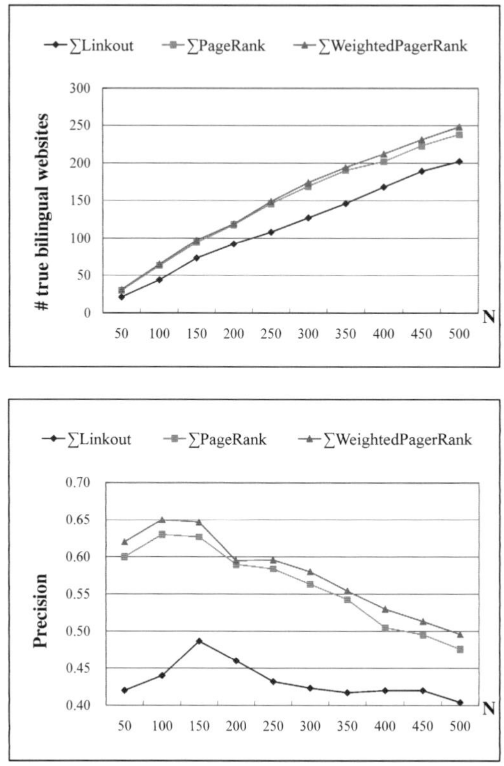

Figure 2: Number and precision of true bilingual websites found per top N outside websites ranked by various criteria.

4 Conclusion

In this paper we have presented an efficient approach to mining bilingual webpages via computing highly credible bilingual URL pairing patterns. With the aid of these patterns learned in an unsupervised way, our research moves on to exploring the possibility of rescuing weak local keys by virtue of global credibility, uncovering deep bilingual webpages by generating candidate URLs using available keys, and also developing an incremental algorithm for mining more bilingual websites that are linked from the known bilingual websites in our seed set. Experimental results show that these several enhanced algorithms improve the precision over the baseline from 94.06% to 99.40% and, more importantly, help discover above 20% more webpage pairs while maintaining a high overall precision.

Acknowledgements

The research described in this paper was supported in part by the Research Grants Council (RGC) of Hong Kong SAR, China, through the GRF grant 9041597 (CityU 144410), National Natural Science Foundation of China through the grant No. 70903032, and Project of the Education Ministry of China's Humanities and Social Sciences through the grant No. 13YJA870020.

References

Sergey Brin and Lawrence Page. 1998. The anatomy of a large-scale hypertextual web search engine. *Computer networks and ISDN systems*, 30(1):107–117.

Peter F Brown, John Cocke, Stephen A Della Pietra, Vincent J Della Pietra, Fredrick Jelinek, John D Lafferty, Robert L Mercer, and Paul S Roossin. 1990. A statistical approach to machine translation. *Computational linguistics*, 16(2):79–85.

Jiang Chen and Jian-Yun Nie. 2000. Parallel web text mining for cross-language ir. In *Proc. of RIAO*, pages 62–77.

Jisong Chen, Rowena Chau, and Chung-Hsing Yeh. 2004. Discovering parallel text from the world wide web. In *Proceedings of the second workshop on Australasian information security, Data Mining and Web Intelligence, and Software Internationalisation-Volume 32*, pages 157–161.

Mark W Davis and Ted E Dunning. 1995. A trec evaluation of query translation methods for multi-lingual text retrieval. In *Fourth Text Retrieval Conference*, pages 483–498.

Miquel Esplà-Gomis and Mikel L Forcada. 2010. Combining content-based and URL-based heuristics to harvest aligned bitexts from multilingual sites with bitextor. *The Prague Bulletin of Mathematical Linguistics*, 93(1):77–86.

William A Gale and Kenneth W Church. 1991. Identifying word correspondences in parallel texts. In *Proceedings of the workshop on Speech and Natural Language*, pages 152–157.

Shihong Huang and Scott Tilley. 2001. Issues of content and structure for a multilingual web site. In *Proceedings of the 19th annual international conference on Computer documentation*, pages 103–110.

Long Jiang, Shiquan Yang, Ming Zhou, Xiaohua Liu, and Qingsheng Zhu. 2009. Mining bilingual data from the web with adaptively learnt patterns. In *Proceedings of the Joint Conference of the 47th Annual Meeting of the ACL and the 4th International Joint Conference on Natural Language Processing of the AFNLP: Volume 2*, pages 870–878.

Chunyu Kit and Jessica Yee Ha Ng. 2007. An intelligent web agent to mine bilingual parallel pages via automatic discovery of URL pairing patterns. In *Proceedings of the 2007 IEEE/WIC/ACM International Conferences on Web Intelligence and Intelligent Agent Technology - Workshops: Workshop on Agents and Data Mining Interaction (ADMI-07)*, pages 526–529.

Xiaoyi Ma and Mark Liberman. 1999. BITS: A method for bilingual text search over the web. In *Machine Translation Summit VII*, pages 538–542.

I. Dan Melamed. 1997. A word-to-word model of translational equivalence. In *Proceedings of the Eighth Conference on European Chapter of the Association for Computational Linguistics*, pages 490–497.

Jian-Yun Nie. 2010. *Cross-Language Information Retrieval*. Morgan and Claypool Publishers.

Douglas W Oard. 1997. Cross-language text retrieval research in the USA. In *Proceedings of the Third DELOS Workshop: Cross-Language Information Retrieval*, pages 7–16.

Philip Resnik and Noah A Smith. 2003. The web as a parallel corpus. *Computational Linguistics*, 29(3):349–380.

Philip Resnik. 1998. Parallel strands: A preliminary investigation into mining the web for bilingual text. In D. Farwell, L. Gerber, and E. Hovy, editors, *Machine Translation and the Information Soup: Third Conference of the Association for Machine Translation in the Americas (AMTA-98)*, pages 72–82.

Philip Resnik. 1999. Mining the web for bilingual text. In *Proceedings of the 37th annual meeting of the Association for Computational Linguistics on Computational Linguistics*, pages 527–534.

Lei Shi, Cheng Niu, Ming Zhou, and Jianfeng Gao. 2006. A DOM tree alignment model for mining parallel data from the web. In *Proceedings of the 21st International Conference on Computational Linguistics and the 44th annual meeting of the Association for Computational Linguistics*, pages 489–496.

Jesús Tomás, Jordi Bataller, Francisco Casacuberta, and Jaime Lloret. 2008. Mining Wikipedia as a parallel and comparable corpus. In *Language Forum*, volume 34.

Sha-ni YE, Ya-juan LV, Yun Huang, and Qun Liu. 2008. Automatic parallel sentences extraction from web. *Journal of Chinese Information Processing*, 22:67–73.

T Yulia and W Shuly. 2010. Automatic acquisition of parallel corpora from website with dynamic content. In *Proceedings of the 7th International Conference on Language Resources and Evaluation (LREC-2010)*, pages 3389–3392.

Ying Zhang, Ke Wu, Jianfeng Gao, and Phil Vines. 2006. Automatic acquisition of chinese–english parallel corpus from the web. In *Advances in Information Retrieval*, pages 420–431. Springer.

Author Index

Association for Computational Linguistics
209 N. Eighth Street
Stroudsburg, Pennsylvania 18360